Integrating China

Anthem Studies in Development and Globalization

INTEGRATING CHINA

Towards the
Coordinated Market Economy

Peter Nolan

ANTHEM PRESS
LONDON · NEW YORK · DELHI

Anthem Press
An imprint of Wimbledon Publishing Company
www.anthempress.com

This edition first published in UK and USA 2007
by ANTHEM PRESS
75-76 Blackfriars Road, London SE1 8HA, UK
or PO Box 9779, London SW19 7ZG, UK
and
244 Madison Ave. #116, New York, NY 10016, USA

British Library Cataloguing in Publication Data
A catalogue record for this book is available from the British Library.

Library of Congress Cataloging in Publication Data
Nolan, Peter, 1949–
Integrating China : towards the coordinated market economy /
Peter Nolan.
p. cm.
ISBN 978–1–84331–237–6 (hardback)
1. China — Economic policy — 2000- 2. Capitalism — China.
3. China — Economic conditions — 2000– I. Title.
HC427.95.N65 2007
337.51 — dc22
2007026385

ISBN–10: 1 84331 237 9 (Hbk)
ISBN–13: 978 1 84331 237 6 (Hbk)

1 3 5 7 9 10 8 6 4 2

Printed in India

For my sister, Catherine, and my brother, Dermot,
and in memory of our sister, Julia

Also from Peter Nolan

Growth Processes and Distributional Change in a South Chinese Province:
The Case of Guangdong
(1983, London: School of Oriental and African Studies, University of London)

with T. J. Byres, *Inequality: India and China Compared, 1950–1970*
(1976, Milton Keynes: Open University Press)

The Political Economy of Collective Farms:
An Analysis of China's post-Mao Rural Economic Reforms
(1988, Cambridge: Polity Press)

State and Market in the Chinese Economy: Essays on Controversial Issues
(1993, Basingstoke: Macmillan)

China's Rise, Russia's Fall: Politics, Economics and Planning in the Transition from Stalinism
(1995, Basingstoke: Macmillan)

Indigenous Large Firms in China's Economic Reform:
The Case of Shougang Iron and Steel Corporation
(1998, London: School of Oriental and African Studies, University of London)

Coca-Cola and the Global Business Revolution: a Study with Special Reference to the EU
(1999, Cambridge: Judge Institute of Management)

China and the Global Business Revolution
(2001, Basingstoke: Palgrave)

China and the Global Economy
(2001, Basingstoke: Palgrave)

China at the Crossroads
(2003, Cambridge: Polity Press)

Transforming China: Globalization, Transition and Development
(2004, London: Anthem Press)

with J. Zhang and C. Liu, *The Global Business Revolution and the Cascade Effect:*
Systems Integration in the Global Aerospace, Beverage and Retail Industries
(2007, Basingstoke: Palgrave)

CONTENTS

ACKNOWLEDGEMENTS

I am grateful to my co-authors with whom several chapters in this book were written.

I am also grateful to Elizabeth Briggs for her expert editing.

AUTHOR AND CO-AUTHORS

Professor Peter Nolan
Sinyi Professor, Judge Business School, University of Cambridge
Chair of Development Studies, University of Cambridge
Director, China Executive Leadership Programme, University of Cambridge
Fellow, Jesus College, University of Cambridge

Dr Jin Zhang
Lecturer in International Business, Judge Business School,
University of Cambridge
Deputy Director, China Executive Leadership Programme,
University of Cambridge
Deputy Director, China Industry Development Research Centre,
Peking University
Fellow, Wolfson College, University of Cambridge

Professor Chunhang Liu
Director, China Industry Development Research Centre, Peking University

Dr Yuantuo Guo
Equity Analyst, Gaohua Securities, Beijing

Dr Huiachuan Rui
Lecturer in International Business, Brunel University

Dr Wang Xiaoqiang
Head of Political and Economic Research Department,
CITIC Pacific, Hong Kong

FOREWORD

The articles in this book were written over a period of more than a decade and a half. They cover a variety of topics relating to China's deepening integration with the global system of political economy. None of the articles has been altered in the light of subsequent events.

Chapter 1 was written in the months immediately following the June 4th events. It was presented at seminars and lectures in numerous locations. Extracts from it were published in various places. The response to the ideas expressed in the article was almost uniformly hostile. Most people in the West believed then that the Chinese Communist Party could not last long, perhaps only a few months. Nor did they believe that it deserved to last long or that it could preside over a successful market economy. They considered that the Soviet Union's path of comprehensive political transformation and high-speed economic liberalisation was the correct path of system reform in communist countries. In fact, the Chinese Communist Party has survived and prospered. The collapse of the Soviet political and economic system destroyed the credibility of large-scale high-speed political and economic reform in China. It paved the way for cautious, experimental economic reform within the framework of stable communist party rule. The most dynamic part of the global market economy is now presided over by the 60 million members of the Chinese Communist Party. This is an unpalatable reality for the chorus of commentators who had argued that only Western democracy could bring successful economic development.

Chapters 2-4 examine different aspects of the challenge presented to China's large-scale firms by the global business revolution, which has been under way since the 1970s. Since China joined the WTO at the end of 2001, its exports have grown at high speed, stimulating rapid growth of employment, and allowing the country to build up large foreign exchange reserves. However, the high-speed growth of foreign direct investment has resulted in a relatively small number of leading global oligopolistic firms dominating many high value-added, high technology and high-branded segments of the economy. Faced with this reality, Chinese policy-makers are nurturing a group of globally competitive, large-scale companies, the core of which is a group of over fifty giant, state-owned firms. They are increasingly benchmarking their performance against that of the world's leading capitalist firms. If the government's strategy is successful, these giant state-owned firms will establish leading international positions in high technology sectors that meet the long-term development needs of the Chinese economy in key sectors, such as energy production and distribution, transport, aerospace, telecommunications, medicine and financial services. Through industrial policy China intends to achieve 'innovation in an open environment'.

Chapter 5 is a study of China in the Asian Financial Crisis. Most commentators consider that China escaped any danger arising from contagion from the crisis thanks to the government controls over the country's capital account. In fact, through the mechanism of Mainland firms' operations in Hong Kong, China was deeply involved in the Asian Financial Crisis. The impact was deepest in Guangdong Province, adjacent to Hong Kong. This chapter analyses the way in which severe repercussions upon the Chinese economy and society were only avoided by drastic policy action. Guangdong's financial flagship, GITIC, was allowed to go bankrupt and its leading financial conglomerate, GDE, was comprehensively restructured, with a large 'haircut' for its creditors. These drastic steps, 'cutting the trees to save the forest', were hugely unpopular with the international creditors, and deeply embarrassed the Guangdong provincial government. However, they allowed the Chinese financial system to survive relatively unscathed. They provided a warning about the urgent need to undertake comprehensive reform of China's financial institutions, and highlighted the dangers of over-rapid integration into the global financial system.

Chapter 6 analyses the wide-ranging challenges that China's political economy faces at the start of the twenty-first century, including widespread environmental deterioration, the challenge of the global business revolution and integration with the global financial system, rising inequality of income and wealth, and surging government corruption. It argues that the only way in which China can surmount these challenges is by 'using the past to serve the present', building on its rich historical experience since ancient times in order to guide the construction of a market economy that operates within the framework of regulation to ensure that collective interests are met. By this means, China can move towards a socially harmonious and sustainable development path. The chapter argues that this is a 'choice of no choice'. In fact, under the leadership of President Hu Jintao and Premier Wen Jiabao, China has undertaken a big strategic policy shift, which involves establishing comprehensive coordination of the market economy in the collective interest. The government has shifted from one-sidedly emphasising output expansion towards achieving balanced growth, giving greatly increased weight to environmental protection, social justice, control over the financial system, and building a group of high technology, globally competitive Chinese firms.

Chapter 7 examines the wider context in which Chinese development is located. It examines the contradictory character of capitalist globalisation. It argues that capitalism is the key propulsive force in technical progress, and that the recent period has seen an unprecedented liberation of this force, as constraints on the market mechanism have been progressively removed. However, it argues that this force is a two-edged sword. Alongside the unprecedented advances have arisen unprecedented challenges that threaten the very survival of the human species. These include the deep threats to the world's ecological system; grotesque global inequalities in the distribution of income and wealth, which have increased during this period in both rich and poor countries; massive international disparities in business power; and the absence of collective control over global finance. These contradictions threaten to interact in an explosive fashion. The deepest immediate danger resides in the possibility of a global financial crisis. At the time of writing (early 2007) a wide range of senior figures in international financial institutions have expressed their fear that the world faces the possibility of a financial crisis that would greatly exceed even that of the early 1930s. It is even possible that the interaction of these contradictions could erupt into violent international conflict. The world's hegemonic power possesses over 7000 nuclear warheads, the lethality of which advances constantly and which could destroy human civilisation in a few minutes.

Chapter 8 examines US-China relations. The forces of global capitalism have exploded beyond national boundaries. However, people's political life remains firmly fixed within nations and groups of nations with differing interests. The critical relationship that will determine the evolution of the global system of political economy in the coming years is that between the United States, the hegemonic country in relative decline, and China, the rising economic power. Their interests are intertwined on almost all major issues of global political economy. It is crucially important that they establish a cooperative rather than a confrontational relationship. They need to understand deeply the challenges that capitalist globalisation poses for both of their societies and for the global system of political economy. The epoch of 'wild' capitalist globalisation is approaching its end. On a wide array of issues it is becoming increasingly clear that the free market cannot solve the challenges that it is creating through its own innate operational mechanism. The most fundamental challenges of capitalist globalisation can only be solved through global regulation. Through cooperative behaviour, the US and China can help to lead the world towards such an outcome and establish a sustainable future for mankind, with a global market economy regulated in the common interest of all human beings. In the absence of such a mechanism, the prospects for humanity are bleak.

Chapter 1

REFLECTIONS ON 4TH JUNE 1989

Peter Nolan

Introduction[1]

The killing of hundreds, perhaps even thousands, of civilians by armed forces in Peking on June 4th 1989 is to be deeply deplored. Such violence is a sign of political failure. However, after the initial emotional shock, one has to attempt to analyse the event coolly to understand why it happened, to consider its significance and anticipate its impact on the future course of China's political economy. The broad thesis of this chapter is that, awful as this event was, it should not have surprised anyone familiar with the political economy of developing countries, especially those observers with more than a superficial knowledge of China. The recent history of virtually all developing countries contains examples of violence by the state against its own citizens. Not even the advanced capitalist countries have been immune in recent times from such actions, albeit on a smaller scale than in China (Kent State and 'Bloody Sunday' spring readily to mind). Not only do China's leaders have to deal with the conflicts characteristic of developing countries in general, but also they are presiding over the turbulent process of de-Stalinisation of their entire system of political economy. Such a process is difficult enough in the relatively advanced, urbanised societies of Eastern Europe. In a backward, hugely populous country with vast regional differences, such as China, the process is incomparably more difficult. The realities of China before June 4th were far removed from the fantasy image created by the Western media and observed through the darkest of glasses by Western tourists insulated in almost every way from the true condition of the Chinese people. June 4th represents a far more complex historical event than the extinguishing of the torch of freedom by an evil, corrupt leadership desperately clinging to power for power's sake.

On a visit to China in the Autumn of 1988 this author everywhere encountered a sense of crisis. He listened to hour after hour of concern expressed at different aspects of the current political economic situation. However, concern and criticism are different from a concrete alternative programme of political economy. His question 'What, then, is your alternative programme for China's political-economic evolution?' was, without exception, met with an inability to answer. One of the most telling banners in Tiananmen before June 4th read: 'Deng Xiaoping: Where is the next stone?' (The reference is to Chen Yun's characterisation of China's economic reforms of the 1980s as analogous to someone crossing the river by touching stones). One could equally turn the question into a rhetorical one and ask the Chinese intellectual community if any of them could really be confident that they knew where the next stone in the reform programme lay? For all its passion, the June 2nd Hunger Strike Declaration (translated in *The Independent* Saturday 10 June 1989) is devoid of such a programme.

Implicit in much of the writing outside China on the subject of June 4th is the idea that no progress of any kind, either economically or politically can be made under the present regime. The Chinese Communist Party (CCP) is argued to have antagonised the whole population by the events in Tiananmen and to be bankrupt, with the internal situation frozen in anticipation of Deng Xiaoping's death in the same way as it was in 1976 in the months between Zhou Enlai's death in April and Mao Zedong's death in September. In the view of many non-Chinese and Chinese observers outside China not just the present leadership, but, indeed the very existence of the CCP as the 'vanguard party', is under the deepest threat in the way that appears to be the case for the Communist Party in Poland. Many people are so pessimistic about the nature of the CCP, crystallised for them in the events of June 4th, that they feel it is both likely and desirable that a period of great turbulence will appear, involving the overturning of the CCP, after which things can begin again with a clean slate. This author is far from convinced that this is a likely scenario and certainly does not believe it is a desirable one. The suffering involved in such a process might be enormous. Moreover, China is not Poland or Hungary. It is much less advanced economically and culturally, and it is not clear that a superior regime to the present one would emerge from such an occurrence. It is ironical that many anti-communists in the West who have, quite rightly, criticised communist countries for dangerous policy 'leaps' should now be supporting such a 'leap' in China.

None of this is intended to condone June 4th. A less divided, more skilful leadership might well have been able to avoid the confrontation. This chapter argues simply that it was a much more complex event than it has been portrayed. Over-simplistic interpretations of it are likely to produce incorrect policy responses with unfortunate consequences, especially for the mass of impoverished Chinese citizens.

1. China's Political Economy Pre-1976

The problems of the 1980s have prompted some people to look back with nostalgia at China's political economy under Mao. How justified is this? Is the solution of China's problems a return to the structures and policies of that epoch?

1.1. Economics

Stalinist administrative planning, with direct control over enterprises, produced some good results. Most notably, 'basic needs' were met for most people in normal times and death rates fell rapidly. By the 1970s China had raised average life expectancy to high levels for a country of its level of income. However, in other fundamental respects the over-centralised system performed badly, achieving high accumulation rates ('macro-economic efficiency') but using capital with great profligacy ('micro-economic inefficiency'). As a result, despite considerable growth of total output, average real incomes grew extremely slowly. Moreover, the system was capable of making huge centrally-determined errors. The greatest of these was the catastrophic Great Leap Forward (1958-59) which resulted in a collapse of output and famine-induced deaths of at least 15 million people.

Fundamental reform of the economic system is on the agenda across almost the whole 'socialist' bloc. Kim Il Sung and Nicholae Ceausescu are left virtually alone as supporters of Stalinist planning. In a fitting gesture Ceausescu received an honorary doctorate from Kim Il Sung in Pyongyang in 1988. Even the 'conservative hardliners' in China today do not support Stalinist economics. It is one of these, Bo Yibo, who in the early 1950s championed China's short-lived New Economic Policy (NEP) with the slogan 'expand the household and become rich'. Another is Chen Yun who for years struggled against Mao's hostility to market forces, and earned himself the title 'China's Bukharin'. Deng Xiaoping states (*People's Daily*, 28 June 1989) that China cannot return to the Stalinist economic system but must press ahead with its reform. He is expressing the collective view of the Chinese leadership. The question is not whether reform should continue but how rapidly and towards what model. Even if there were complete consensus about the model towards which the Chinese economy should move the process of moving to this from the Stalinist system would still be immensely complex.

At the end of the Maoist epoch in the mid-1970s it became clear that China had an extremely low average standard of living compared to what might have been achieved with different policies. It is unrealistic to imagine that China could have grown as rapidly as the East Asian NICs (Newly Industrialising Countries) since the 1950s. However, the huge success of China's neighbours fuelled an acute sense of lost opportunity. Not only was the average living standard in China still extremely low, but a new openness in reporting after 1976 revealed that perhaps one-third of the Chinese population was still living in the direst poverty, little changed since the mid-1950s. This was a world far removed from the fairy-tales of model communes. The principal goal for any Chinese leadership for a long time to come ought to be raising the mass of the Chinese population out of poverty.

1.2. Politics

Pre-1976 China was ruled by a highly centralised Communist Party practising a form of 'barracks socialism' little different from the other 'socialist' countries in respect to the Party's internal organisation and relationship to society. The party penetrated deep into the fabric of socio-economic life. The main decisions about the occupancy of leading positions were the outcome of high-level power struggles and the main lines of policy were determined by those who emerged successful from these struggles. Regular purges were conducted against opponents of Party policies in the course of which large numbers of people were imprisoned and killed. Long-running struggles were conducted against national minorities. In Xinjiang in the 1970s major battles were fought between the People's Liberation Army and the local Uighur population with heavy loss of life.

In normal times individual liberties were greatly restricted. The Party controlled culture tightly and people had very little freedom of movement. The Chinese population was almost entirely insulated from the international flow of people and ideas. During the Cultural Revolution, launched by Mao from his position of supreme power, individual liberties were even more tightly restricted and xenophobia even more pronounced. Moreover, for a period of time at the height of the movement, there was a widespread breakdown of civil order, extensive factional fighting, great insecurity and much loss of life.

2. An Assessment of the Post-1978 Reforms

The action in and around Tiananmen Square on June 4th is of very different historical significance from the violent events in Hungary in 1956 and Czechoslovakia in 1968. The most obvious difference is that in the former case the armed forces were internal and in the latter cases they were external. However, the contrast is much deeper than that, and differentiates China also from the bloody suppression of student protesters in 'socialist' Burma in 1988. In Hungary, Czechoslovakia and Burma the violent suppression came from a regime committed to maintaining traditional Stalinist economics and politics. In China, the military action against its own citizens came after more than a decade of de-Stalinisation in the economy, considerable de-Stalinisation in culture and even a certain amount of political change. Moreover, the regime was committed to continue with economic de-Stalinisation. China's difficulties in the late 1980s arose because of the enormous advances that had occurred, promoted by the leadership, with Deng Xiaoping at it head.

2.1. Economics

Huge reforms were effected in the Chinese economic system in the 1980s. The most important of these were de-collectivisation of agriculture, opening up to international trade, investment and economic ideas, greatly increased independence for small-scale non-farm enterprises and the beginnings of reform of large-scale state enterprises. In the USSR, despite the high international profile of Gorbachev's *perestroika*, little economic de-Stalinisation had in fact occurred by 1989. The changes in China brought immense improvements in efficiency, reflected in a radically changed growth pattern. Their most important result was a sharp improvement in popular living standards: food consumption increased to a level much above that of pre-1976; consumer durable ownership rose at an exceptionally rapid rate and, after long years of neglect, the amount of housing space per person rose by around 50 per cent over the decade. Few developing economies, let alone ones the size of China, have experienced such a rapid rise in the standard of living. Moreover, the growth was deep-rooted, affecting, to some degree, all regions and social strata. Consequently, the number and proportion of people in poverty fell strikingly, constituting the biggest single success of the whole programme. Despite these great advances, the average standard of living in China still remained extremely low.

To some degree the growth was exceptional because it was taking up the 'slack' from poor resource use under Mao. However, the new, enduring growth momentum had been created with the release of long-suppressed market forces. This was especially so in densely populated east coast areas such as the Pearl River Delta and Southern Jiangsu with long traditions of production and trade for domestic and international markets. Growth in these areas in the 1980s was truly explosive and seemed to have attained a momentum of its own.

2.2. Politics

In certain fundamental respects, nothing changed politically in China in the 1980s. The CCP maintained its position as the 'vanguard' party with a monopoly of political power. Arrests and imprisonments of those designated as political opponents continued on a wide scale during the anti-'spiritual pollution' and 'bourgeois liberalisation' campaigns. Massive erosion of individual rights occurred during the 'One Child Family' campaign, which reached a crescendo in 1983, when large numbers of women were arrested for the 'crime' of being pregnant with a second child and underwent forcible abortions. In the campaigns to combat crime large numbers of people were executed, often in public, not infrequently in order to meet local execution quotas. It is estimated by Amnesty International that at the peak of the campaign in 1983, 'several thousand' people were executed in just a few months.

However, these fundamental continuities should not blind one to the important changes that took place. Serious efforts were made by the leadership to divorce the Party from interference in the economy, to introduce a comprehensive framework of economic law and legal protection of individual rights, to professionalise government administration and to democratise local government. These efforts were far from wholly successful, but the fact that the attempts were made and some progress achieved was extremely significant. In cultural matters Party control was dramatically weakened compared to pre-1976. The boundaries of permissible topics and approaches were pushed back at great speed in the 1980s. In both high and mass culture not only did the variety of indigenous products grow explosively but China once again, as in the 1920s and 1930s, was opened up to a huge range of international cultural influences. In an electronic age and one with mass international tourism new ideas penetrated China at an extremely rapid pace. The existence of the large overseas Chinese community also helped to push this process along. Compared to the USSR under Gorbachev, China in the 1980s was much more liberal in allowing and financially supporting its intellectuals, especially students, to travel internationally. This provided yet another important avenue for the transmission to China of ideas outside the control of the Party.

3. The Causes of 4th June 1989

The mass movement of May 1989 in China's cities, which culminated in the declaration of martial law and, eventually, in the confrontation in and around Tiananmen Square can only be understood against the wider background of tensions associated with de-Stalinisation.

3.1. The ti-yong Struggle

The relationship between the economic and political aspects of de-Stalinisation is immensely complex. It is most likely that China will be able at some point to raise average incomes to a reasonably high level, at which time it is likely that the Chinese people will either have been given or will take into their own hands the individual liberties and democratic rights that are taken for granted in the advanced capitalist countries. However, it is far from clear what is either the likely or, indeed, the desirable route by which China attains this distant goal.

The Chinese leadership's approach towards this question was fairly united and reasonably clear for most of the 1980s. It parallels in certain respects the debate among late nineteenth century Chinese philosophers about Westernisation. Their argument was about whether it was possible to have Western technology (*yong*, i.e. 'useful') while keeping Chinese ideas (*ti*, i.e. 'essence'). Few, if any, of China's leaders in the 1980s have much understanding or sympathy with Western liberal values. Moreover, even if they did, it is not inconceivable that they might regard these as inappropriate to China's transition from Stalinism. They all have personal experience of the chaotic conditions of China pre-1949, and experienced too the anarchy of the Cultural Revolution. Their response to the events of the 1980s in general and 1989 in particular stems not just from the desire to retain power for its own sake but also from a deep-rooted fear that without strong leadership, undemocratic in Western liberal terms, China could easily collapse into political turmoil – *da luan*. The image of China as a 'sheet of loose sand' held together by the CCP is not one invented to serve the propaganda purposes of a despotic government, but is one held deeply by the leadership and which touches a chord in the psychology of the Chinese population, especially those of an older generation than the students in Tiananmen Square whose formative years were the 1980s.

There is, undoubtedly, a connection between capitalist markets, individual freedom and political rights. The eighteenth century Scottish political economist, John Millar, was not alone in his belief that economic progress would lead to greater 'personal independence, and to higher notions of general liberty' (quoted in A.O. Hirschman, *The Passions and the Interests*, Princeton, Princeton University Press, 1977, p.89). Two centuries later, writing in respect to the student movement in Peking, the *Economist* wrote: 'The experiences of Japan, South Korea, and, above all Taiwan, show that the freer the markets, and the wider the prosperity they generate, the greater the demands of ordinary people to have more say in the running of their country' (27 May 1989).

However, the point at which market development and rising incomes result in a broadly-based demand for democratic rights is not easy to determine. Indeed, de Tocqueville was far from convinced that 'a close tie and a necessary relation exist between ... freedom and industry' (quoted in Hirschman, ibid. p.122). He argued that, on the contrary, the basis for an authoritarian pattern of economic progress was laid in the fact that 'the taste for material enjoyments ... develops more rapidly than the enlightenments and habits of liberty' (quoted in Hirschman, ibid. p.123). Indeed, what is striking about the relationship between economic development and political democracy is that hardly a single country advanced from low to moderate levels of income under democratic systems in Western liberal terms. Britain in the late eighteenth and early nineteenth century, Meiji Japan, much of Continental Europe in the wake of the defeat of the 'revolutions' of 1848, South Korea, Taiwan and Hong Kong in the 1960s and 1970s, all achieved their initial growth under more or less undemocratic governments. The apparent exception is the United States, but, of course, its industrialisation began from an already high level of average income built on violent expropriation of the assets of the indigenous population. In most cases, liberal political democracy followed rather than preceded the achievement of moderate income levels.

In a predominantly peasant, low income country where most work is extremely laborious, it is questionable whether the large majority of the population has much interest in political democracy. Indeed, there is a possibility that the early establishment of formally democratic institutions might lead to their manipulation by powerful regions, urban intellectuals, industrial interests and bureaucrats, to the disadvantage of the peasant majority. While the peasant majority might show little interest in democratic ideals, the dilemma for all developing countries is that a substantial part of the urban population does, indeed, have such an interest from quite early in the development process. The difficulty with setting up such institutions, at an early stage, is that the political bargaining between different interests (regions, peasants, bureaucrats, intellectuals, workers, managers, etc.) may in respect to key economic issues (the internal terms of trade between farm and non-farm products, tax policy, regional policy, labour laws, attitudes to international trade, etc.), lead either to compromises, or to capitulation to sufficiently powerful interests, which may produce a slower rate of growth than that which is possible given other conditions relevant to the country's growth. A strong, autonomous state is far from a sufficient condition for raising poor countries out of poverty, but it may well be necessary to enable the state to take the tough decisions which are necessary to achieve rapid national growth. One cannot stress sufficiently strongly that successful growth is the surest way to produce an eventual move to mass demands for democracy and the cultural preconditions for making democracy a reality, as the experience of a succession of East and Southeast Asian countries has demonstrated in recent times.

If these considerations apply to poor countries in general, it may be argued that they apply even more strongly to poor 'socialist' countries attempting to liberalise their economies. The shift from an administered to a market economy involves many extremely difficult decisions which threaten different vested interests. As the market economy develops, the scope for individual economic and cultural freedom can, and should, widen rapidly. However, this is a different matter from political democracy, and the over-rapid advance might compromise the state's capacity to take the necessary decision for the interest of the mass of the population. The Soviet Union in the 1920s demonstrated that it is not impossible to combine economic and cultural liberalisation with tight political control. This doesn't prove that this is always either possible or desirable, but it does suggest that it is not entirely unfeasible.

3.2. The Nature of the Demands of the Protesters in May 1989

One view argues that the demands of the students were precise and moderate: recognition of an independent students' organisation, dialogue between the government and the students' independently elected representatives, freedom of the press and an end to corruption. It is argued that had government responded quickly to these demands in the early days of the movement, the protests would not have escalated. Dialogue with the students plus serious promises to end corruption and to provide a freer press might well have defused the situation. Failing that, normal anti-riot actions could well have brought the street protest to an end, though there is reason to believe Li Peng's alleged claims that China lacked large stocks of tear gas, possessed no rubber bullets, that lack of suitable water hydrants prevented the use of water cannon in Tiananmen Square, and that China's armed forces were poorly trained in urban riot control. The escalation was permitted mainly by indecision among the leadership caused by differences of view. This indecision effectively allowed the rules of the political game to be changed. Where previous student protests had been met with tough police action in this case it was not.

However, although there is a lot to this view, there are some problems with it. In a one-party communist state the students' demands were not as moderate as they appear to a Western audience. The demand for a free press and for independent student organisations were head-on attacks upon the idea of a vanguard party. What appears to outsiders as a relatively innocuous protest, to China's leaders appeared as a revolution against Party rule. If that was so in the early stages, it became even more so in the late stages. The widespread demand that Li Peng should resign, the demands by some demonstrating workers' groups for independent trade unions and, finally, the construction of a Chinese 'Statue of Liberty' opposite Chairman Mao's portrait, could not be interpreted as anything other than the deepest of challenges to the traditional notions of Party rule.

China's urban population in general and intellectuals in particular had obtained enormously increased freedom in the 1980s. To focus demands carefully upon further advances (e.g. a freer press rather than a 'free press') which the leadership might have been prepared to meet required an impossible level of political skill and organisation among the protesters. Once the movement became a large-scale, inchoate street protest, it was extremely difficult to control peacefully and it is not hard to see why the government considered it to be much more of a threat to its power than did the Western public. Similar situations in other developing countries produced similar responses from the government against mainly student protesters with similar loss of life and subsequent large-scale arrests – Mexico in 1968, Thailand in 1976 (Thannasat University) and South Korea in 1980 (Kwangju) come quickly to mind. In fact, in most developing countries such urban disturbances are met with state violence at a much earlier stage. In 'democratic' India, not only has the state killed many thousands of opponents of the regime (e.g. Naxalites in the 1960s, Sikhs in the 1980s) in major battles, but it has regularly attacked and killed smaller groups of protesters, showing little compunction about opening fire and rarely warranting even a footnote in the Western press.

3.3. *Economic Liberalisation and Social Tension*

Until the mid-1980s China's movement away from the Stalinist economy met with success on almost all sides. Increasingly in the second half of the 1980s the reforms ran into difficulties. After explosive growth in the early 1980s the agricultural growth rate fell to around its long-term trend rate, and grain production stagnated. To some degree this reflected difficulties in maintaining cooperative institutions, but, more importantly, it reflected the failure of the state to raise substantially the relative price of farm sales. The state was afraid that this would exacerbate urban discontent – the 'Polish problem' was never far from its mind.

Reform of state-owned industry proved much harder than the reform of agriculture and small-scale non-farm enterprises. Without a number of inter-connected changes state industry would not become more efficient, but these changes involved many problems. Without a 'hard budget constraint' it was hard to see how enterprise managers could be forced to act competitively. However, the threat of bankruptcy implied by this was extremely ominous for both workers and managers. In China, as in other 'socialist' countries, there was massive over-manning and a slow work pace. Workers in this sector formed an 'aristocracy of labour' with lifetime tenure, often jobs guaranteed for their children, labour insurance, housing provision, and other benefits. Although a Bankruptcy Law was, indeed, passed, it was hardly ever implemented for fear of the social consequences and large numbers of loss-making enterprises were kept afloat through state subsidies. To stimulate state enterprises to function more competitively required not only the 'stick' of the threat of bankruptcy, but also the 'carrot' of profits related to enterprise performance. It proved extremely difficult to prevent the local Party apparatus from taxing heavily those enterprises that earned high profits. A major justification for state intervention to tax away the profits of successful enterprises and subsidise loss-making ones was the continued distortion of prices which failed to bear much relationship to supply and demand, so that enterprise profits and losses could be argued to bear little relationship to efficiency. Reforming prices at a single stroke would have caused chaos. Instead, China opted for a 'dual track' system in which, for any given product, the part of output sold at free market prices would be gradually increased and the proportion sold at state fixed prices correspondingly reduced. Unfortunately, this is a system which strongly encourages corruption since the relevant proportions are determined by negotiation between the enterprise and the administrators.

In its desire to encourage better use of, and more interest in, raising budgetary revenue, the central authorities in the 1980s decentralised control over a large part of state revenue to local authorities. Unfortunately, the main interests of local authorities were parochial and short-term (in a rapidly-changing situation both their own positions and the system of budgetary decentralisation were uncertain). Consequently, there was a relative squeezing of state investment in areas of high long-term social returns such as large agricultural projects, education, transport and power supply. Not only did the structure of investment leave much to be desired, but the rate of investment remained extremely high. In the half-reformed economy, with the future uncertain, it made sense for state enterprises and local authorities to pressure banks to provide credit for as much construction as possible, upon which future employment and income streams would depend: 'investment hunger' remained deeply built in to the system.

One of the proud achievements of the post-1949 government was that there was an extremely stable price level. In the 1980s inflation reappeared to the great consternation of the leadership. Undoubtedly there were cost-push forces at work as the prices of formerly underpriced products were raised intentionally and the cost increases often passed on in higher prices of final products. However, ultimately prices can usually only rise generally if the money supply increases much faster than the rate of growth of real output. This is indeed what happened, with money supply accelerating to an average annual growth rate in the 1980s of over twice that of the growth rate of real output. This reflected a variety of political pressures. At the local level, it reflected the power of local Party officials to pressure banks to make loans. It reflected too the pressure on officials at all levels to supply funds to prevent enterprises going bankrupt and to subsidise urban women for those increases in urban food prices which did take place. The revenue share handed to the central government fell in the 1980s, while the budget deficit grew significantly in relation to total budgetary outlays.

Overall indicators of income distribution did not shift greatly in the 1980s but a considerable change in both ideology and occupancy of income positions took place. The sharp change in ideology from 'serve the people' to 'take the lead in getting rich' was profoundly de-stabilising. Although China still had a lot of state intervention to control income inequalities the leadership failed to provide a coherent ethic justifying both the existence of and the need for, limits on income inequalities. The appearance of high pre-tax incomes in certain areas and among certain groups of people caused great jealousy ('red eye disease') after long years of Maoist egalitarianism. More importantly the economic reforms provided considerable opportunities for corrupt incomes. This applied both at the local level, especially through the dual track price system, and in dealings with the international economy, in which well-placed officials and individuals in domestic companies could take advantage of the increased connections with the outside world filtered through a still heavily administered system in which market forces only partially operated. Moreover, as inflation began to bite in the late 1980s those on fixed incomes looked angrily upon those with flexible incomes, of which none were more flexible than those earned via corruption.

Few people with much knowledge of the Chinese scene did not appreciate that these difficulties were bubbling up in the 1980s. They form the backcloth to the massive debouchment of the urban population into the streets of China's major cities in May 1989. However, identification of this complex, inter-related set of problems and devising a feasible political-economic strategy for solving them is quite a different matter. The decisions that were needed, and still need to be taken are easy to state in economic terms: raise farm purchase substantially, impose a hard budget constraint upon enterprises, control the growth of the money supply, push steadily away from the dual track price system, remove the local Party apparatus from interference in enterprise affairs, shift the balance of investment towards projects with high long-term social returns, etc. However, behind each of these 'economic' policies lie great political difficulties. It is hard to see how 'more democracy' could have contributed to their solution. Indeed, a rapid move towards greater democracy in Western liberal terms might easily have made it less easy to enact some of the requisite policies. What was required at a minimum was firm, fair, and extremely clear-sighted leadership capable of explaining in great clarity to the Chinese people the difficulties of the second phase of the reforms. Unfortunately, China's aged leadership was not well-equipped for the Herculean task, Deng Xiaoping possessed the necessary credentials but his great age reduced his capacity to lead China successfully through the difficult transition period which might be of many years duration.

4. Prospects

Behind the Chinese Communist Party lies the People's Liberation Army. The vast popular demonstrations of May 1989 would not have happened if the leadership had been united and had early on either compromised with the students and/or opposed them forcefully. If the leadership has the will to continue to rule China in an authoritarian fashion, then it is most unlikely that they will be unable to do so. Should that be the case, what are the prospects? The choices are clear; the leadership can return to Stalinism, it can try to stand still, or it can attempt to push forward with the reforms.

The chances of a return to Stalinism are small. Even the most conservative, elderly group in the leadership, who were wheeled in from 'retirement' to defeat Zhao Ziyang, mostly support a combination of plan and market, rather than obliteration of markets. Moreover, it is debatable whether this group will really control economic policy in the immediate period ahead.

The most worrying, and also the most likely, scenario is that the whole system of political economy will mark time. The force of the urban demonstrations may well have reduced the freedom of manoeuvre of whoever rules China in the period ahead. If the Chinese leadership was afraid of the 'Polish problem' before May 1989, then it can be imagined that they will be much more so now. It seems even less likely in this atmosphere that the leadership will dare to risk the urban discontent that would stem from a sharp improvement for farmers of the internal terms of trade and of allowing state enterprises to go bankrupt, or that they would be able to risk the antagonism from local Party officials that would come from a sharp re-centralisation of budgetary powers.

Even control of the money supply may be at least as hard in the wake of June 4th as it was before it because of the array of vested interests that need to be tackled if this problem is to be solved. In the absence of measures to force enterprises to operate in a competitive environment or to control the money supply, pressing ahead with reform of the dual track price system would be extremely difficult to accomplish without great inflationary consequences. If the system which provided great opportunities for corruption was still in place only hard penal measures against those convicted of offences might control it. In the wake of June 4th the leadership desperately needs a united Party to support it. It seems most unlikely that it would dare to mount a serious assault on those very Party members to punish them severely for using their position to take advantage of the opportunities offered to earn corrupt incomes.

The outcome of this, the most likely scenario, is not that growth would cease. Strong forces for growth have been released in the 1980s which would continue to operate. International trade and foreign investment will not stop, though official capital flows may be reduced. However, growth would be unbalanced, with continuing problems in agriculture, infrastructure and large-scale industry, and it would be hard to control inflation. The same social tensions as in the late 1980s would exist, and they would be 'solved' through authoritarian state action. Given sufficient determination among the leadership, it would be unwise to believe that such a scenario could last for only a short period of time. Even Deng Xiaoping's death might not see the end of such a set-up. The photo of the newly 'elected' Standing Committee of the Politburo (*People's Daily*, 25 June 1989) shows not just its six members, but symbolically, in their centre stands Yang Shangkun: the connection between Party and Army is strong and will outlive Deng.

However, there is a third, more positive, scenario possible under continued authoritarian rule. The assumption that a regime which commits acts of violence against many of its citizens is incapable of taking difficult decisions necessary for rapid development is contradicted by many examples. In recent times, Brazil, Mexico, Indonesia, Thailand, South Korea and Taiwan, to name but a few, have all experienced rapid growth under authoritarian, repressive rule. It must be stressed that a large number of developing countries have had authoritarian rule, without rapid growth. The point of these observations is, simply, to suggest that, while this author does not believe it to be the most likely outcome, the possibility should not be discounted that even after June 4th, even with a great deal of discontent among the urban population, China may be able to tackle many of the problems that afflicted it in the late 1980s. It is conceivable that, emboldened by the head-on clash of June 4th, the economic and political crises of 1988-89 may force the leadership to take the kind of actions which few thinking people in China do not perceive as being necessary. It needs to publicly and honestly face up to the nature of the crisis. Ideally, it needs to present a credible and honest account of why the events of June 4th took place. It needs to construct a clear, transitional programme for the next five years, outlining the hardships that will be involved, explaining the likely costs and gains to different social interests involved in pressing ahead with economic reforms. It needs to construct an ethic for sharing the hardships of the transition period. None of this means establishing Western liberal democracy in China in the early 1990s. It means establishing, under continued one-Party rule, a coherent overall strategy of political economy for the difficult second phase of the economic reforms. Such a strategy which placed overall social interest in the first place would be the surest way to establish genuine popular support for the regime. One has, however, only to begin to explore these possibilities to realise how difficult it is likely to be. It means, effectively, changing the CCP from an administrative apparatus with a great deal of self-interest into a genuinely 'developmental state' with socialist values. In a time of national crisis, a comparably great transformation happened to the Kuomintang in its move from the mainland to Taiwan. Who in the 1930s could possibly have imagined that the corrupt, ramshackle regime of Chiang Kaishek could have been so transformed after 1949? Who could have imagined that a general, Chiang Kaishek, and his son, Chiang Chingkuo, who had studied in the USSR for 12 years and been the long time head of Taiwan's secret police, could have presided over Taiwan's extraordinarily successful marriage of plan and market – literally a 'planned free market economy' (*jihuaxing de ziyou jingji*) – whose success laid the material and cultural foundations for the eventual move out of martial law towards liberal democracy? In a time of great crisis too, this appears to have happened in Vietnam. In response to the virtual collapse of their economy, with its enormous development potential, the Vietnamese leadership purged its own ranks and pushed ahead in 1988-89 with a far-reaching set of reforms of the kind that China needs but has so far shied away from. Vietnam appears to have become the only reforming 'socialist' economy to have really imposed a 'hard budget constraint' upon enterprises and to have resisted the political pressures that lead to loss of control over the money supply.

It is, of course, possible to paint other possible scenarios, though they appear to this author to be much less likely than those outlined above. Although there is much rural discontent at farm purchase prices, local corruption and unredeemed state IOUs for farm purchase prices, it is unlikely that most of the Chinese peasantry would form a movement to topple the CCP from its monopoly of power. However, the main focus of political action, even in a developing country, is the cities. There is in the urban areas great popular cynicism about, and discontent with, the Party, especially in the wake of June 4th. It is not impossible that an event such as the death of Deng Xiaoping or the establishment of a democratically elected government in Hong Kong, could trigger renewed mass protests in mainland cities. The outcome of this might be a transition to multi-party democracy. More likely is a period of prolonged turbulence, in the last resort, perhaps even the fracturing of China into more or less autonomous regions. The latter set of outcomes would be worse for most Chinese people in fundamental ways than even the present situation. However, history doesn't work through rational, carefully-debated decision making, especially in developing countries. In the last resort even though it is far from likely, a new Chinese revolution against the Chinese Communist Party is not impossible.

5. Policies Towards China

There are loud calls for economic and cultural sanctions against China. Such calls must be very puzzling to the Chinese leadership. They have, even since 1976, committed violent acts against their own citizens with no response forthcoming from the West. Moreover, they must be surprised that they should be singled out for sanctions while exactly comparable events in Mexico, Thailand and South Korea, and not too dissimilar actions in India, Indonesia and elsewhere provoked little response. There is strong hypocrisy in those who call for sanctions against China today, but did not do so in these other cases. If one had applied rigorously the policy of sanctions against regimes that conducted violent acts against their own citizens of an order comparable with that in China in early June 1989, a large part of the developing world would at any point over the past 40 years have been cut off from the benefits of economic and cultural contacts with the advanced countries.

It might, however, be argued that sanctions should, indeed, have been applied in all such cases, or even that 'two wrongs don't make a right', and whatever happened in the past or in other cases, sanctions should be imposed today against China in a gesture of disgust at the leadership's barbarous behaviour. It is most important to argue these issues coolly and to separate a response which provides emotional catharsis to the citizens of developed countries from that which produces the best results for the mass of the citizens in the country which has committed barbarous acts. In this respect this author finds much to learn from the position of Mrs. Helen Susman, life-long opponent of both apartheid and of sanctions against South Africa.

It is, of course, hard to make sanctions work. The usual result is that they channel profits to one part of the international economy, that which is prepared to deal with the regime at the expense of those that are not. There are, however, stronger arguments against sanctions. The first priority in really poor countries is raising mass incomes for the direct improvement in welfare it provides. To the degree that sanctions work and prevent that goal being achieved, this author opposes them. Moreover, the best way to attain a truly democratic society is through raising income levels in the wake of which people will tend much more to wish to take the affairs of their country into their own hands. Broadly speaking, the more that international capital, labour and knowledge contribute to modernisation the stronger also will such developments be. Arguments could have been convincingly made to impose sanctions against Thailand, South Korea, Taiwan and, even, Singapore, in the past 25 years. Had they been imposed and been effective, it is most unlikely that the mass of the citizens of these countries would be enjoying as high a standard of living as they do today or have made so much progress towards democracy.

Xenophobic nationalism is, probably, a stronger force in China than in most developing countries. The barbarous acts of June 4th should be condemned loudly and clearly, in the same way as previous barbarities in China and elsewhere should have been condemned but too often were not. However, economic and cultural isolation of China would be likely to retard development and to reinforce domestic repression with a regime buoyed in such actions by the external hostility. It is not a coincidence that many of the most repressive episodes in modern world history (e.g. the USSR under Stalin, China in the Cultural Revolution, Kampuchea under Pol Pot, North Korea under Kim Il Sung) have occurred in countries isolated from the civilising effects of contact with the international community.

Notes

1.   This paper was written shortly after the Tiananmen events of June 1989. Parts of it were published in a variety of different publications.

Chapter 2

THE GLOBAL BUSINESS REVOLUTION AND DEVELOPING COUNTRIES

Peter Nolan, Jin Zhang and Chunhang Liu

1. Contrasting Views on Globalisation and Industrial Structure

The nature and determinants of industrial structure are among the most important issues in economics. In the history of economics, there have been radically contrasting views on the basic determinants of industrial structure. For most of the twentieth century, industrial structure was heavily influenced by state industrial policy. Since the 1980s, the end of communist central planning and of inward-looking development strategies in poor countries, together with widespread privatisation and liberalisation, ushered in the epoch of 'globalisation'.[1] This provides an opportunity to test the validity of the competing views of the determinants of industrial structure under free market conditions.

There is a substantial empirical literature analysing the nature and determinants of industrial structure prior to the epoch of modern 'globalisation'.[2] However, there is still a dearth of empirical analysis of the nature and causes of the trends in industrial structure in the epoch of globalisation, and of the implications of these trends for both theory and policy. The assembly and interpretation of evidence on this issue is critical for understanding the current epoch.

1.1. Mainstream View

The 'mainstream', 'neo-classical' view of the competitive process believes that the perfectly competitive model best describes the essence of capitalist competition. Departures from it are viewed as exceptional and typically arising from government intervention, including protection and nationalisation. At the heart of the mainstream view is the self-equilibrating mechanism of market competition. It is believed that the basic driver of the capitalist process, competition, ensures that if any firm enjoys super-normal profits rivals will soon enter to bid away those profits and undermine any temporary market dominance that the incumbent enjoys. The neo-classical approach emphasises the importance of competition among small firms as the explanation for the prosperity of the advanced economies. Milton Friedman, for example, believed that there is 'a general bias and tendency to overemphasise the importance of the big versus the small': 'As I have studied economic activities in the United States, I have become increasingly impressed with how wide is the range of problems and industries that can be treated as if they were competitive' (Friedman, 1962:120-3).

Mainstream economists tend to believe that managerial diseconomies of scale set in after firms reach a certain size. The classic expression of this view was contained in Marshall's *Principles of Economics*:

> [H]ere we may read a lesson from the young trees of the forest as they struggle upwards through the benumbing shade of their older rivals. Many succumb on the way, and a few only survive: those few become stronger with every year, they get a larger share of light and air with every increase of their height, and at last in their turn they tower above their neighbours, and seem as though they would grow on for ever and for ever become stronger as they grow. But they do not. One tree will last longer in full vigour and attain a greater size than another; but sooner or later age tells on them all. Though the taller ones have a better access to light and air than their rivals, they gradually lose vitality; and one after another they give place to others, which though of less material strength, have on their side the vigour of youth...[I]n almost every trade there is a constant rise and fall of large businesses, at any one moment some firm being in the ascending phase and others in the descending (Marshall, 1920: 315-6).

Despite the fact that during the epoch of globalisation, mergers and acquisitions have reached new heights,[3] it is widely argued that global concentration levels have not increased.[4] It is observed that there is a high rate of disappearance of companies from the *Fortune 500* (Wolf, 2004: 226). Based mainly on the analysis of shareholder returns, mainstream economists believe that mergers and acquisitions mostly fail.[5] The explanation that is usually advanced for mergers and acquisitions is the pursuit of power and wealth by CEOs, who are alleged to pursue their own interests at the expense of shareholders, rather than industrial logic. It is argued also that in the epoch of globalisation markets have become so large that it is hard for any firm or small group of firms to dominate a given sector.

In recent years, the argument has gained ground that advances in information technology have created the possibility for a radical change in the nature of the firm. Activities that it was formerly rational to carry out within the firm can now be performed by networks of small firms connected by the internet (Castells, 2000). This is widely thought to herald the rise of a new form of 'Post-Fordist' economic system based around 'clusters' of small businesses that can both compete and cooperate at different times (Piore and Sabel, 1984; Porter, 1990). This view appears to be strongly reinforced by the rapid rise in the extent of outsourcing activities that were formerly carried on within the firm. In Coasian terms (Coase, 1988) the boundaries of the firm have shifted. Many researchers argue that the large corporation is being 'hollowed out', and rapidly becoming an 'endangered species': 'While big companies control ever larger flows of cash, they are exerting less and less direct control over business activity. They are, you might say, growing hollow' (Malone and Laubacher, 1998: 147).

The spread of global markets has greatly reinforced the belief that 'catch-up' at the level of the firm is the normal path of capitalist development. In this view, there are limitless opportunities for firms from developing countries to 'catch-up' if they compete on the free market of the 'global level playing field'. This view is expressed powerfully in Thomas Friedman's book (Friedman, 2005), *The World is Flat*: 'The explosion of advanced technologies now means that suddenly, knowledge pools and resources have connected all over the planet, levelling the playing field as never before, so that each of us is potentially an equal – and competitor – of each other' (Friedman, 2005).[6] The view that the 'World is Flat' is strongly reinforced by the explosive growth of China during the epoch of globalisation. The world is widely thought to have become 'flat' for individuals, countries and firms from developing countries, due to liberalisation, privatisation and the information technology revolution.

1.2. Non-Mainstream View

From the earliest stages in the development of modern capitalism, there were economists who believed that capitalism contained an inherent tendency towards industrial concentration. Marx, in *Capital* Vol. 1, argued that there was a 'law of centralisation of capital' or the 'attraction of capital by capital'. The driving force of concentration was competition itself, which pressured firms to cheapen the cost of production by investing ever larger amounts of capital in new means of production and in 'the technological application of science', which in turn creates barriers to entry. In the early 1970s, on the eve of the modern epoch of globalisation Hymer (1972) visualised the possible outcome of the capitalist process if existing restrictions on merger and acquisition were lifted:

> Suppose giant multinational corporations (say 300 from the United States and 200 from Europe and Japan) succeed in establishing themselves as the dominant form of international enterprise and come to control a significant share of industry (especially modern industry) in each country. The world economy will resemble more and more the United States economy, where each of the large corporations tends to spread over the entire continent, and to penetrate almost every nook and cranny (Hymer, 1972).

In fact, Marshall's *Principles of Economics* provides numerous reasons to explain 'the advantages that a large business of almost any kind, nearly always has over a small one' (Marshall, 1920: 282). These included economies in procurement, transport costs, marketing, branding, distribution, knowledge, human resources, and management (Marshall, 1920: 282-4). By contrast, his explanation of 'managerial diseconomies of scale' resorts to an analogy ('the trees in the forest') without logic or evidence.

Penrose's path-breaking book, *The Theory of the Growth of the Firm,* addresses directly the issue of possible limits to the growth of the firm. Like Marshall, she identifies a number of potential advantages that can be enjoyed by the large firm (Penrose, 1995: 89-92). She considers that the most significant advantages for the large firm are those that she terms 'managerial economies'. Penrose concludes that there are no theoretical limits to the size of the firm: 'We have found nothing to prevent the indefinite expansion of firms as time passes, and clearly if some of the economies of size are economies of expansion, there is no reason to assume that a firm would ever reach a size in which it has taken full advantage of all these economies' (Penrose, 1995: 99).

Chandler has demonstrated the central role of the large, oligopolistic firm in technical progress in the business history of today's high-income countries. This was, in its turn, central to the whole growth dynamic of modern capitalism. He has shown that the modern industrial enterprise 'played a central role in creating the most technologically advanced, fastest growing industries of their day'. These industries, in turn, were 'the pace-setters of the industrial sector of their economies'. They provided an underlying dynamic in the development of modern industrial capitalism (Chandler, 1990: 593). Chandler emphasises the paradox that even as the number of firms in a given sector shrinks, competition between increasingly powerful firms can intensify: 'market share and profits changed constantly, which kept oligopolies from becoming stagnant and monopolistic' (Chandler and Hikino, 1997: 31).

The succession of studies which purport to show the irrationality of mergers and acquisitions is almost entirely based on the analysis of the consequences for shareholder value in the short term. The much smaller number of studies which analyse the long-term impact of mergers and acquisitions on business survival and growth show a different story (Chandler, 1990; Nolan, 2001a and 2001b; Boston Consulting Group, 2004). They suggest, rather, that well-selected and well-executed mergers and acquisitions that have a clear strategic purpose can increase the business capability of the firm concerned. They can strengthen the firm's presence in given geographical markets, increase their access to technologies they formerly did not posses, acquire scarce human resources, add valuable brands to their portfolio, and enable long-term savings through economies of scale and scope in procurement, research and development, and marketing.

2. The Evidence: The Global Business Revolution[7]

This section examines four sectors in order to see the degree to which there are common patterns of industrial concentration across a wide range of industries. At one extreme is the commercial aircraft industry. A single large commercial aircraft costs over US$ 200 million. At the other extreme is the soft drink industry. A single serving of a soft drink or a beer costs only around one dollar. In between are the automobile and telecommunications industries. Between them they comprise a large segment of modern economies, and embrace a wide range of technologies.[8]

2.1. Aerospace[9]

Large commercial aircraft and advanced military aerospace equipment contain bundles of the world's most advanced technologies. The design, assembly, marketing and upgrading of this equipment embodies powerful economies of scale and scope. The design of a new aircraft requires enormous investments with significant up-front costs during the launch stage. While the cost of failure is high, so is the reward for success. A successful new plane can lock up its chosen market segment for over twenty years, producing sales of US$ 25-40 billion and huge profits. Due to the 'bet-the-firm' nature of new aircraft launches, every new aircraft design therefore requires rigorous market analysis based upon the company's deep knowledge of its customers. The industry has large economies of scale in assembly, which come from spreading planning efforts and high tooling costs over large outputs of one type of aircraft. There are economies achieved through learning effects, obtained in the course of producing more units of a given aircraft model. Having a family of aircraft with common platforms enables the manufacturer to spread given R&D outlays over a larger number of aircraft, and to obtain economies of scale in procurement of components, and to achieve large operating benefits for customers. Branding is critical in the aerospace industry. A large installed base itself is the best demonstration of product reliability, operating efficiency and technology leadership.

By the late 1960s, the United States' commercial aeroplane industry had reduced to just three main producers: Boeing, McDonnell Douglas, and Lockheed. The competitive pressure from Boeing on its rivals was intense. By the mid-1990s, Lockheed had ceased production of the Tristar and McDonnell Douglas was in deep financial difficulties in its commercial aeroplane division. In 1997 came the path-breaking merger of Boeing and McDonnell Douglas. Following the merger Boeing accounted for over four-fifths of the world's total commercial aircraft in service. From the 1950s to the 1970s, there were several European companies each manufacturing large jet airliners (by the standards of the time).[10] By the late 1960s it was apparent that none of them was able to compete with Boeing. In 1970, France and Germany decided to join forces to build a family of large commercial aeroplanes that could challenge Boeing's dominance, and preserve a wide array of high technology supplier industries within Europe. They were later joined by Britain and Spain. Without massive support from the respective governments, Airbus could never have become established. By the early 2000s, Airbus had overtaken Boeing in the market for large commercial aircraft. The two companies are now locked in head-to-head duopolistic rivalry. Boeing has staked much of its future on the medium-sized 787 ('Dreamliner'), while Airbus has done the same with the super-large A380. The USSR possessed a highly sophisticated aerospace industry that produced thousands of large jet passenger planes.[11] If the USSR had followed a suitable path of system reform, the Soviet aircraft industry could have become a formidable challenger to the West's leading companies in both civilian and military sectors (Nolan, 1995). Today, the industry is in ruins.[12]

The systems integrators, Airbus and Boeing, have huge procurement budgets, totalling more than US$ 29 billion annually in Boeing's case. They focus increasingly on coordinating and planning the supply chain, rather than direct manufacture. As much as 60-80 per cent of the end-product value of aerospace products is now derived from the external supply network (Murman et al, 2002: 18). Airbus pioneered the concept of final assembly of large sub-systems.

However, Boeing has taken the lead over Airbus in reorganising its supply chain. In each aircraft programme, Boeing selects risk-sharing partners that develop and design important subsystems of the aircraft. These require massive R&D investments. Boeing's top suppliers invest hundreds of millions of dollars on R&D annually and they own increasing amounts of the intellectual property embedded in the aircraft. As aircraft technology becomes more complex and the cost pressure increases, the systems integrators have pushed more development and design activities down the supply chain to their subsystems integrators.

In 2000, Boeing started to implement the Toyota Production System (TPS), converting its production system from batch processes to assembly line processes. TPS requires just-in-time delivery of parts, which in turn called for changes in suppliers' operations. In 1999, Boeing centralised the procurement function and radically pruned the number of suppliers. Between 2000 and 2005, it reduced direct suppliers from 3600 to 1200. In the supplier structure for the new B787, Boeing deals directly with just seven or eight first tier suppliers. The reduction in the number of direct suppliers allows Boeing to form closer collaboration with its direct suppliers and maintain tight control over the aircraft design and assembly as technology and cost requirements continue to increase.

They way in which Airbus and Boeing reorganised the institutional structure of the supply chain in order to reduce the number of suppliers and nurture large-scale subsystems integrators constitutes a form of industrial policy, with the systems integrators picking and nurturing 'winners'. They each penetrate deeply into their respective supply chain. Surrounding each of them is an 'external firm' in which control by the core systems integrator extends across the boundary of the legally-owned entity: 'If we are to succeed in the face of increasing global competition and greater demands for cost improvements from our customers, then *our entire extended enterprise* must operate under Lean principles and a Lean philosophy.' (Mike Sears, former Boeing CFO)(Sears, 2001).

In order to meet the demands of the systems integrators, the major subsystem and key component suppliers themselves need to invest heavily in research and development, and to expand in order to benefit from cost reduction through economies of scale and scope. A powerful merger movement has taken place at all levels of the supply chain and the level of concentration in the upper reaches of the aircraft industry supply chain has increased rapidly. Through continuous merging and acquiring 'core businesses' that meet their strategic goals, and through divesting 'non-core businesses' in order to 'upgrade' their asset portfolio, a group of giant subsystems integrators have established or strengthened their competitive position in businesses covering one or more aircraft subsystems. All of these suppliers are headquartered in, and have their main production facilities in, developed countries, especially the United States. Leaders in their respective industries, all of them are global giants themselves with billions of dollars in revenues and large R&D outlays (Table 1). They dominate every major subsystem of the aircraft.

Table 1. Leading Aerospace Subsystems Integrators

Company	Revenues (2005, US$ billion)	R&D spending (2004-05, US$ million)
GE	157.2	2961
of which: GE aero engines	11.0	n.a.
United Technologies	42.7	1203
of which: Aerospace division	15.0	n.a.
Honeywell	28.9	478
BAE Systems	20.2	2042
Finnemeccanica	15.1	1893
Thales	13.4	569
Rolls-Royce	10.9	519
Snecma	8.9	980
Smiths	5.1	252
Goodrich	4.5	237
Rockwell Collins	2.8	210
Cobham	1.5	90

Sources: *Fortune*, 31 July 2006 and DTI, 2005

Engines are by far the most expensive aircraft subsystem, requiring enormous development costs and R&D outlays. There are now only three engine makers that are able to produce large modern jet aircraft engines that meet the continuously advancing demands of Boeing and Airbus. These are GE, Rolls-Royce, and United Technologies (Pratt & Whitney). Aircraft structures are dominated by a handful of companies, including Vought Aircraft (which is the sole supplier of major structures for the B747), BAE Systems (which is the sole supplier of wings for Airbus), Finnemeccanica (Alenia), Mitsubishi Heavy Industries, Fuji Heavy Industries and Kawasaki Heavy Industries. Honeywell is by far the most powerful firm in the supply of avionics systems, including communication and navigation systems, flight instrument systems, flight management systems, as well as traffic alert and collision avoidance technologies. It is also at the forefront of power distribution, pneumatic and landing systems. Honeywell was selected to supply the core avionics systems for both the A380 and the B787. Smiths Industries, Goodrich, and Rockwell

Collins are major competitors in the supply of avionics and other control systems. Each of them supplies subsystems to both Boeing and Airbus, and each has positions on both the A380 and B787. The supply of landing gear, wheel and braking systems is dominated by Snecma's Messier-Bugati and Messier-Dowty subsidiaries, and by Goodrich. Each of these supplies complete landing subsystems to both Boeing and Airbus. Between them they have close to 80 per cent of the global market for brakes on commercial aircraft (company websites).

Even the smaller subsystems on the large aeroplanes are dominated by a small number of powerful subsystems integrators. The wiring systems on large commercial aircraft are immensely complex. Snecma (through its subsidiary Labinal) is the world leader in the supply of wiring systems. It supplies the main part of the wiring systems for both the A380 and the B787. Jamco is sole supplier to Boeing for aircraft lavatories. Meggitt supplies the fire and smoke detectors for almost all large commercial aircraft. Recaro and B/E Aerospace account for most of the market for seats on large commercial aircraft. Many critically important components and materials are supplied by specialist aerospace divisions of giant global firms. Michelin, Goodyear and Bridgestone are the only firms capable of supplying tyres for large commercial aircraft. Saint-Gobain is the sole supplier of aircraft glass to Airbus. Alcoa and Alcan account for most of the world's supply of aluminium for aircraft assembly. Each A380 will use around one million Alcoa 'lockbolts'.

2.2. Automobiles

The global stock of automobiles has grown from around 150 million in 1950 to around 800 million in 2000, and is predicted to rise to around 1600 million in 2030 (DaimlerChrysler, 2005). In 1960 there were forty-two independent automobile assemblers in the 'Triad' regions of North America, Western Europe and Japan. By 2005, that number had shrunk to just twelve firms, through an intensive process of merger and acquisition. The top five auto assemblers now account for 58 per cent of total automobile output in the Triad regions and the top ten account for 83 cent of total vehicle output (DaimlerChrysler, 2005). Even the leading automobile firms face threats to their survival arising from the intensity of oligopolistic competition.

To survive in this ferocious competition, the leading assemblers must spend large amounts on R&D, in order to make vehicles lighter in weight, and to improve fuel efficiency, safety, durability and reliability. Each of the main automobile assemblers spends between US$ 2-8 billion annually on R&D (DTI, 2005). They also each spend several billion dollars each year on building their brands. They each spend several tens of billions of dollars annually on procurement of materials and components. GM, for example, has an annual procurement spend of around US$ 80 billion. As the leading automobile assemblers have grown in terms of the scope and size of their markets since the 1970s, so also has the intensity of pressure they have imposed upon their supply chains. The pressure upon suppliers is felt most visibly in terms of price. The price pressure on North American assemblers has been so intense in recent years, that several of them have become large loss makers and entered bankruptcy under Chapter 11.

However, the relationship is far from arms length. There is a deep interaction between the direction of the core strategic suppliers' R&D and the needs of the assemblers. The leading auto assemblers have put intense pressure on leading components suppliers to invest large amounts in R&D to meet the assemblers' needs. The fourteen giant components suppliers in the *Fortune 500* have an average annual R&D spend of over US$ 1 billion, and the industry leaders, Bosch, Delphi and Denso, each spends over US$ 2 billion on R&D (DTI, 2005). The assemblers have selected a group of powerful subsystem integrator firms, that are able to partner them in their global expansion: 'We're looking for the top suppliers to help us grow in the market place. As we grow, they will grow with us' (GM website). The leading auto assemblers work together to plan the supplier firm's investment in new production locations close to the assemblers. Leading components suppliers such as Bosch, Delphi, Valeo, and Michelin, each have more than a hundred production plants across the world, close at hand to the assembly plants.

The strategic suppliers themselves are deepening their relationship with their own suppliers beyond a simple price relationship. For example, Delphi, is developing a group of its own seventy to eighty key 'strategic suppliers': 'These are the suppliers we'd like to grow with, they understand our cost models, where we are going, and being increasingly willing to put more of their research and development and engineering money behind projects for us' (*FT*, 30 June 2003).

The auto components industry has been through a dramatic transition during the past two decades, under intense pressure from the 'cascade effect'. The number of components makers expanded from an estimated 20 000 in 1950 to over 40 000 in 1970. However, by 1990 the number had fallen to under 30 000. During the epoch of revolutionary growth and consolidation of the vehicle assemblers, the number of components makers shrank to fewer than 5000 in 2000, and is predicted to fall still further, to fewer than 3000 by 2015 (DaimlerChrysler, 2005).

A handful of components makers have emerged, mainly through merger and acquisition, to dominate the upper reaches of the auto components supply chain. The combined revenues of the fourteen giant auto components firms in the *Fortune* 500 amounts to a total of around US$ 291 billion (*Fortune*, 31 July 2006), which amounts to around 55-60 per cent of the total estimated spending by the auto assemblers on procurement.[13] In each segment of the vehicle, a handful of subsystems integrators, each with their own supply chains, dominate the global market. For example, three firms (Michelin, Bridgestone and Goodyear) account for 55 per cent of total world production of auto tires (*FT*, 6 June 2006); three firms (Asahi, Saint-Gobain and NSG) account for 75 per cent of the world output of auto glass (Pilkington, 2005); three firms (GKN, NTN and Delphi) account for 75 per cent of the global market for constant velocity joints (GKN and NTN, *Annual Reports*, 2005); two firms (Bosch and Delphi) account for around three-quarters of the world's production of diesel fuel injection pumps (*Ward's Auto World*, January 2000); two firms (Johnson Controls and Lear) account for over one-half of all the automobile seat systems supplied to auto assemblers in Europe and North America (Lear and Johnson Controls websites, 2006); and two firms (Bosch and Continental) account for around 50 per cent of the global total of ABS/ESC[14] brake systems (Continental and Forbes, websites, 2005).

In addition, the pressure from the cascade effect has been a major stimulus for the high-speed consolidation in the steel industry, and, to a lesser extent in the aluminium industry. Following their merger, in 2006 ArcelorMittal accounted for an estimated 26 per cent of the total global production of automotive steel, and the top five firms (ArcelorMittal, Nippon Steel, JFE, US Steel, and ThyssenKrupp) accounted for 54 per cent of global auto steel production (Mittal, 2006). In the aluminium industry, the top five firms (United Company Rusal, Alcoa, Alcan, Chalco and Hydro) now account for 44 per cent of total global production, and the top ten for 57 per cent (*FT*, 31 August 2006).

2.3. Telecommunications

Privatisation and liberalisation of the telecommunications services industry in the 1990s unleashed a wave of international expansion and consolidation. A small group of super-large telecomms services companies emerged from this process. By 2005, the top ten telecomms firms had revenues of between US$ 35 billion and US$ 95 billion. They were all headquartered in high-income economies. They had mainly built extensive international operations. Where permitted, they had participated heavily in the acquisition of formerly state-owned telecomms assets in developing and former communist countries.[15] The giant telecomms firms benefited from advantages of scale, through their ability to build global brands, offer global services, and lower costs through large procurement budgets. The leading telecomms firms such as NTT, Verizon, Deutsche Telekom and Vodafone have annual procurement budgets of US$ 15-25 billion. Their intimate knowledge of the final customer helped to place them in a position to integrate their supply chains in order to meet their needs.

Alongside the transformation of the telecomms services industry, the telecomms equipment industry experienced high-speed institutional change in the 1990s. Under intense pressure to meet the technical demands of the telecomms service providers, with their enormous procurement budgets, the telecomms equipment industry witnessed intense consolidation as the industry leaders sought increased scale, in order especially to increase their R&D capability both through direct spending and the acquisition of smaller companies with specialist technical knowledge. By 2002, the top ten telecomms equipment makers, all with their headquarters in the high-income countries, accounted for 57 per cent of the total global telecomms equipment market (Xing, 2004). In the mobile handsets market, which only emerged as a mass market in the late 1990s, the sector is already highly concentrated. In 2006, the top five firms in the sector, all with headquarters in the high-income countries, accounted for 81 per cent of the global market, and the top two alone (Nokia and Motorola) account for 56 per cent of the global market (*FT*, 29 September 2006).

Institutional change in the industry entered a new phase in 2005-06, stimulated by technical change. New technologies have created the possibility for 'convergent' services that offer a combination of 'triple play', including video, voice and data, which can be provided by broadband and include VoiP ('voice-over-the-internet protocol' telephony). The new technologies have created the possibility for a new form of telecommunications firm providing all these services in a combined 'bundled' package to customers. The telecomms industry is being restructured at high speed, with fixed line, mobile, cable, satellite, internet and media companies all participating in the 'convergent' institutional restructuring of the industry. This places intense pressure on the telecomms equipment makers to meet the needs for 'converged technologies' of the giant telecomms services companies in the new epoch of telecommunications: 'Equipment suppliers are being forced to offer end-to-end solutions to a consolidating base of carrier customers that are in the middle of major network transformations...As carrier consolidation continues to drive increased vendor instability, existing players will need to seek merger and partnership opportunities to compete within the new market structure' (*FT*, 7 April 2006).

In 2005-06 a new round of industry consolidation was unleashed among the telecomms equipment makers in order to meet the intense pressure to supply new converged technologies. In rapid succession, Cisco acquired Scientific Atlanta, Ericsson acquired Marconi, Alcatel merged with Lucent, and Nokia and Siemens merged their telecomms equipment divisions. Following the hectic round of mergers and acquisitions, the top three firms in the sector (Ericsson/Marconi, Nokia/Siemens, and Alcatel/Lucent) accounted for 75 per cent of total global sales of wireless telecomms equipment (*Communications Weekly*, 26 June 2006), and were poised to dominate the epoch of convergent technologies. The top five telecomms equipment makers each spend US$ 2-5 billion on R&D, amounting to between 10-17 per cent of their revenue (DTI, 2005).

Pressure from the cascade effect in the telecomms industry does not end with the leading telecomms equipment suppliers. Semiconductors are a critically important part of the technical progress in the equipment industry, just as they are in the computer and consumer electronics industries. The level of industrial concentration in the industry is high. The leading semiconductor firms typically supply products for the whole range of industries using their products, enabling them to benefit from 'economies of scope' in applying new technologies across several closely-related sectors. The top ten firms, all with headquarters in the high-income countries, account for 49 per cent of the total global market for semiconductors (*DigiTimes.com*, March 2006). However, within individual subsectors, the level of industrial concentration is even higher. Meeting the needs of the world's leading telecomms equipment makers necessitates large scale and a high level of spending on R&D. In the supply of integrated circuits to the wireless telecommunications industry, the top five firms accounted for 44 per cent of total global sales revenue in the sector in 2005, and the top ten firms, all with headquarters in the high-income countries, for 65 per cent (*IC Insights*, 16 November 2005).

The impact of the cascade effect penetrates even deeper down the industry supply chain. The manufacture of silicon wafers has witnessed high-speed consolidation as the firms in the sector struggle with the large capital costs and high level of R&D spending required to meet the exacting demands of the semiconductor makers. Following the latest round of industrial concentration in the sector, the top two firms in the sector, one American and one Japanese, account for 63 per cent of total global revenue in the sector (*FT*, 21 September 2006). The sector supplying the equipment to manufacture semiconductors is even more highly concentrated. The leading firm in the sector, Dutch-based ASML, accounts for 57 of global sales in the sector (*FT*, 19 January 2006).

2.4. Beverages[16]

Since the 1980s, the global beverage industry has witnessed high-speed consolidation. In the carbonated soft drinks sector, just two firms now account for around three-quarters of total global sales. In the broader category of non-alcoholic drinks, just five firms account for over one-half of the global market. The beer industry lags some way behind, but the trend towards consolidation is clear, with the emergence of super-large global firms, such as Anheuser-Busch, SABMiller, and InBev.[17] The closely-related food industry has undergone its own process of consolidation, resulting in the emergence of a group of super-large international firms, such as Nestlé, Unilever and Sara Lee. The beverage and food industry are both experiencing intensifying pressure from the emergence of giant retailers, such as Wal-Mart, Metro, Carrefour, and Tesco.[18]

The massive procurement expenditure on material inputs and services by the world's leading beverage producers has increased the pressure for consolidation from the higher reaches of the supply chain. In many areas, the cascade effect pressures on the supply chain from the beverage industry are applied simultaneously by the food industry. This cascade effect has stimulated a wave of consolidation in the beverage industry's supply chain. Moreover, as the higher reaches of the supply chain have struggled to meet the global needs of the world's leading beverage companies, the process of consolidation within their ranks has produced further 'cascade' pressure on the supply chain of these firms, as they struggle to lower costs, and achieve the technical progress necessary to meet the fierce demands of the world's leading system integrators who stand at the centre of their respective supply chains.

The global consumer packaging industry is a huge industry, worth about US$ 300 billion annually. The top ten global packaging firms account for between 40 and 80 per cent of global markets, depending on the sector. The world's leading beverage firms interact closely with the leaders of the packaging industry to work together for ways to meet their needs better through innovations in product and process technologies. Key pressures on the packaging industry have included cost and weight reduction, improved customer safety, increased product life and enhanced appearance. Technical progress has also been achieved through contributions from the primary material suppliers in the aluminium, steel, PET resin industries, as well as in the suppliers of machinery. The world's leading beverage firms have interacted with this process at every step, acting as 'systems integrators' for the overall process of technical progress, and nurturing institutional change so that leading suppliers have sufficient scale to meet the beverage companies' strict requirements.

Over 200 billion beverage cans are consumed annually. Since the late 1980s, the world's metal can industry has rapidly consolidated. Three firms now stand out as the global industry leaders,[19] with a combined global market share of 57 per cent (FT, 2 November 2005). The metal can industry is a major consumer of both aluminium and steel, and places intense pressure on the steel and aluminium industries to achieve technical progress, improve product quality and lower costs. The other major users of primary metals have also consolidated at high speed during the global business revolution, including the automobile, aerospace, construction and household durable goods industries. They also place intense pressure on the steel and aluminium industries, which have experienced intense consolidation. The top five firms produce 44 per cent of total world production of aluminium (*FT*, 31 August 2006), and an even higher share of the aluminium sheet for beverage cans. In the steel industry, leading steel firms focus on high value-added, high technology products for global customers, including steel for beverage cans. Although the top ten firms account for 'only' around 27 per cent of total global output by weight, following the merger of Arcelor and Mittal Steel, they account for around three-fifths of total global sales revenue from the steel industry (Nolan and Rui, 2004).

Glass bottles are still the main form of primary packaging in the beer industry, and, despite its relative decline, the glass bottle remains an important form of packaging for soft drinks, especially in developing countries. Following successive rounds of merger and acquisition in the 1990s, the glass bottle industry has become highly consolidated. The two super-giants of the industry (Owens-Illinois and Saint-Gobain) now account for around 68 per cent of total glass bottle production in Europe and North America (Owens-Illinois and Saint-Gobain, *Annual Reports*). Between them they produce more than 60 billion glass bottles annually.

PET (plastic) bottles were developed in the late 1960s, and quickly became the most important form of primary packaging in the soft drinks industry, though they still have a less important place in the beer industry. In recent years the industry has become increasingly concentrated. By 2003, excluding the production by beverage companies for self-consumption, the top four firms accounted for almost two-thirds of the total production of PET bottles in both North America and Europe. Much of the technical progress in the PET bottle industry has been achieved by the specialist machine builders, which make two different types of machinery, namely 'pre-forms' and the equipment that 'blows' the pre-forms into their final bottle form. Each of these sectors is dominated by specialist high technology firms. One firm alone (Husky) accounts for around three-quarters of the total global market for high volume PET injection machines (Husky, *Annual Reports*), while another specialist firm (Sidel)[20] has a near monopoly on the purchase of advanced blowing equipment by the world's leading beverage companies.

In the supply of beverage filling line equipment, the high value-added, high technology segments of the market supplying the world's leading beverage companies are dominated by just two firms (KHS and Krones), the product of remorseless M&A, which together account for almost nine-tenths of global sales of high-speed beverage bottling lines (KHS and Krones, *Annual Reports*). The world's leading beverage companies have bought machines almost exclusively from these two companies because of their high levels of reliability, low operating costs, high speed, more consistent filling height, and low rates of damage to bottles and product. Each of them spends heavily on research and development.

The advertising and communication sector, which is crucial for branding global businesses, has witnessed intense M&A activity, alongside the global expansion of their main customers. The world's top ten spenders each spend an average of US$ 2-3 billion per company annually. They account for a large share of the revenues of the leading advertising and marketing firms. In addition, the advertising and communication companies must engage with increasingly powerful global media companies, such as Disney, News International, Time Warner, and Viacom, with which they place their products. The advertising and communication industry has become polarised into a small number of immensely powerful firms and a large number of small firms. By 2001, the top four firms in the sector[21] accounted for almost three-fifths of total global advertising revenue.

The world's leading beverage companies are among the largest purchasers of trucks.[22] Their truck fleets are enormous, amounting to hundreds of thousands of trucks for the industry leaders. The world's leading truck manufacturers experience intense pressure from their global customers to lower costs and improve technologies. This intensifies the pressure to increase scale in order to achieve greater volume of procurement and push down costs across their own value chains, including suppliers of truck components (engines, brake systems, tyres, exhaust systems, seats, informatics, and ventilation systems) and materials (steel, aluminium and plastics). Greater scale also enables them to achieve faster technical progress through economies of scope (coordinated technical progress that can be used in different divisions of the company), in order to provide the customer with more reliability, lower fuel costs, greater safety and more effective ability to meet pollution control requirements. Since the 1980s, industrial concentration in the truck industry has greatly increased. By the late 1990s, the world's top five truck makers accounted for one-half of total global sales in terms of the number of units sold (DaimlerChrysler, 2005) but an even higher share of the total market value, as the leading truck companies tended to produce far higher technology vehicles. In 2003 industry leader Daimler-Chrysler's truck division alone had revenues of US$ 36 billion and operating profits of US$ 1.1 billion, and spent US$ 1.3 billion on research and development.

3. Interpreting the Evidence

3.1. Systems Integrators

The period of the global business revolution has witnessed massive asset restructuring, with firms extensively selling off 'non-core businesses' in order to develop their 'core businesses' and upgrade their asset portfolio. The goal for most large firms became the maintenance or establishment of their position as one of the handful of top companies in the global market-place. Although the intensity abated in the wake of the collapse of the late 1990s stock market bubble, the merger and acquisition process has continued at a high level in recent years. An unprecedented degree of industrial concentration has been established among leading firms in sector after sector. By the 1980s, there was already a high degree of industrial concentration within many sectors of the individual high-income countries (Pratten, 1971, Prais, 1981). However, the global business revolution saw for the first time the emergence of widespread industrial concentration across all high-income countries, as well as extending deeply into large parts of the developing world.

By the early 2000s, within the high value-added, high technology, and/or strongly branded segments of global markets, which serve mainly the middle and upper income earners who control the bulk of the world's purchasing power, a veritable 'law' had come into play: a handful of giant firms, the 'systems integrators', occupied upwards of 50 per cent of the whole global market.[23]

3.2. Cascade Effect

The process of concentration through simultaneous de-merger of non-core businesses and merger of core businesses is cascading across the value chain at high speed. In sector after sector, leading firms, with powerful technologies and marketing capabilities, actively select the most capable among their numerous suppliers, in a form of 'industrial planning', adopting 'aligned suppliers' who can work with them across the world. Thus, across a wide range of activities a cascade effect is at work in which intense pressures developed for first tier suppliers of goods and services to the global giants to themselves merge and acquire, and develop leading global positions. These, in their turn, pass on intense pressure upon their own supplier networks. The result has been a fast-developing process of concentration at a global level in numerous industries supplying goods and services to the systems integrators.

3.3. Planning and Coordination: the External Firm

If we define the firm not by the entity which is the legal owner, but, rather, by the sphere over which conscious coordination of resource allocation takes place, then, far from becoming 'hollowed out' and much smaller in scope, the large firm can be seen to have enormously increased in size during the global business revolution. As the large firm has 'disintegrated', so has the extent of conscious coordination over the surrounding value chain increased. In a wide range of business activities, the organisation of the value chain has developed into a comprehensively planned and coordinated activity. At its centre is the core systems integrator. This firm typically possesses some combination of a number of key attributes. These include the capability to raise finance for large new projects, and the resources necessary to fund a high level of R&D spending to sustain technological leadership, to develop a global brand, to invest in state-of-the-art information technology and to attract the best human resources. Across a wide range of business types, from fast-moving consumer goods to aircraft manufacture, the core systems integrator interacts in the deepest, most intimate fashion with the major segments of the value chain, both upstream and downstream. This constitutes a new form of 'separation of ownership and control', in which the boundaries of the firm have become blurred.

3.4. Competition

From a mainstream perspective, 'greater competition' is equated with a larger number of firms in a given sector. In the non-mainstream, view, 'greater competition' is equated with increased intensity of competition between powerful oligopolistic firms. Far from stifling 'competition', powerful oligopolies can produce increasingly intense competition as giant global firms struggle with other such firms, applying greater resources in R&D and marketing, and leveraging greater procurement budgets to lower costs and stimulate technical progress across the supply chain.

3.5. Challenges for Developing Countries

The high-income economies contain just 15 per cent of the world's total population. Firms headquartered in these countries account for 94 per cent of the companies listed in the 'Fortune 500', which ranks firms by sales revenue (Table 2). They account for 96 per cent of the firms in the 'FT 500' list of the world's leading firms, ranked by market capitalisation. They account for almost 100 per cent of the firms included in the list of the world's top 700 firms ranked by expenditure on research and development, which is a critical indicator of the distribution of global business power. There is not a single firm from the low or middle-income countries in the list of the world's 'top 100 brands' (Sorrell, 2004). Firms from developing countries are joining the 'global level playing field' at a point at which the concentration of business power has never been greater. In developing countries that have liberalised their business systems, oligopolies have rapidly been established not only by the world's leading systems integrators in each of the industries analysed in this chapter,[24] but also in the upper reaches (at least) of the supply chain of these industries. Whether this makes a positive or a negative contribution to 'development' is beyond the scope of this chapter.

Table 2. Dominance of the Global Business Revolution by Firms Based in High-Income Countries

	Population (2000)		GNP (2000) (a)		GNP (2000) (b)		Fortune 500 companies (2003) (c)		FT 500 companies (2003) (d)		Top 700 companies by R&D spend (2002-03)	
	million	%	$b	%	$b	%	No	%	No		No	%
HIEs	903	15	24 828	80	24 781	55	472	94	480	96	69	100
L/MIEs	5152	85	6 336	20	20 056	45 (e)	28	6 (f)	20	4 3	7	neg

Notes: HIEs=High-Income Economies
L/MIEs=Low/Middle-Income Economies
(a). at official rate of exchange
(b). at PPP dollars
(c). ranked by the sales revenue
(d). ranked by market capitalisation
(e). China=14, India=4, Brazil=3, Russia=3, Mexico=1, Malaysia=1, Venezuela=1, Thailand=1
(f). Russia=7, China*=4, India=3, Mexico=3, Brazil=2, India=1
*all floated in Hong Kong
Sources: FT, 27 May 2004; World Bank, 1998 and 2002; Fortune, 26 July 2004; DTI, 2003

4. Conclusion

Mainstream, neo-classical economists consider that opening up developing economies to global competition provides broad opportunities for indigenous firms to catch up with firms headquartered in the high-income countries. Their view is based on the belief that the basic tendency of capitalism is competition with strict limits to growth of firm size: they believe that by forcing weak firms to compete with strong ones, the weak can learn from the strong, imitate them and overtake them. They believe that the epoch of global free trade and free movement of capital, allied with the revolution in information technology, has produced wide possibilities for firms from poor countries to catch up with those with their headquarters in rich countries. In other words the world of vastly expanded global markets is 'flat'.

In fact, the epoch of the global business revolution since the 1980s has witnessed an unprecedented degree of industrial consolidation and concentration of business power at a global level. Alongside a huge increase in global output in the sectors analysed in this chapter, the number of firms has shrunk and the degree of global industrial concentration has increased greatly. The 'commanding heights' of the global business system are almost entirely occupied by firms from high-income countries. This presents a deep challenge for indigenous firms and policy-makers from developing countries.

The most easily visible part of the structure of industrial concentration is the well-known firms with powerful, globally recognised technologies and/or brands. These constitute the 'systems integrators' or 'organising brains' at the apex of extended value chains. As they have consolidated their leading positions, they have exerted intense pressure across the whole supply chain in order to minimise costs and stimulate technical progress. The close coordination by the systems integrators of legally independent firms across the supply chain constitutes a new form of separation of ownership and control.

However, the challenge is even deeper than it at first appears. This chapter has examined the value chains in four industrial sectors, with widely different products. It has shown that they have striking similarities in the way in which the core systems integrators have stimulated a comprehensive transformation of industrial structure across the whole supply chain. At every level there has taken place an intense process of industrial concentration, mainly through merger and acquisition, as firms struggle to meet the strict requirements that are the condition of their participation in the systems integrators' supply chains. This 'cascade effect' has profound implications for the nature of competition. It means that the challenge facing firms from developing countries is far deeper than at first sight appeared to be the case. Not only do they face immense difficulties in catching up with the leading systems integrators, the visible part of the 'iceberg', but they also face immense difficulties in catching up with the powerful firms that now dominate almost every segment of the supply chain, the invisible part of the 'iceberg' that lies hidden from view beneath the water.

At the dawn of the twenty-first century, the reality of the intense industrial concentration among both systems integrators and their entire supply chain, brought about through pressure from the 'cascade effect', presents a comprehensive challenge for both indigenous firms and policy-makers from developing countries.

Notes

1. This is the second epoch of modern 'globalisation'. The first epoch was brought to a halt by the wars of the twentieth century, the rise of communism and the inward-looking economic policies of non-communist developing countries.
2. Pratten (1971)analysed industrial structure in a number of UK industries. Prais (1981) analysed industrial structure in several industries in the UK, Germany and the United States. Chandler (1990) analysed industrial structure in the United States, Great Britain and Germany. Chandler (1997) extended the analysis to include small European nations, and Italy, Spain, France, Japan, South Korea, Argentina, the USSR and Czechoslovakia. Scherer (1996) analysed the structure of a number of industries in the United States.
3. Global mergers and acquisitions rose from an annual level of around US$ 260 billion in the early 1990s to a peak of US$ 3173 in 2000, falling to US$ 1060 billion in 2002. Thereafter, mergers and acquisitions rose to US$ 2507 billion in 2005 (Moore, 2006), and it seemed likely that the total for 2006 would exceed the previous peak of 2000.
4. See, for example, Wolf, 2004: 'Global M&A activity rose more than five-fold between 1995 and 2000. Yet the surge in cross-border M&A does not seem to have increased concentration' (Wolf, 2004: 224).
5. Meeks, 1977, is the classic study of this topic. The view that 'most mergers fail' is repeated remorselessly among mainstream academics of all ideological persuasions.
6. Friedman's book is a best-seller. It was hugely popular among participants at the Davos Economic Forum in 2006, and won the Financial Times/Goldman Sachs 'Business Book of the Year' award.
7. For a more extensive analysis of the issues contained in this section, see Nolan, 2001a and 2001b.
8. In 2005 the *Fortune 500* companies in these sectors had a combined revenue of US$ 3.8 trillion.
9. The issues in Section 2.1 are analysed in more detail in Nolan, Zhang and Liu, 2007. Due to limitations of space, this section focuses only commercial aircraft. However, the military aircraft industry has also witnessed intense consolidation during the past decade, with equally profound consequences for the supply chain.
10. These included the UK's de Havilland (Comet), Vickers (VC10), Hawker Siddeley (Trident), and BAC (BAC 111), Germany's VFW (VFW 614), France's Sud Aviation (Caravelle), and the Netherlands' Fokker.
11. Tupolev alone produced almost 2000 Tu-134s and 154s, which placed it roughly on a par with McDonnell Douglas, though far short of Boeing. Antonov and Ilyushin also produced large commercial aircraft.

12.   President Putin is reconstructing a unified Russian aerospace industry with majority state ownership, but it remains to be seen how successful this endeavour will be in catching up with the global industry leaders.

13.   This is a rough estimate based on the fact that GM spends around US$ 80 billion on procurement, and accounts for around 16 per cent of total global automobile sales.

14.   Anti-locking Brake Systems and Electronic Stability Control Systems, respectively.

15.   There still are important restrictions on the international expansion of the leading telecommunications firms, notably in China and India, and, to some extent, still within Western Europe.

16.   Unless otherwise indicated, data in this section are taken from Nolan, Zhang and Liu, 2007. For a detailed study of the 'cascade effect' in the global beverage industry see Nolan, 2008 (forthcoming).

17.   In the United States, the top three firms account for around four-fifths of the market. In Japan and Europe, the top two or three firms account for over 70 per cent of the respective markets.

18.   There are now more than thirty giant retail groups with annual revenues of more than US$ 10 billion, including seven super-giants with revenues of over US$ 50 billion (*Fortune*, 26 July 2004).

19.   These are Ball, Crown and Rexam.

20.   In 2003, Tetra Laval, the Swedish/Swiss packaging giant, acquired Sidel. With the weight of Tetra Laval behind it, Sidel will be in an even better position to maintain its leading position in the global PET pre-form blowing industry.

21.   WPP, Omnicom, Interpublic, and Publicis.

22.   Either directly, or through their 'third party' logistics suppliers. Most beverages are delivered to customers by truck.

23.   Even in less well-known sectors, the share of systems integrators has typically become very high. For example, the global market share of the top two firms in the financial information sector stood at 86 per cent and at 77 per cent in electronic games; the share of the top three firms stood at 71 per cent in legal publishing and at 62 per cent in artificial joints; the share of the top five firms stood at 77 per cent in recorded music; and the share of the top six firms stood at 60 per cent in water management (Nolan, 2001a).

24.   The telecomms services sector remains the most protected of these sectors at the level of the systems integrators, but even in those countries which protect their telecomms services sector the supply chain in this industry is comprehensively dominated by the global leaders in telecommunications equipment production.

References

Boston Consulting Group, *Growing through acquisitions* (Boston: BCG Publishing, 2004)

Castells, M., *The rise of the network society* (2nd edn.) (Oxford: Blackwells, 2000)

Chandler, A., *Scale and Scope: the Dynamics of Industrial Capitalism* (Cambridge, Mass.: Harvard University Press, 1990)

Chandler, A., and T. Hikino., 'The large industrial enterprise and the dynamics of modern economic growth', in Chandler, A., F. Amatori and T. Hikino (eds), *Big Business and the Wealth of Nations* (Cambridge: Cambridge University Press, 1997)

Coase, R. H., *The Firm, the Market and the Law* (Chicago: University of Chicago Press, 1988) (originally published 1937)

DaimlerChrysler, 'Challenges, measures and opportunities' (DaimlerChrysler, 2005)

Department of Trade and Industry (DTI), *The UK R&D Scoreboard 2003* (Edinburgh: DTI, 2003)

Department of Trade and Industry (DTI), *The UK R&D Scoreboard 2004* (Edinburgh: DTI, 2004)

Department of Trade and Industry (DTI), *The UK R & D Scoreboard 2005* (London: DTI, 2005)

Financial Times (FT), various issues

Fortune magazine, various issues

Friedman, M., *Capitalism and Freedom* (Chicago: University of Chicago Press, 1962)

Friedman, T., *The World is Flat: a Brief History of the Twenty-first Century* (New York: Farrar, Straus and Giroux, 2005)

GKN, *Annual Report* (2005)

Husky, *Annual Reports* (various years)

Hymer, S., 'The multinational corporation and the law of uneven development' (1972) reprinted in Radice, H. (ed.) (1975)

KHS, *Annual Reports* (various years)

Krones, *Annual Reports* (various years)

Malone, T. W. and R. L. Laubacher, 'The dawn of the e-Lance economy', *Harvard Business Review* (September-October 1998)

Marshall, A., *Principles of Economics* (London: Macmillan, 1920) (originally published 1890)

Marx, K., *Capital, Vol. 1* (New York: International Publishers, 1967 edn.) (originally published 1867)

Meeks, G., *Disappointing marriage* (Cambridge: Cambridge University Press, 1977)

Mittal, A., 'Leading the steel industry' (September 2006)

Moore, D., ' M& A environment' (Morgan Stanley, 2006)

Murman, E. *et al.*, *Lean Enterprise Value: Insights from MIT's Lean Aerospace Initiative* (New York: Palgrave, 2002)

Nolan, P., *China's Rise, Russia's Fall: Politics, Economics and Planning in the Transition from Stalinism* (Basingstoke: Macmillan, 1995)

Nolan, P., *China and the Global Business Revolution* (Basingstoke: Palgrave Macmillan, 2001a)

Nolan, P., *China and the Global Economy* (Basingstoke: Palgrave Macmillan, 2001b)

Nolan, P., and H. Rui, 'The cascade effect and the Chinese steel industry' (mimeo, 2004)

Nolan, P., J. Zhang and C. Liu, *The Global Business Revolution and the Cascade Effect: Systems Integration in the Global Aerospace, Beverage and Retail Industries* (Basingstoke: Palgrave Macmillan, 2007)

Nolan, P., *Coca-Cola and the Transformation of the Chinese Business System* (Basingstoke: Palgrave Macmillan, 2008) (forthcoming)

NTN, *Annual Report* (2005)

Owens-Illinois, *Annual Reports* (various years)

Penrose, E., *The Theory of the Growth of the Firm* (Oxford: Oxford University Press, 1995, 2nd edn.)

Pilkington, *Annual Report* (2005)

Piore, M., and C. Sabel, *The Second Industrial Divide: Possibilities for Progress* (New York: Basic Books, 1984)

Porter, M., *The competitive advantage of nations* (London: Macmillan, 1990)

Prais, S. J., *Productivity and industrial structure* (Cambridge: Cambridge University Press, 1981)

Pratten, C., *Economies of Scale in Manufacturing Industry* (Cambridge: Cambridge University Press, 1971)

Radice, H. (ed.), *International firms and modern imperialism* (Harmondsworth: Penguin Books, 1975)

Saint-Gobain, *Annual Reports* (various years)

Sears, M., 'The Bottom Line on Lean: a CFO's Perspective,' a speech given on the Lean Aerospace Initiative, 10 April 2001

Scherer, F. M., *Industry, Structure, Strategy and Public Policy* (New York: HarperCollins College Publishers, 1996)

Sorrell, M., 'The advertising and marketing services industry: outlook good and getting better', in WPP, *Annual Report, 2004* (2005)

Wolf, M., *Why Globalization Works: The Case for the Global Market Economy* (New Haven and London: Yale University Press, 2004)

World Bank, *World Development Report, 1998* (New York: Oxford University Press, 1998).

World Bank, *World Development Report, 2002* (New York: Oxford University Press, 2002).

World Bank, *World Development Indicators*, 2004 (Washington DC: World Bank, 2004)

Xing, Weixi, 'Globalisation and Catch-up in the Chinese Telecommunications Industry: the Case of Huaei' (Judge Business School, University of Cambridge, Doctoral Dissertation, 2005)

Chapter 3

THE GLOBALISATION CHALLENGE AND THE CATCH-UP OF DEVELOPING COUNTRIES: THE CASE OF THE BREWING INDUSTRY

Peter Nolan and Yuantao Guo

1. Introduction

The role that big businesses perform in the national economy has triggered numerous theoretical interests, which can be broadly categorised into two schools. The mainstream school prefers small and medium-sized enterprises (SMEs) to big businesses because the former in a perfect competition is believed to bring about allocative efficiency, whereas the latter is believed to be more often than not associated with monopoly or oligopoly, and to deviate from allocative efficiency. Big businesses in the form of monopolistic and oligopolistic firms are believed to hinder free competition. According to Marshallians, big businesses will lose their dominant positions in the long run (Marshall, 1920: 315-6).

In contrast, the non-mainstream approach argues that big businesses (often monopoly or oligopoly) could benefit the economy in the long run. The Schumpeterian theorem demonstrates through a process of creative destruction, monopolies or oligopolies are more conducive to growth than perfect competition (Schumpeter, 1976). Scherer (1996) points out that monopolistic or oligopolistic competition exists in a wide array of industries in the United States. Whether or not oligopolies and monopolies cause lower welfare depends on individual industries. Nolan *et al.* (2002) demonstrate that in the era of the global big business revolution, the number of players in industry after industry has fallen dramatically and global competition among oligopolistic firms has been vastly intensifying. In terms of a giant firm's limit, Edith Penrose (1995) suggests that a firm's size has no theoretical limits because a firm can always expand with the aid of managerial resources and research capabilities. From an historical perspective, the rise and spread of big businesses is argued to be the major engine of the economic transformation of advanced economies throughout the nineteenth and the twentieth century (Schmitz, 1993; Chandler, Amatori and Hikino, 1997) and plays a critical role in the catch-up process of successful industrialised latecomers (Amsden, 1997; Chang, 2002).

Clearly, polarised views have strong implications for developing countries like China, which cautiously searches for future direction whilst at the crossroads of a critical transitional period. The following sections reveal the applicability of the mainstream versus non-mainstream views in explaining the transformation of the global and Chinese brewing industry in the globalisation era and explore its implications.

2. The Globalisation Challenge

(a) Industrial Concentration and 'Cascade Effect'

The industrial concentration is embedded in the nature of the capital. In the early stage of modern capitalism, Karl Marx (1961, Vol. 1: 626-7) had noticed that capital tended to concentrate in successful industrial capitalists' hands because the larger capitals (firms) had advantages such as larger production scales and cheaper products. Since the late nineteenth century, there has been a continuing process of industrial concentration, through which large firms have grown into global giants (Porter, 1986).

In the current era of globalisation, the worldwide concentration has become unprecedented in terms of both its magnitude and speed. The extraordinary speed and scale of cross-border mergers and acquisitions (M&As) have significantly facilitated Multinationals' (MNC) global expansion (Nolan, 2001). There is an unprecedented increase in the intensity of oligopolistic global competition. The current era has witnessed a 'full flowering of the in-built tendency of the capitalist system to concentration' (Nolan et al., 2002: 91). Unlike the M&A mania in the 1980s in which financial buyers often bought companies and then sold out in exchange for short-term profits, the 1990s merger fever was mainly driven by companies in similar industries in pursuit of higher market shares, pricing power and economies of scale

(*Fortune*, 11 January 1999). Large MNCs have become the most important and powerful globalising force and the major locus of transnational economic and political practices (Sklair, 2002).

The concentration among giant MNCs has led to a 'cascade effect', i.e. a correspondingly intensified concentration among their suppliers at the global level in numerous industries supplying goods and services to giant MNCs, which in themselves are identified as core systems integrators (Nolan *et al.*, 2002). Only those suppliers who have large scale, powerful technological potential and strong global marketing capabilities can be aligned as long-term strategic suppliers of large MNCs. This intense pressure has not only resulted in massive consolidation among upstream suppliers, but also caused consolidation among downstream service providers (Nolan, 2001).

(b) Value Chain Integration and Systems Integrators

The value chain theory has been explored by a large body of business literature (e.g. Porter, 1986; Ruigrok and van Tulder, 1995; Dicken, 1998). Simple comparative advantages such as factor-cost differences that arise from production locations and scale economy cannot be sustained for too long. To maintain a sustainable leading position, a firm must coordinate within the value chain (Porter, 1986). As such, the ability to manage the value chain becomes an important aspect of competitiveness. A large MNC is regarded as the 'core of networks of supply and distribution', or 'a spider of an industrial web' (Ruigrok and van Tulder, 1995: 65). As core systems integrators, they stand at the centre of the value chain that is comprehensively planned and co-coordinated by themselves (Nolan, 2001). The core systems integrators not only plan raw material procurement from strategic first tier suppliers and arrange global distribution and logistics, but they also conduct R&D and develop global brands. Across all these activities, they 'interact in the deepest, most intimate fashion with the major segments of the value chain, both upstream and downstream' (Nolan, 2001: 42). The function of global giant firms has developed from direct manufacturing towards a 'brain' function - systematically integrating resources in the value chain and across the world. As such, a much wider array of firms and sectors beyond the production domains of the core systems integrators are closely intertwined. In this sense, modern global giant firms have become 'external' firms and their boundaries have become blurred (Nolan, 2001).

(c) Brand

Successful brand management has a powerful 'virtuous circle effect' on firms' competitiveness in that a strong brand image can lead to larger market share and higher operating margins. The increased cash flow can be further used to maintain and expand market share or to develop brands in other geographical locations (MSDW, 1998). Large MNCs are at a greater advantage than SMEs because they have stronger financial resources, more powerful bargaining power and better distribution channels which can be used to enhance brand image. In many circumstances, they could nurture a homogenised global culture for their brands through huge advertising inputs, tremendous marketing efforts and various sponsorships (Nolan, 1999). In the fast moving consumer goods (FMCG) industry, in particular, packaging innovation has become a very powerful means to strengthen the brand image. Consequently, global giants from advanced economies have obtained a considerable level of sustainability[1], which reaches as high as twenty-three years for the aerospace/defence industry, sixteen years for capital goods and fourteen years for the consumer industry (MSDW, 1998: 6).

(d) Technology and Innovation

Technology is widely regarded as an engine for enhancing firms' competitiveness. Schumpeter (1976: 83) regards it as 'the fundamental impulse that sets and keeps the capitalist engine in motion'. Freeman (1982) argues that companies who fail to innovate will eventually have to go out of business. Brooks and Guile (1987) assert that technological changes determine the structure of industry both at the national and global levels through their impact on the economies of production and information flow. Competitive advantages such as lower costs and production differentiations cannot be sustained for too long and only cumulative investments in R&D and constant technological upgrading can ensure the sustainable competitiveness of firms (Porter, 1990). But technological innovations require carriers (Dicken, 1998: 145). Giant MNCs, as the pillar carriers, enable technological innovation to be made, due to their extraordinary amounts of investment in R&D.

(e) Summary

Global giant firms from advanced economies have significantly intensified global competition. Big businesses have not lost their dominant positions but rather gained tremendous competitive advantages over SMEs, which imposes serious challenges to firms from developing countries (Nolan, 2004a, 2004b). The following section investigates the transformation of the brewing industry in the current era and its implications for latecomers from developing countries.

3. The Global Brewing Industry

(a) Industrial Concentration

Research has found that as a conventional capital-intensive industry, brewing illustrates a remarkable relation between production scale and efficiency (Hawkins and Radcliffe, 1971; Cockerill, 1977; Prais, 1981). Large brewers also enjoy scale economy in advertising (Tremblay, 1985; Scherer, 1996). In practice, scale economy takes place in brewers' interaction with suppliers in the value chain, which ranges from procurement, production, sales and advertising to marketing and logistics. The scale advantages that large brewers possess not only take place at individual plant level but also at the firm level across the globe. In the current era, leading global brewers' production scales have been enormously increased. The 'state-of-the-art' technology adopted in Anheuser-Busch's highly modernised breweries not only dramatically increases efficiency, but also ensures that each of its beers has the same crisp and clean taste (Anheuser-Busch, *Annual Report*, 2002: 8). The scale related competitiveness creates a huge entry barrier for latecomers from Least Developed Countries (LDCs) to enter the global playing field. The entry barrier to the low-end beer market may be relatively easy to overcome but competing in the premium market on the global playing field is extremely tough, if not impossible, for players from LDCs. In most circumstances, it is rather unrealistic for them to attempt to challenge global giants' dominance.

Giant brewers' battle for dominance has never ceased. The brewing industry in most industrialised economies underwent significant structural change between the 1950s and 1980s, resulting in enlarged brewery size, reduced brands (Müller and Schwalbach, 1980) and a high level of concentration (Gourvish, 1995). Since the 1990s, leading brewers in advanced economies have launched aggressive global campaigns. The global consolidation has become a 'key factor shaping global development as brewing companies achieve greater scale and their beer brands grow in more international markets' (Interbrew, 2003: 2). The industry has witnessed explosive cross-border M&As in which giant brewers act as 'consolidators'. A number of mega-mergers[2] among large brewers has drastically altered the dynamic matrix of the global competition. Strategic partnerships have gained increasing popularity in the global consolidation. Large brewers with well-established brands and strong positions in emerging markets become desirable acquisition targets.

(b) Value Chain Integration and Systems Integrators

Vertical integration into the value chain has a long history in many beer markets. Retail tied houses used to serve as a means of securing markets (Gourvish and Wilson, 1994). However, the competition environment has changed so dramatically that tied houses are no longer critical for leading brewers because of vastly increasing free trade and the popularity of national brands (Hawkins and Radcliffe, 1971). Giant brewers are indeed disposing of tied houses. The industrial trend suggests that the focus of the value chain integration has changed to tighter control and more efficient management of the value chain. With the aid of the most advanced IT, global giant brewers' enormous bargaining power plays a substantial role in integrating both the up- and downstream value chain.

The fact that giant brewers purchase in bulk to exploit scale economy provides them with privileged bargaining power in relation to their suppliers, which range from barley suppliers in the upstream, to production equipment suppliers in the midstream, and to packaging suppliers in the downstream. They enjoy not only lower purchase prices but also better communication with suppliers. Giant brewers have been actively pushing ahead the technological improvement of associated machinery and packaging industries through close interactions with core suppliers. The concentration among large brewers has resulted in a 'cascade effect' on the wholesalers in the downstream. In the United States, for example, brewers' concentration from the 1950s to the 1990s caused rapid concentration among malt wholesalers and beer distributors (*BI*, November 1995; *BW*, 15 September 2000). Giant brewers also possess huge bargaining power and substantial influence on service providers like logistics firms, advertising agencies and promotional goods manufacturers, etc.

(c) Brand

A strong brand portfolio and sustainable sales growth constitute key competitive advantages in consumer industries (MSDW, 1998). Tremblay and Tremblay (1995) have found that large brewers' escalating advertising expenditures increase their market power. Leading global brewers consistently build up and upgrade global images of core premium brands through intensive sales and promotion efforts, in many circumstances even through nurturing consumption culture. For instance, the success of Budweiser, the best-selling beer globally, is significantly attributed to Anheuser-Busch's substantial advertising and promotional expenditures, which went up from US\$ 164 million in 1995 (*BI*, January 1996) to US\$ 822 million in 2002 (Anheuser-Busch, *Annual Report*, 2002: 36). Giant brewers have also introduced tight quality control systems and built up advanced communication infrastructures within their global production networks to maintain the global image of a couple of core brands. The low-end markets with lower profitability are in general segmented whilst the high-end markets are concentrated in the hands of a few global giants.

(d) Technology and Innovation

Beer is traditionally regarded as a low technology sector. However, recent decades have seen considerable production innovations (Gourvish, 1998). Highly complicated technologies have been used to improve the processes of ingredients selection and filling as well as speeding up the brewing process. Beer packaging has undergone dramatic innovation, evolving from wooden kegs and glass bottles to metal cans, aluminium cans, PET (polyethylene terephthalate) and PEN (polyethylene naphthalate) bottles. Packaging has become lighter, user friendly and environmentally friendly. Packaging innovation is becoming a more and more important means to enhance beers' brand image and a brewer's competitiveness.

Leading global brewers take the lead in packaging innovations through enormous R&D endeavours. Anheuser-Busch's Packaging Innovation Center (*Annual Report*, 1998) adopts the most advanced technologies in the industry to produce high quality and low cost beverage cans. Interbrew (Company Website) introduced the world's first 'monolayer barrier enhanced PET bottle' in 2003, which adopted a single-layer, barrier-enhanced resin technology to offer outstanding protection against oxygen and light while keeping the carbonation inside the bottle. The technology significantly improved the freshness and quality of beers while keeping bottles light and unbreakable. Giant brewers are also adopting advanced technologies to monitor packaging systems, as suggested by Heineken's inspection system which uses spin-and-brake technology to investigate tiny particles in filled and capped glass bottles (*BW*, 15 September 2002).

It is not the case, however, that all global giants have developed in-housed packaging innovation, but rather, in most cases, they have pushed ahead technological development with the aid of global leading production and packaging equipment manufacturers such as Crown, Ball, Krones and

Owens-Illinois, etc. The huge bargaining power that global giant brewers possess and the giants' eagerness for reducing costs through the adoption of the latest advanced technologies induce close cooperation between giant machinery manufacturers and giant brewers. Subsequently, the introduction of the finest technology in both production and packaging dramatically increases giant brewers' efficiency, enables them to lead the industrial trend and also stimulates the technological development of associated machinery and packaging industries.

(e) Summary

The mainstream's critics on big businesses mentioned earlier, to a certain extent face challenge in explaining the transformation of the global brewing industry. Not only have global giants, most of whom are oligopolies or monopolies, adopted the most advanced technologies in production, packaging and management, but they have also pushed associated suppliers to match their high standards on technological innovation. In contrast to what the Marshallians have claimed that big businesses' dominance will end in the long run, the boundary of giant brewers is expanding to an unprecedentedly wide geographical reach. From the global perspective, big businesses do not deter competition but rather compete fiercely against one another in the hope of achieving global dominance. There is a clear trend of concentration across the world rather than the boom of small and medium-sized brewers.

Giant brewers from advanced economies have gained enormous competitive advantages, which build up huge entry barriers to their territories. Their large-scale acquisitions of, and strategic alliances with, large successful brewers in developing countries dramatically deepens their global dominance and may deprive latecomers of catch-up opportunities because many emerging national giants in developing countries can easily be swallowed up before they actually grow strong enough to challenge global giants' dominance. The following section examines the challenge to the Chinese brewing industry and Chinese brewers.

4. The Chinese Brewing Industry

China has become the largest beer producer, accounting for approximately 17 per cent of the global sales volume. From 1949 to 2003, China's beer production increased from just 7 million litres to 25 400 million litres; and per capita production from less than 1 litre to 19.1 litre (China Light Industry

Almanac). Nonetheless, large indigenous players face huge challenges from highly competitive global giants, as we shall see soon.

(a) Industrial Concentration

(i) Scale versus Concentration

Under the planned economy, China had only a few dozen brewers. A vast number of small and medium-sized breweries emerged in the 1980s. At its highest, there were once over 700 brewers (China Light Industry Almanac). The industry has been overheated and saddled by a number of structural weaknesses.

First, scale is always an important contributor to competitiveness in brewing but the crux is that the bulk of indigenous brewers operate on a small scale which bears little comparison with global giants. For instance, by the end of the 1990s brewers whose annual production reached over 200 million litres only accounted for 4 per cent of the total number of brewers; brewers whose annual production was between 100 and 200 million litres accounted for just 5.3 per cent of the total number of brewers; and 78 per cent of brewers operated at a scale below 50 million litres (China Light Industry Almanac 2000: 218). Tsingtao is the largest indigenous brewer but it is still too small to bear comparison with leading global brewers.

Although China is the world's largest beer market in volume terms, the mass production was/is not achieved through exploiting scale economy, but rather the aggregate production of a vast number of small players. The profitability of the industry is extremely low. The ratio of profits before tax upon production of the industry dropped from 4.7 per cent in 1993 to 2.2 per cent in 2003, suggesting a 7.3 per cent annual decline. Due to poor profitability, return on assets (ROA) declined from 3 per cent in 1993 to 1.3 per cent in 2003, representing an 8 per cent annual decline. The loss-makers accounted for 34 per cent of the total number of brewers in 2003. Such a ratio reached as high as 42.5 per cent in the peak year of 1999.[3]

A certain level of concentration is the basic requirement for realising scale economy in the brewing industry. Concentrated markets with a higher Herfindahl-Hirschman Index generate higher profits, whereas fragmented markets suffer from lower profits. Compared to most advanced markets, the Chinese market is segmented and its profitability, measured by earnings before interest and tax (EBIT), is considerably lower. For instance, the industrial EBIT of South Korea, where Hite Brewery and Oriental Brewery dominate, is as high as over 30 per cent. The same ratio for the Australian market where Foster's and Lion Nathan dominate is above 25 per cent and for the US market where Anheuser-Busch, SABMiller and Coors dominate is over 20 per cent. In contrast, the same ratio for China stays around 6 per cent (Guo, 2005). This lower profitability has become a significant competitive disadvantage when Chinese brewers compete with global giants since lower profitability results in lower capital reserves. Many endeavours aimed at improving competitiveness could be handicapped by this financial constraint. The structural weakness has become a barrier to the catch-up of indigenous brewers (ibid).

Second, the industrial growth was/is by and large led by volume growth instead of price mix. The majority of Chinese beers are sold as economy products. Domestic beers compete severely against one another in low-end markets. Many rely heavily on price-cutting to win market share, which consequently further jeopardises profitability and impedes them from accumulating capital to make technological improvements.

Third, the existence of too many loss-makers, most of which are SMEs, jeopardises the industry's profitability and distorts the distribution of social resources. The industry faces a tough dilemma: it suffers from overcapacity but most loss-makers do not easily go out of business. This particular phenomenon is to a certain extent caused by local protection, or in many cases, by the conflict of interest among/between the central government, local governments and individual bureaucrats: 'many local governments would like loss-makers to exist by offering certain assistance because any potential social turmoil caused by downsizing may damage local governors' political careers' (interview, China Brewing Industry Association).

(ii) Concentration Pace

The industrial concentration began in the mid-1990s when a few large players equipped with better facilities and supported by preferential industrial policies launched their national campaigns. Foreign brewers' rapid penetration served as another strong stimulus. As the concentration speeded up, the market share of the top ten players increased from a mere 14.2 per cent in 1990 to 52.8 per cent in 2003; and the share of the top three rose from 5.5 per cent to 32 per cent. Tsingtao Brewery and Yanjing Brewery have made tremendous efforts to lead concentration. However, successful large indigenous brewers are becoming subsidiaries of global giants. Eight out of the ten largest brewers of the 1990s were partly or entirely acquired by foreign rivals (Tables 1 and 2).

The concentration is still at an early stage. In less affluent regions the market is still highly segmented. However, the concentration among the top ten domestic

Table 1. The Top Ten Brewers in China, 1990

Brewers	Production (million litres)	Market Share (%)	Headquarters	Remarks
Zhujiang	133.0	2.0	Guangzhou, Guangdong province	24% of Zhujiang Brewery was bought by Interbrew in 2002 for US$ 19.5 million
Shenyang	126.5	1.9	Shenyang, Liaoning province	China Resources Brewery (CRB) holds 94% of Shenyang Brewery
Tsingtao	100.5	1.5	Qingdao, Shandong province	Anheuser-Busch holds 27% of Tsingtao Brewery
Qianjiang	95.9	1.5	Hangzhou, Zhejiang province	It entered into an agreement with CRB in March 2004 to reorganise Qianjiang into a JV. CRB will hold 70% of the JV and Qianjiang the remaining 30%
Yanjing	94.6	1.4	Beijing	No foreign ownership involved at present
San Miguel (Guangzhou)	88.0	1.3	Guangzhou, Guangdong province	Headquartered in the Philippines. San Miguel is one of the largest beverage and food conglomerates in Asia
Beijing	76.8	1.2	Beijing	It was established in 1941 and dominated about 80% of the Beijing market in the 1980s. It was bought by Japanese leading brewer Asahi in 1996 and renamed Beijing Beer Asahi Co.
Dongxihu	72.8	1.1	Wuhan, Hubei province	It was restructured as a JV with Danone in 1997. CRB acquired Danone's 60% holdings in 2001

Brewers	Production (Million litres)	Market Share (%)		Remarks
Laizhou	71.8	1.1	Laizhou, Shandong province	Yanjing Brewery acquired 80% of the company in 2000
Yantai	69.9	1.1	Yantai, Shandong province	Asahi acquired 53% of the company in 2000
Top Ten	929.8	14.2		
Chinese Market	6 545	100		

Sources: Annals of Tsingtao Brewery; China Food Industry Almanac 1991:259-1; author's own research.

Table 2. The Top Ten Brewers in China, 2003

Brewers	Production (million litres)	Market Share (%)	Headquarters	Remarks
Tsingtao	3338.0	13.1	Qingdao, Shandong Province	Anheuser-Busch bought 22.5% of Tsingtao Brewery in 2002 for about RMB 1.5 billion (US$ 182 million) and now holds 27% of the company
China Resources	2540.0	10.0	Hong Kong	A JV between SABMiller (49%) and China Resources Enterprises (51%)
Yanjing	2230.0	8.8	Beijing	No foreign ownership involved at present

Brewers	Production (million litres)	Market Share (%)	Headquarters	Remarks
Harbin	1170.0	4.6	Harbin, Heilongjian province	Anheuser-Busch bought 100% of Harbin Brewery in 2004
Henan Golden Star	938.0	3.7	Zhengzhou, Henan province	No foreign ownership involved at present
Chongqing	910.0	3.6	Chongqing	19.5% of Chongqing Brewery was acquired by S&N for about RMB 525 million in 2003
Zhujiang	882.0	3.5	Guangzhou, Guangdong province	24% of Zhujiang Brewery was bought by Interbrew in 2002 for US$ 19.5 million
Sedrin	578.0	2.3	Putian, Fujian province	No foreign ownership involved at present
Lion Group	411.3	1.6	Malaysia	Is is a diversified Malaysian conglomerate. Interbrew bought out Lion's brewing operations in China in 2003 and 2004 for a cash consideration of over RMB 2 billion (US$ 263 million)
Huiquan	405.9	1.6	Huian, Fujian province	Yanjing Brewery is its largest shareholder after the purchase of 38% of Huiquan Brewery in 2003
Top Ten	13 403.2	52.8		
Chinese Market	6 545	100		

Sources: Beer Science and Technology, March 2004:72; author's own research

players could be extremely tough in that, firstly, local protection remains a barrier. Secondly, top domestic brewers in general do not want to be taken over by domestic rivals. In many cases, they would prefer to be acquired by foreign rivals. The reasons for pro-foreign takeover are complicated but the premium takeover price that a global giant generally pays, the prestige of being part of a global giant, and the job security, personal welfare and career development of senior management are significant factors. Thirdly, the fact that two out of the top three and six out of the top ten brewers have had global giants as their significant shareholders is one of the greatest barriers to creating a single indigenous giant. In fact, when the sales value instead of volume is used to rank the top ten and when global giants' shares in large indigenous brewers are also taken into consideration, the bulk of the top ten are indeed already in the hands of global giants. In this sense, the battle among indigenous brewers is becoming a battle among global giants. Fourthly, post China's entry into the WTO, preferential industrial policies are increasingly weakening. Large indigenous brewers have to rely on themselves to compete in the market place. Compared with previous decades, leading indigenous brewers are subject to more challenging threats, of which the risk of being swallowed up by global giants is the most obvious. Another associated issue is how the concentration improves the competitiveness of the industry as a whole. If the concentration is just a simple integration of small brewers into large brewers, whereby scale synergy and technological improvement are insufficient, the benefits from the concentration can be vastly discounted. In many circumstances, acquired small brewers could even become long-term liabilities to large acquiring brewers.

(b) Leading Multinationals' Penetration

Leading global brewers started to build footholds in China in the early 1990s and their penetration intensified dramatically in the late 1990s. China is now a fierce battlefield among giant brewers, which have very strong presence in almost all affluent regions. SABMiller holds a dominant position in the Northeast and Sichuan province. Anheuser-Busch holds a strong position in Hubei and Heilongjiang provinces. InBev is building up a strong position in Zhujiang River Delta (ZRD) and Yangtze River Delta (YRD). Japanese brewers converge on YRD, ZRD, Shandong and Fujian provinces. Heineken is the largest player in Hainan province and competes intensively in YRD. Carlsberg strategically targets the Northwest and Southwest. However, neither the huge market nor the rapid penetration guarantees a successful performance. What counts could be the mode of entry. In the past few years, China has witnessed a great number of foreign acquisitions and increasing strategic alliances between foreign and large indigenous brewers.

(i) Greenfield Investment

Lion Nathan, the second largest Australian brewer, was the first foreign brewer to set up a Greenfield plant in China. But its heavy investments in Suzhou, a strategic city in the YRD region, has been making substantial losses, which was to a large extent caused by the difficulties associated with Greenfield investments. Lion Nathan was unfamiliar with methods of running a business in China. As the first Greenfield investor in the Chinese beer market, it had no previous experiences to draw lessons from. Consequently, the company mismanaged fundamentals and brand positioning (Lion Nathan Presentation, 2002). It eventually had to sell off its China brewing businesses to China Resources Brewery (CRB) in early 2005. Lion's experience demonstrates the enormous difficulties and huge costs of entering China without the collaboration of domestic partners; it also sheds light on an increasing pattern of foreign acquisitions being simultaneously accompanied by strategic alliances between foreign and leading domestic brewers.

(ii) Strategic Alliance

The most successful foreign brewers are those who have local partnerships, among which InBev, SABMiller and Anheuser-Busch stand out.

InBev (formerly Interbrew), the largest brewer in volume terms globally, acquired 24 per cent of Zhujiang brewery, the seventh largest Chinese brewer, for a cash consideration of US$ 19.5 million in 2002. InBev takes a rather active role in the partnership not only because it is the second largest shareholder of Zhujiang, but also because it is one of the forces behind transforming Zhujiang into a public company by sharing its experience in the capital market. The partnership is rewarding to InBev: Zhujiang's solid market position and the local government's support provide InBev with a favourable platform for further expansion in Southern China. It will be interesting to see how the Zhujiang/InBev alliance develops, given that Interbrew (now InBev) prefers a 'majority participation in any of its acquisitions, or at least a contractual assurance this will be the case over time' as well as a 'full decision control' over its acquired companies (Dezutter, 1997: 140).

SABMiller. SABMiller, the third largest brewer globally and one of the most profitable foreign brewers in China, carries out its expansion through CRB, a JV set up in 1993 between SABMiller and China Resources Enterprise (CRE). Since its establishment, CRB has been expanding through frenetic acquisitions of successful local brewers in SABMiller's strategic regions – the Northeast, which is one of the highest per capita beer consumption regions and Sichuan province, which is the most heavily populated. CRB is now the largest player in these two regions and the second largest player nationwide. Since the acquired brewers are leading regional players whose brands enjoy strong local loyalty, SABMiller does not replace them with its global core brands. More importantly, SABMiller's successful entry is substantially attributable to the local partnership since tough issues can be easily solved through CRE, as commented on by Chris Barrow, the Managing Director of SABMiller Asia:

> Our partners are China experts. They have experience of doing business there. As a result they have amazing contacts that can cut the red tape surrounding many issues: they can bring their other commercial operations to bear in a number of areas; they have access to people, they know the market and understand the rate of change required. We have been able to harness our knowledge of the beer industry with their knowledge of China and come up with an awesome team (quoted in Everatt, 2000: 10).

Anheuser-Busch. The largest indigenous brewer, Tsingtao Brewery, sold convertible bonds valued at US$ 182 million in 2002 to Anheuser-Busch (Tsingtao Brewery, 2002), the second largest brewer globally. The transaction eventually increased Anheuser-Busch's share holding in Tsingtao from 4.5 per cent[4] to 27 per cent. Tsingtao's current largest shareholder, Qingdao State Assets Administrative Office (QSAAO) holds just 3.6 per cent more. Tsingtao hopes to gain assistance from AB in its attempt to enhance competitiveness, improve profitability, maintain its domestic leadership, and enter into the global top ten. For Anheuser-Busch, China is strategically important for its global expansion. Having Tsingtao as a strategic partner serves as a critical step to the participation in the concentration process of the Chinese brewing industry, since Anheuser-Busch may 'piggyback' on Tsingtao's nationwide production bases, sales network and successful operational experience which has been accumulated over the years but has not been easily obtainable by foreign brewers.

The impact of such an alliance goes far beyond the surface of the alliance itself in that the alliance (Tsingtao Brewery, 2002) provides Anheuser-Busch with plenty of room to further take over Tsingtao. First, it provides Anheuser-Busch with opportunities to take part in Tsingtao's operational decision-making since Anheuser-Busch has representatives on Tsingtao's Board, the Supervisory Board and key Board committees which involve almost all the core areas of Tsingtao's daily operation. The participation of Anheuser-Busch's representatives, who are specialists in both the global and the Chinese brewing industry, could bring about considerable change in the power structure of Tsingtao's Board.

Second, Anheuser-Busch has strategically secured its position as Tsingtao's largest non-government shareholder. It is entitled to anti-dilution rights if Tsingtao issues new shares. It is also entitled to outstripping QSAAO's shareholding in Tsingtao once QSAAO's holding drops below 27 per cent. Such terms leave potential for Anheuser-Busch to become Tsingtao's largest shareholder and this is the most challenging scenario that Tsingtao will have to face.

Third, that Anheuser-Busch becomes Tsingtao's exclusive foreign strategic partner provides Anheuser-Busch with dramatic competitive advantages in the face of other foreign brewers' severe competition in China.

Fourth, the term that QSAAO cannot sell its holding in Tsingtao to any persons or entities engaged in the brewing or beverage business, except to QSAAO's wholly owned domestic SOE subsidiaries which are acceptable to Anheuser-Busch, deprives QSAAO of a great deal of flexibility in dealing with Tsingtao. Such a term blocks the possibility of any indigenous brewer teaming up with Tsingtao through the acquisition of QSAAO's shareholding. Consequently, the likelihood of forming a gigantic indigenous brewer through mergers between Tsingtao and other large domestic brewers becomes very remote, if not impossible.

Fifth, it is still early to conclude the extent of support that Tsingtao will receive from Anheuser-Busch. The technological and managerial assistance from Anheuser-Busch is still at its initial stage. There has been little 'material' exchange in R&D areas. In terms of Tsingtao's global campaign, Anheuser-Busch has clearly pointed out that it has no intention of expanding Tsingtao's business in the US (Tsingtao Brewery Investment Agreement, 2002), the most profitable beer market globally. In this regard, Tsingtao's expectation of leveraging Anheuser-Busch's strength in its global expansion appears rather unrealistic.

In a nutshell, the strategic alliance between large indigenous brewers and leading global giants is bound to have a huge influence on the Chinese brewing industry. The competition among/between foreign and domestic brewers will significantly tighten up; extremely complicated competitive and cooperative relationships among all associated parties, foreign and domestic, are being developed. To a certain extent, it could be just a matter of time before large indigenous brewers, even including Tsingtao, become the *de facto* subsidiaries of global giants.

(iii) Competitiveness

Foreign brewers equipped with better facilities and advanced technologies are competitive. Table 3 shows that the number of foreign brewers declined from 126 in 1996 to 108 in 2002, but their share in the total number of brewers went up from 17 per cent to 21.6 per cent. Their assets had accounted for 37.4 per cent of the total assets of the Chinese industry and their production (in value terms) had accounted for 38 per cent of the industrial production.

Most foreign brewers pursue a strategy of focusing on premium brands, whereas most domestic brewers produce and market low value-added economy products. Industrial analysts estimate that about 80-90 per cent of the premium segment is controlled by foreign brands. Anheuser-Busch's Budweiser is the number one premium brand (Anheuser-Busch *Annual Report*, 2003), holding about 50 per cent of China's premium market. Leading global giant brewers' profitability and productivity are much higher than those of Chinese brewers, including the leading players like Tsingtao. Tsingtao is the largest indigenous player but its size is dwarfed by global giants. For instance, the total assets of InBev, Anheuser-Busch and SABMiller are respectively 21, 13 and 12 times Tsingtao's; their sales revenues are 12, 18 and 13 times those of Tsingtao's (Table 4). Competing in the global marketplace with such a small size can be extremely tough in such a conventional capital-intensive industry.

(c) Value Chain Integration and Systems Integrators

Emerging national giants expand territories through aggressive acquisitions. But an effective integration of the production, marketing, logistic network and brand structure of acquired brewers is far more challenging than acquisition itself. Large indigenous brewers like Tsingtao and Yanjing obtain bargaining power in relation to raw materials suppliers but have limited power over wholesalers on the sales side. This is because the market is not highly consolidated to allow large brewers to control wholesalers and brewers fail to keep instantaneous communication with wholesalers through the adoption of the latest IT. For instance, at Tsingtao there is no online database on the wholesaler and retailer sides to allow it to grab the latest sales data; no satellite or internet-based training programme targeting wholesalers or retailers. The feedback from wholesalers is far from adequate. In contrast, global giants' integration of the downstream value chain is substantially facilitated by advanced IT. Anheuser-Busch (*Annual Report*, 2002: 3) provides wholesalers in its home market with satellite-based training, and its internet-based communication systems

Table 3. Foreign Brewers in China

Year	No of Foreign Brewers (a)	Foreign Brewers/ Total Brewers (%)	Foreign Brewers Production/ Total Production (%) (b)	Foreign Brewers Assets/ Total Assets (%)
1996	126	170	36.0	35.1
1997	120	17.2	37.0	38.4
1998	101	17.5	37.1	38.8
1999	95	17.2	37.5	38.8
2000	101	18.7	36.7	37.3
2001	103	20.3	25.9	37.6
2002	108	21.6	38.0	37.4
2000/ 1996 CAGR	−2.5	4.0	1.4	1.0

Notes: (a) Refers to Greenfield investements and JVs from foreign countries, Taiwan province, Macao and Hong Kong
(b) Refers to production value
Sources: Compiled from and calculated based on data from China Food Industry Almanac, various years; author's own research

Table 4. Comparison between Leading Multinationals and Tsingtao, Asahi and Yanjing 2004

Companies	Beer Sales (hl mn)	Total Assets (US mn)	Net Sales (US$ mn)	EBIT (US$ mn)	Net Profit (US$ mn)	EBIT Margin (%)	Net Margin (%)	ROA (%)	EBIT/Assets	Productivity (US$)	Global Brands
InBev	234	25 198	11 610	1 775	974	15.3	8.4	3.9	7.0	155 431	Stella Artois, Skol, Brahms, Antarctica
Anheuser-Busch	160	16 173	17 160	3 361	2 240	19.6	13.1	13.9	20.8	545 895	Budweiser, Bud Light, Michelob
SABMiller (a)	159	15 225	12 901	1 749	1 344	13.6	10.4	8.8	11.5	317 227	Miller, Castle Lager, Pilsner Urquell
Heineken	122	14 117	13 557	1 391	728	12.5	5.4	5.2	12.0	219 609	Heineken
Carlsberg	92	8 104	6 553	452	164	6.9	2.5	2.0	5.6	207 793	Carlsberg
Molson Coors (b)	60	11 175	6 174	685	356	11.1	5.8	3.2	6.1	417 162	Canadian, Coors
S & N	50	12 665	8 490	870	517	10.2	6.1	4.1	6.9	540 275	Newcastle, John Smith's, Kronenberg
Grupo Modelo (c)	43	6 589	4 019	1 179	555	29.3	13.8	8.4	17.9	90 135	Corona, Modelo
Tsingtao	37	1 187	931	68	34	7.3	3.7	2.9	5.7	33 111	Tsingtao
Asahi	26	12 182	14 065	986	298	7.0	2.1	2.4	8.1	893 092	Asahi
Yanjing	26	892	565	47	33	8.4	5.8	3.7	5.3	55 077	Yanjing

Notes: hl=hectolitres; productivity=sales per employee; EBIT margin=operating profits/net sales; net margin=net profits/net sales; ROA=net profits/total assets.
(a) March 2004 to March 2005 data used for SABMiller and the rest for fiscal year ended in December.
(b) Coors and Molsom merged in February 2005; 2004 proforma data used.
(c) Anheuser-Busch holds a 50% equity ownership in Grupo Modelo.

Sources: Company *Annual Reports*; Molson Coors, 2004; Molson Coors 2005, management interview; author's own research.

generate sales data and customised sales tools almost instantaneously. Compared with global giants, indigenous brewers, including those top players, still have a long way to go before becoming a truly 'core systems integrator' or 'spiders of industrial web' in both the domestic and global competition arenas.

(d) Brand

We have seen that brand serves as one of the most important competitive advantages in the beverage industry. The implications for different markets, however, vary considerably. In China, the mass market is price driven but the emerging middle class is concerned more about brand image and beer quality (Euromonitor, March 2004). With the aid of brand value creation activities such as vigorous advertising, sponsorships, community schemes and packaging innovation, etc., global giant brewers concentrate on key high-end brands, targeted at consumers with higher purchasing power. It is only in recent years that domestic players started paying attention to brand management. A few emerging national giants, particularly Tsingtao Brewery and Yanjing Brewery, have just started to build up a nationwide brand system. In contrast, 'most small and medium-sized domestic brewers have not started building up a concrete brand system. Instead, they launch a large number of brands. Once a particular brand is no longer welcome in the market, they simply introduce new brands to replace the old ones' (interview, China Brewing Industry Association).

(e) Technology and Innovation

For a lengthy period from the 1950s to the 1980s, indigenous brewers' progress in innovation and technological improvements was extremely slow. It was recorded in the Annals of Tsingtao Brewery (1993: 89) that 'from 1903, the founding year of the (Tsingtao) Brewery, to 1979, the technical equipment at Tsingtao had remained at the original standard'. It was, however, during this lengthy period that global giants consolidated their home markets and quickly went global. Persistent technological improvement and innovations have played an indispensable role in the trajectory of global giants' national and global campaigns. The Chinese government in the late 1980s once assisted a couple of indigenous brewers[5] to improve their production standards and to improve the much-needed development of the brewing machinery manufacturing industry. Nonetheless, the endeavours were far from sufficient to thoroughly improve the overall underdevelopment of the brewing industry and its associated industries in the value chain.

The mid-1990s has witnessed aggressive penetration from global giants. To survive and compete, large indigenous brewers were pressured to draw attention to innovation, technological improvements and R&D. Large player like Tsingtao and Yanjing (interviews) have planned to allocate roughly 2-4 per cent of their annual revenues to R&D. They have also made progress in new products development. Given all this progress, however, Chinese brewers still face catch-up gaps. For instance, Tsingtao (*Annual Report*, 2002) is struggling to stabilise the taste of Tsingtao Beer brewed in different domestic locations. The bulk of domestic brewers, in particular small and medium-sized players, are incapable of quickly raising technological and technical standards: 'many are short of capital to make innovations or introduce advanced equipment… They can only compete in the low-end segment but foreign brewers take the risk of remaining in the high-end market even at the expense of losing money in the initial years due to their financial strengths and advanced technologies which reduce the unit costs' (interview, China Brewing Industry Association).

As far as packaging innovation - an important competitive advantage in the beverage industry - is concerned, foreign brewers take the lead both globally and in the Chinese market. For instance, Anheuser-Busch has been a consistent innovator. In 2001, Budweiser introduced China's first embossed beer bottle, along with other innovations such as vertical labels, fluted beer cans and large-mouth can openings (Anheuser-Busch website). In contrast, the Chinese brewers' response is considerably slower. At present, no indigenous brewers have adopted PET or PEN bottles. Tsingtao did not pay serious attention to packaging innovation till very recently. All indigenous brewers face huge catch-up gaps in incorporating the latest packaging developments but the under-development of the domestic packaging manufacturing industry, in particular, the glass bottle manufacturing industry, has considerably slowed down the catch-up of large indigenous brewers.

(f) The WTO Impact

The brewing industry does not belong to 'protected industries' following China's entry into the WTO. The tariff cut[6] of the WTO impact is very limited. It does not bring about a substantial increase in imports because most brewers would rather set up local operations to avoid high transportation costs. The most challenging aspect of the WTO impact lies in the fact that foreign firms and indigenous firms are being subject to the same regulations. Direct and indirect state intervention will have to reduce substantially. The likelihood of domestic brewers relying on government support to enhance their competitiveness is diminishing. Once the same level of income taxation regime is carried out, the profitability of a couple of emerging national giants, in particular Tsingtao Brewery and Yanjing Brewery that have been supported by preferential tax regulations, could reduce sharply.

More importantly, the property right reform, aimed at reducing government's shareholding in SOEs, is set to have the most far-reaching impacts on large indigenous firms in that this scheme will substantially raise the likelihood of large SOEs being taken over by competitive global giants. Large indigenous brewers, in particular the top ten players, are on the verge of being swallowed up. The decreasing benefits from industrial policies and a loose control on strategic alliances speed up the process of large indigenous brewers becoming global giants' overseas subsidiaries *per se*.

(g) Summary

The Chinese brewing industry has achieved substantial growth in the past two decades but is besieged by serious structural and non-structural weaknesses. Chinese brewers as a whole have to fill large catch-up gaps in a wide array of areas. Some traditional advantages are diminishing: the traditional sales networks are being challenged by increasingly popular modern trade; global giants have penetrated premium end-user markets like high street restaurants, hotels and bars; good relationships with local governments will no longer matter as much as they did following China's WTO obligations; indigenous brewers' successful experiences are being passed onto global giants through so-called strategic alliances; global giants have also quickly adjusted their strategies according to past lessons learned.

Foreign brewers' ambitious penetration, in the form of explosive M&As and increasing strategic alliances, is radically altering the competition matrix and speeding up concentration. Large domestic brewers face tremendous challenges. The so-called strategic alliance increases the likelihood of large indigenous brewers being swallowed up by global giants. On the global playing field, Chinese brewers are not in a position - now or in the near future - to compete with global giants. The burning issue that large Chinese brewers face at the current stage is, however, not going global, but rather securing their backyard in the face of ambitious foreign penetration.

5. Conclusions

In the globalisation era, the worldwide concentration led by giant multinationals has widely spread to almost each industry. Many people understand that in high-tech industries such as aeroplanes, automobiles, pharmaceuticals and computer sciences, etc., latecomers from developing countries face huge entry barriers and catch-up gaps. In industries where products are simple, there seems to be space for small-scale and low value-added local firms to survive. However, the adoption of the advanced technologies and the severe global competition, as we have seen in this chapter, has immensely increased the catch-up hurdle for local firms in developing countries; and these sectors also tend to be controlled in the hands of leading MNCs in a similar way that high-tech sectors do. This chapter explores a beverage sector where the entry barrier is relatively lower, but paradoxically the catch-up task remains huge. Global giant brewers have obtained huge competitive advantages and surpassed players from LDCs in a wide array of aspects. Large indigenous brewers in China are at a disadvantage and face imminent threat from global players.

Many people confuse the catch-up at the country level and at the firm level. The former is fundamentally different from the latter in that a country could make impressive economic progress through enhanced productivity made directly and indirectly by MNCs instead of indigenous firms. There exists a high likelihood of a country catching up but its indigenous firms not doing so[7]. A striking phenomenon is that many emerging national giants which in themselves were fostered by the Chinese government through decades of hard struggles are being acquired by foreign rivals in the form of so-called strategic alliances. Should this trend continue, which is very likely, there exists a fairly high possibility that foreign rivals will gradually become national giants' *de facto* owners. Consequently, building up the so-called national champions is much tougher than before; and may even face a challenge of crumbling. This is not only a particular phenomenon in the brewing industry, but also a challenging phenomenon in many other industries.

In sum, even in the low-tech sectors such as FMCG sectors where the entry barrier is relatively lower, the task of catching-up for developing countries at the firm level remains very difficult. The catch-up task at the firm level becomes even more challenging when large MNCs speed up the industrial concentration and increasingly introduce advanced technologies to the low-tech sectors.

Notes

1. It is measured by the number of years a competitive rival would take to catch up. The higher the sustainability, the tougher it is for latecomers to catch up.
2. Miller was acquired by South African Breweries (SAB) in 2002 and the combined company was renamed SABMiller. Interbrew and Ambev merged as InBev in March 2004. Coors and Molson merged in February 2005. Refer to Table 4 for global ranking.
3. Calculations based on data from China Food Industry Almanac, various years; and China Light Industry Almanac.
4. Acquired on the Hong Kong Stock Exchange in 1993.
5. For example, Tsingtao Brewery, Yanjing Brewery and Zhujiang Brewery.
6. Beer tariff has been reduced from 42 per cent in 2002 to nought per cent in 2004 (Ministry of Foreign Trade and Economic Cooperation, 2001: 171).
7. This point of view is contributed by Professor Peter Nolan.

References

Amsden, A. H., 'South Korea: Enterprising Groups and Entrepreneurial Government', in A. Chandler, F. Amatori and T. Hikino (eds), *Big Business and the Wealth of Nations* (Cambridge: Cambridge University Press, 1997)

Anheuser-Busch, *Annual Reports* (1998, 2002, 2003)

Annals of Tsingtao Brewery (Qingdao: Qingdao Publishing House, 1993)

Beer Science and Technology (pi jiu ke ji), (March 2004)

Beverage Industry (BI), 'Future Beer Wholesalers Consolidation Seen Ahead', 86: 11 (1995)

Beverage Industry (BI), 'Big Beer Ad Expenditures Stable', 87: 1 (1996)

Beverage World (BW), 'A Full House', 119: 1694 (2000)

Beverage World (BW), 'Heineken Takes Bottles for a Spin', 121: 9 (2002)

Brooks, H. E. and B. R. Guile, 'Overview', in H. E. Brooks and B. R. Guile (eds), *Technology and Global Industry: Companies and Nations in the World Economy* (Washington, DC: National Academy Press, 1987) 1-15

Chandler, A., F. Amatori and T. Hikino, 'The Large Industrial Enterprise and the Dynamics of Modern Economic Growth', in A. Chandler, F. Amatori and T. Hikino (eds), *Big Business and the Wealth of Nations* (Cambridge: Cambridge University Press, 1997)

Chang, H. J., *Kicking Away the Ladder: Development Strategy in Historical Perspective* (London: Anthem Press, 2002)

China Food Industry Almanac (*Zhong guo shi pin gong ye nian jian*) (1985 to 2002) (Beijing: China Food Industry Publishing House)

China Light Industry Almanac (*Zhong guo qing gong ye nian jian*) (1990 to 2003) (Beijing: China Light Industry Publishing House)

Cockerill, A., 'Economies of Scale, Industrial Structure and Efficiency: The Brewing Industry in Nine Nations', in A. P. Jacquemin and H. W. De Jong (eds), *Welfare Aspects of Industrial Markets* (Leiden: Martinns Nijhoff Social Science Division, 1977) 279-301

Dezutter, B., 'Experiences of Investing in Eastern Europe: A Study of a Multinational Brewing Company', *European Business Review*, 97: 3 (1997) 139-44

Dicken, P., *Global Shift* (London: Paul Chapman Publishing Ltd, 1998)

Euromonitor, Alcoholic Drinks in China (March 2004)

Everatt, D., *South African Breweries International: Devising a Chinese Market Strategy* (Western Ontario: Richard Ivey School of Business, 2000)

Fortune, 'The Year of the Mega Merger' (11 January 1999)

Freeman, C., *The Economics of Industrial Innovation* (London: Pinter Press, 1982)

Gourvish, T. R., 'Mergers and the Transformation of the British Brewing Industry, 1914-80', in Y. Cassis, F. Crouzet, and T. R. Gourvish (eds), *Management and Business in Britain and France: The Age of the Corporate Economy* (Oxford: Oxford University Press, 1995) 191-203

Gourvish, T. R., 'Concentration, Diversity and Firm Strategy in European Brewing, 1945-90', in T. R. Gourvish and R. G. Wilson (eds), *The Dynamics of the International Brewing Industry Since 1800* (London and New York: Routledge, 1998) 80-92

Gourvish, T. R. and Wilson, R. G., *The British Brewing Industry 1830-1980* (Cambridge: Cambridge University Press, 1994)

Guo, Y., 'The Global Big Business Revolution and the Challenge for Catch-up by Large Firms from Developing Countries: the Case of the Chinese Brewing Industry' (Judge Business School, University of Cambridge, Doctoral Dissertation, 2005)

Hawkins, K. and R. Radcliffe, 'Competition in the Brewing Industry', *Journal of Industrial Economics*, 20: 1 (1971) 20-41

Interbrew Company Presentation, 'Working Together to Move Beer Forward' (Interbrew UK, April 2003)

Lion Nathan Company Presentation, 'Lion Nathan China' (15 November 2002)

Marshall, A., *Principles of Economics* (London: Macmillan, 1920) (originally published 1890)

Marx, K., *Capital, Vol. 1* (Moscow: Foreign Languages Publishing House, 1961) (originally published 1867)

Ministry of Foreign Trade and Economic Cooperation, Compilation of the Legal Instruments on China's Accession to the World Trade Organization (Beijing: Law Press, 2001)

Molson Coors, Official Merger Notification Between Molson and Coors (December, 2004)

Molson Coors, Company Presentation to Analysts, New York (March 2005)

Morgan Stanley Dean Witter (MSDW), *The Competitive Edge* (New York: Morgan Stanley Dean Witter Research, 1989)

Müller, J. and J. Schwalbach, 'Structural Change in West Germany's Brewing Industry: Some Efficiency Considerations,' *Journal of Industrial Economics*, 28: 4 (1980) 353-67

Nolan, P., *Coca-Cola and the Global Business Revolution: a Study with Special Reference to the EU* (Cambridge: Judge Institute of Management Studies, 1999)

Nolan, P., *China and the Global Business Revolution* (Basingstoke: Palgrave Macmillan, 2001)

Nolan, P., D. Sutherland and J. Zhang, 'The Challenge of the Global Business Revolution', *Contributions to Political Economy*, 21: 1 (2002) 91-110

Nolan, P., *Transforming China: Globalization, Transition and Development* (London: Anthem Press, 2004a)

Nolan, P., *China at the Crossroads* (Cambridge: Polity Press, 2004b)

Penrose, E., *The Theory of the Growth of the Firm* (Oxford: Oxford University Press, 1995)

Porter, M. E., 'Competition in Global Industries: A Conceptual Framework', in M. Porter (ed.), *Competition in Global Industries* (Boston: Harvard Business School Press, 1986)

Porter, M. E., *The Competitive Advantage of Nations* (London: Macmillan, 1990)

Prais, S. J., *Productivity and Industrial Structure in the Brewing Industry: A Statistical Study of Manufacturing Industry in Britain, Germany and the United States* (Cambridge: Cambridge University Press, 1981) 110-37

Ruigrok, W. and R. van Tulder, *The Logic of International Restructuring* (New York: Routledge, 1995)

Scherer, F. M., *Industry Structure, Strategy and Public Policy* (New York: HarperCollins College Publishers 1996) 391-423

Schmitz, C. J., *The Growth of Big Business in the United States and Western Europe, 1850-1939* (London: Macmillan, 1993)

Schumpeter, J. A., *Capitalism, Socialism and Democracy* (London and New York: Routledge, 1976) (originally published 1943)

Sklair, L., *Globalization: Capitalism and Its Alternatives* (Oxford: Oxford University Press, 2002)

Tremblay, V. J., Strategic Groups and the Demand for Beer, *Journal of Industrial Economics*, 34: 2 (1985) 183-96

Tremblay, V. J. and C. H. Tremblay, Advertising, Price, and Welfare: Evidence from the US Brewing Industry, *Southern Economic Journal*, 62: 2 (1995) 367-81

Tsingtao Brewery, *Annual Report* (2002)

Tsingtao Brewery Investment Agreement 'Strategic Investment Agreement between Tsingtao and Anheuser-Busch' (2002)

Chapter 4

THE GLOBAL INDUSTRIAL CONSOLIDATION AND THE CHALLENGE FOR CHINA: THE CASE OF THE STEEL INDUSTRY

Peter Nolan and Huaichuan Rui

1. Introduction

1.1 Mainstream View

The 'mainstream', 'neo-classical view of the competitive process believes that the perfectly competitive model best describes the essence of capitalist competition. Departures from it are viewed as exceptional. In this view, there are limitless opportunities for firms from developing countries to 'catch-up' if they are forced into competition on the free market of the 'global level playing field'. At the heart of the mainstream view is the self-equilibrating mechanism of market competition. It is believed that the basic driver of the capitalist process, competition, ensures that if any firm enjoys super-normal profits rivals will soon enter to bid away those profits and undermine any temporary market dominance that the incumbent enjoys. The neo-classical approach emphasises the importance of competition among small firms as the explanation for the prosperity of the advanced economies. Milton Friedman, for example, believes that there is 'a general bias and tendency to overemphasize the importance of the big versus the small' (Friedman, 1962: 120-3).

Mainstream economists argue that managerial diseconomies of scale set in after firms reach a certain size. The classic expression of this view was contained in Marshall's *Principles of Economics* (1920: 315-6), in which he likens the competitive process to the 'trees in the forest'. The forest canopy never grows above a certain height. Large trees eventually lose their vigour and are replaced by newcomers: '[I]n almost every trade there is a constant rise and fall of large businesses, at any one moment some firm being in the ascending phase and others in the descending. Mainstream economists believe that 'mergers mostly fail' (Meeks, 1977). Such studies are usually based on an analysis of short-term returns to shareholders. The explanation that is usually advanced for mergers is the pursuit of power and wealth by CEOs, who are alleged to pursue their own interests at the expense of shareholders. Mainstream economists typically consider that mergers and acquisitions undermine national industrial competitiveness (Porter, 1998).

In recent years, the argument has gained ground that advances in information technology have created the possibility for a radical change in the nature of the firm. Activities that it was formerly rational to carry out within the firm can now be performed by networks of small firms connected by the Internet (Castells, 2000). This is widely thought to herald the rise of a new form of 'Post-Fordist' economic system based around 'clusters' of small businesses that can both compete and cooperate at different times (Piore and Sabel, 1984; Porter, 1990). This view appeared to be strongly reinforced by the rapid rise in the extent of outsourcing activities that were formerly carried on within the firm. In Coasian (1988) terms the very boundaries of the firm have shifted. Many researchers argue that the large corporation is 'hollowing out', and rapidly becoming an 'endangered species': 'While big companies control ever larger flows of cash, they are exerting less and less direct control over business activity. They are, you might say, growing hollow' (Malone and Laubacher, 1998: 147).

The spread of global markets has greatly reinforced the belief that 'catch-up' at the level of the firm is the normal path of capitalist development. It is argued that markets have become so vast that it is hard to imagine that any firm or small group of firms could dominate any given sector.

1.2 Non-Mainstream View

From the earliest stages in the development of modern capitalism, there were economists who believed that capitalism contained an inherent tendency towards industrial concentration. Marx (1967), in *Capital* Vol. 1 argued that there was a 'law of centralisation of capital' or the 'attraction of capital by capital'. The driving force of concentration was competition itself, which pressured firms to cheapen the cost of production by investing ever larger amounts of capital in new means of production and in 'the technological application of science', which in turn creates barriers to entry. In the early 1970s, on the eve of the modern epoch of globalisation Hymer (1972) visualised the possible outcome of the capitalist process if existing restrictions on merger and acquisition were lifted: 'Suppose giant multinational corporations (say 300 from the United States and 200 from Europe and Japan) succeed in establishing themselves as the dominant form of international enterprise and come to control a significant share of industry (especially modern industry) in each country. The world economy will resemble more and more the United States economy, where each of the large corporations tends to spread over the entire continent, and to penetrate almost every nook and cranny'.

Marshall's *Principles of Economics* provides numerous reasons to explain 'the advantages that a large business of almost any kind, nearly always has over a small one' (Marshall, 1920: 282). These included economies in procurement, transport costs, marketing, branding, distribution, knowledge, human resources, and management. By contrast, his explanation of 'managerial diseconomies of scale' resorts merely to an analogy ('the trees in the forest') without logic or evidence. Penrose's path-breaking book, *The theory of the growth of the firm*, addresses directly the issue of possible limits to the growth of the firm. Like Marshall, she identifies a number of potential advantages that can be enjoyed by the large firm. She considers that the most significant advantages for the large firm are those that she terms 'managerial economies'. Penrose concludes that there are no theoretical limits to the size of the firm: 'We have found nothing to prevent the indefinite expansion of firms as time passes, and clearly if some of the economies of size are economies of expansion, there is no reason to assume that a firm would ever reach a size in which it has taken full advantage of all these economies' (Penrose, 1995: 99).

Chandler has demonstrated the central role of the large, oligopolistic firm in technical progress in the business history of today's high-income countries. This was, in its turn, central to the whole growth dynamic of modern capitalism. He has shown that the modern industrial enterprise 'played a central role in creating the most technologically advanced, fastest growing industries of their day'. These industries, in turn, were 'the pace-setters of the industrial sector of their economies' (Chandler, 1990: 593). They provided an underlying dynamic in the development of modern industrial capitalism. Chandler emphasises the paradox that even as the number of firms in a given sector shrinks, competition between increasingly powerful firms can intensify: 'market share and profits changed constantly, which kept oligopolies from becoming stagnant and monopolistic' (Chandler and Hikino, 1997: 31).

The succession of studies which purport to show the irrationality of mergers and acquisitions are almost entirely based on the analysis of the consequences for shareholder value in the short-term. The much smaller number of studies which analyse the long-term impact of mergers and acquisitions on business survival and growth show a different story (Chandler, 1990; Nolan, 2001; and Boston Consulting Group, 2004). They suggest, rather, that well-selected and well-executed mergers and acquisitions that have a clear strategic purpose can increase the business capability of the firm concerned. They can strengthen the firm's presence in given geographical markets, increase its access to technologies it formerly did not posses, acquire scarce human resources, add valuable brands to its portfolio, and enable long-term savings through economies of scale and scope in procurement, research and development, and marketing.

1.3 The Global Business Revolution

In the 1990s, most constraints on firm growth were removed. Vast regions of the world were opened for competition. Privatisation was enacted across almost all countries. Cross-border restrictions on mergers and acquisitions were removed from all but a few sectors. The period provided a unique opportunity to test competing views of the competitive process. The period since the 1980s has seen an unprecedented intensity of mergers and acquisitions, with resulting high levels of concentration in a wide range of sectors, providing strong support for the non-mainstream view of the fundamental forces determining the nature of industrial structure. The concentration process was most obvious among the leading global giant firms, which we call 'systems integrators', who possess a combination of leading brands and technologies, multi-billion dollar procurement budgets and superior human resources. By the early twenty-first century, a virtual 'law' was becoming apparent. Unrestrained global competition resulted in a handful of firms accounting for one half or more of total global markets.

However, the depth of the challenge that firms from developing countries face on the 'global level playing field' is even deeper than appears to be the case at first sight due to the profound changes taking place through the 'cascade effect'. The small number of 'systems integrators' that dominate global markets place intense pressure on their supply chain to meet their global needs, which requires achieving the requisite scale necessary to build a global network of plants, to undertake the requisite investment in R&D, and to achieve the requisite reduction in unit costs through large volume of procurement. This intense pressure has meant that an explosive process of industrial concentration has taken place in the upper reaches of the global value chain. The invisible changes taking place 'below the water level' of the 'iceberg' of industrial concentration are at least as powerful as those that are more easily visible 'above the water level'.

The steel industry has traditionally been thought of as highly fragmented and low technology, offering large opportunities for firm level 'catch-up' in developing countries such as China. However, as shown below, the impact of global consolidation among 'systems integrators' and the resulting 'cascade effect' has compelled intense pressures on Chinese steel firms. Between December 2004 and August 2006, we conducted a case study on Baosteel and had interviews with fifty-two top and medium level executives in Chinese steel firms, multinational iron ore producing firms, and Chinese government and industry association officials. The interviews were conducted in Mandarin Chinese and English, and all interviewees were promised individual anonymity. From these interviews we have been able to collect valuable data used in the following sections of this chapter, to support our views in this first section.

2. Forces of Consolidation

2.1 Accumulated Problems of the World Steel Industry by the 1990s

Steel is an important industry, and is likely to remain so, far into the future. Although it accounts for only about 0.5 per cent of world gross domestic product, customers of steel companies are responsible for nearly 20 per cent of global output. In 2004, US$ 500 billion worth of steel was consumed in sectors ranging from car-making to construction (*FT*, 29 Sep 2004). World steel output increased from 135 Mt in 1947 to 716 Mt in 1980. In the following decade and a half output stagnated due especially to the collapse of the USSR. In the late 1990s, global growth resumed, rising from 752 Mt in 1995 to 1116 Mt in 2005 (Table 1).

Table 1. World Steel Output and Average Growth Rates 1947-2005

Year	Output (Mt)	Years	average growth rate (% per annum)
1947	135	n. a.	n. a.
1970	595	1947-70	6.2
1975	644	1970-75	1.6
1980	716	1975-80	2.2
1985	719	1980-85	0.1
1990	770	1985-90	1.4

Year	Output (Mt)	Years	average growth rate (% per annum)
1995	752	1990-95	−0.5
2000	848	1995-00	2.4
2003	965	2000-03	4.4
2005	1132	2004-05	6.2

Source: IISI, 2006.

In the wake of World War II steel was regarded as a strategic industry. It was widely protected by the state. In many countries a national champion state-owned steel company was nurtured which dominated the domestic market. Even after widespread privatisation of steel firms from the 1970s onwards, the extent of cross-border merger and acquisition was very limited. Even at the end of the 1990s, the industry was regarded as one with a low level of industrial concentration.

2.2 The Impact of the Cascade Effect upon the World Steel Industry since the 1980s

A value chain comprises all the intervening steps leading from 'upstream' raw material processing to an ultimate 'downstream' sale of the final product. In order to minimise costs across the whole value chain, systems integrators deeply penetrate their respective value chains both upstream and downstream, as stated above. Steel has an important place in the supply chain of many industries, with customers in construction, defence, machinery (including automobiles), and home appliances. Its own supply chain includes iron ore, coke, coking coal, water, and logistics. Since the 1990s most of these industries have consolidated rapidly, internationalised and achieved high levels of technical progress. For example, in the automobile industry, which is one of the main customers for steel, intense competitive pressures have stimulated consolidation among systems integrators. These include the merger of Daimler and Chrysler, Ford's acquisition of Volvo Motors and Jaguar, GM's acquisition of Saab, and Renault's acquisition of a controlling share of Nissan. By 2003 the top five automotive manufacturers accounted for over 60 per cent of global production. On the upstream side of the steel industry, in the iron ore industry, intense consolidation meant that by 2003 three giant firms (Rio Tinto, BHP

Billiton, and CVRD) produced almost half of the world's total iron ore output and accounted for 70 per cent of the global seaborne iron ore trade.

Finance is an essential part for any industry to create and add value. Steel firms also make efforts to attract funding for investment. However, the world financial market has also been highly globalised (Smith, 2002) and financial resources tend to flow to those firms with the best returns. From 1989 to 2000, the world steel industry's average total shareholder return was negative. It was also lower than the total shareholder returns of other basic-materials industries (Stikova and Maug, 2004). As a result, steel firms were relatively starved of external sources of finance. This was an important stimulus to consolidation in the steel industry, which it was hoped would improve returns and attract more financial resources to the industry.

Steel firms cannot escape the pressure of the cascade effect from either the upstream or the downstream side. They have been forced to interact with a diminishing number of larger customers and suppliers, each with massive bargaining power, adopting new methods of procurement and logistics organisation. Since the 1980s there has been large scale movement of manufacturing into low and middle-income countries. Steel firms have faced the choice of either following their traditional customers or losing them (Morooka, 2002). Steel firms can only join and retain their place in the world's leading manufacturers' supply chains by meeting their intense and remorselessly advancing technology, price, and service requirements:

> Competitive pressure is leading manufacturers to seek out ways to optimise added value, reduce costs and enhance their offer to meet different requirements around the world. To this end, purchasing is becoming increasingly centralised, with outsourcing based on close relationships with sub-contractors, and an accelerating pace of technical innovation through partnerships (Arcelor, 2003: 35).

The only counterweight to the enormous leverage of corporations who make up the buyers is to 'think big, merge or buy out others, thereby expanding capacity and expunging competition' (Wheelan, 1999). As we will see below, this is the fundamental reason that the top ten steel firms in recent years have entered a period of intense merger and acquisition, as well as forming strategic alliances with both customers and suppliers.

3. Consolidation and its Consequences

3.1 Consolidation

Between 1995 and 2005, the world steel industry entered a period of intense merger and acquisition. No fewer than eight new names appeared in the list of the world's top ten steel firms (Table 2), each of which emerged from mergers and acquisitions. The progress can be illustrated by the fact that in 1993 the top ten producers supplied only around 150 Mt but the figure had doubled to approximately 300 Mt by 2005. There is a consensus of opinion in the world's steel industry that the consolidation process will continue unabated. In 2003 and 2004, both Chief Executives of Arcelor and Mittal Steel, the world number one and number two by then, forecasted that within a decade, there would emerge one or two giant firms with a capacity of 100-120 Mt, and several firms with a capacity of 50-100 Mt. They believed that this handful of 'truly global players' would have a footprint in all the major regions (SSS, 2003; Mittal, 2004). Interestingly, in 2006 we have witnessed the merger of these two giant firms. In order to better understand the dramatic consolidation in the steel industry, we demonstrate the growth path of the two leading firms below.

Table 2. Steel Firms' Rank and their Output 1995-2004 (Mt)

Rank	1995		1998		2002		2004	
1	Nippon	27.8	Posco	25.6	Arcelor	44.0	Mittal	57
2	Posco	23.4	Nippon	25.1	LNM	34.8	Arcelor	43
3	British Steel	15.7	Arbed	20.1	Nippon	29.8	Posco	32
4	Usinor	15.5	Usinor	18.9	JFE	28.9	Nippon	32
5	Riva Group	14.4	LNM Group	17.1	Posco	28.1	JFE	30
6	US Steel	12.1	British Steel	16.3	Bao-steel	19.5	Nucor	20
7	NKK	12.0	Thyssen Krupp	14.8	Corus	16.8	US Steel	20
8	Arbed	11.5	Riva Group	13.3	Thyssen Krupp	16.4	Thyssen Krupp	20
9	Kawa-saki	11.1	NKK	11.5	US Steel	14.4	Bao-steel	20

Rank	1995		1998		2002		2004	
10	Sumi-tomo	10.7	USX	11.0	Nucor	12.4	Corus	19
Top ten total A		154.2		173.7		245.1		293
World total B		752		777		902		1000
A/B(%)		20.5		22.3		27.1		29.3

Sources: *FT,* 29 Sep 2004; IISI, 2003, 2004; *Annual Reports* of individual companies, various years; Osiris, 2004.

Arcelor. In 2001 Arcelor overtook Nippon Steel to become the largest steel firm in the world as the result of a merger between Europe's three largest steel firms. For European steel firms, there were severe difficulties arising from the movement of manufacturing capacity out of Europe, compounding the difficulties caused by a stagnant market. The main growth opportunities for large European steel firms lay in expanding capacity in distant markets, but this also required increased scale. The merger provoked a great deal of debate among competition experts. However, the EU competition authorities and the three relevant governments approved the merger on the grounds that it would facilitate substantial synergies between the companies and lower costs.

The three-way merger created the world's largest steel group with 110 000 employees and a capacity of 46 Mt. The new firm had a powerful position in the world's high value-added steel market. After the merger Arcelor became the world's biggest producer of flat carbon, long carbon and stainless steel (Arcelor, 2003). However, only a short while later, the competitive landscape in the global steel industry altered once again in a dramatic fashion with the formation of the Mittal Group.

The Mittal Steel Company. The Group was arguably the only truly global steel corporation, and the most successful acquirer of under-performing steel-making facilities around the world. It began life in only 1976 under the name 'Ispat'. It acquired the United States' sixth largest firm in 1998, making itself the world's eighth largest steel maker with an annual output of 12.5 Mt. The acquisition provoked intense discussion about the tendency towards internationalisation in an industry that for decades had been organised mainly on national lines (*FT,* 18 and 19 March 1998). After the year 2000, the company began a series of acquisitions in Central and Eastern Europe. In October 2004, the company (in the name of LNM) launched a further move in its global expansion with the US$ 4.5 billion acquisition of the United States'

International Steel Company. This merger created the world's largest firm, the Mittal Steel Company. By 2005 Mittal Steel had shipments of 63 Mt and revenues of over US$ 28.1 billion. It employed 224 000 people in 16 countries.

On the completion of this acquisition, Mittal Steel's chairman announced that the company's goal was to produce 100 Mt of steel annually within five years and that it would seek further acquisitions in Asia (*FT*, 26 October 2004). However, Mittal accomplished this goal even earlier than expected through its historical hostile takeover with Arcelor in 2006. The 25.8 billion euro (US$ 32.3 billion) deal will establish the new company ArcelorMittal by middle 2007, which will control 10 per cent of the world steel market with more than 320 000 employees operating in 61 plants across 27 countries (ArcelorMittal, 2006). The significance of this merger is far beyond the expected synergies, estimated at US$ 1.6 billion (Mittal Group, 2006). As well reflected in the latest summary by Mr. Mittal himself (2006), this merger has opened 'the ultimate phase of consolidation' in the world steel industry, won 'undisputed global leadership' with 'unmatched strength', therefore matched 'the concentration level of main customers [and suppliers] to regain pricing power' and will eventually achieve sustainable advantage and growth (Mittal, 2006: 17-24). ArcelorMittal's market strength is shown in Figure 1, which shows that for the first time, an auto steel firm has caught up with the market power of the leading auto assemblers. Moreover, the new entity could mobilise its entire global resources to expand in emerging markets, as reflected in its intention to acquire more firms in China, including Baosteel (see below).

Figure 1. Matching Concentration Level of Main Customers to Regain Pricing Power

Automotive producers
global market share   Automotive Steel producers
global market share

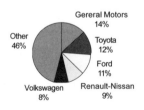 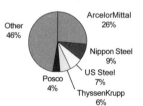

Top 5 producers represent
54% of market   Top 5 producers represent
53% of market

Source: Mittal, 2006:18.

3.2 Consequences of Consolidation

We have seen that under intense pressure from the cascade effect arising from global industrial concentration, since the 1980s leading steel firms have entered a period of intense consolidation. The share of the top ten steel firms rose from 21 per cent in 1995 to over 29 per cent in 2004 (see Table 2). Of the top ten steel firms in 1995, only Nippon Steel had an output of over 20 Mt, but by 2004, nine of the top ten firms had an output over 20 Mt.

High Value Products and Industrial Concentration

Even more significant than the increased levels of industrial concentration in terms of tonnage of steel is the fact that the leading steel firms account for an even larger share of global markets in terms of value of sales revenue (Table 3). The total market for global steel rose from around US$ 250 billion in 1995 to US$ 300 billion in 2003, with the share of the top ten firms rising from almost 51 per cent to over 55 per cent in the same years. In other words, the world's leading steel firms make products with higher unit values, due mainly to the fact that their products are specialised and technologically advanced to meet the demands of leading global customers. Indeed, within different sub-sectors of the steel industry, levels of concentration are even higher. For example, stainless steel accounts for only 2.5 per cent of the world's steel production by weight, but it accounts for 12.5 per cent of the global steel turnover by sales value (*Metallurgy Management*, 2004). In 2003 the five largest stainless steel makers accounted for 44 per cent of total world output (MEPS, 2004). As a result, the world steel industry is fast becoming bifurcated, one section producing low quality, low value-added products, typically for local firms, and the other producing high value-added, high profit margin products for global firms.

Table 3. Share of the Top Ten Steel Producers in Sales Value (Rank By Output) (Million US$)

	1995		2003	
Rank	Firms	Sales value	Firms	Sales value
1	Nippon Steel	22 969	Arcelor	31 836
2	Posco	11 181	LNM	12 000
3	British Steel	11 032	Nippon	16 479
4	Usinor	15 719	JFE	22 672
5	Riva Group	4 474	Posco	14 930
6	US Steel	6 872	Baosteel	14 548
7	NKK	18 711	Corus	14 640
8	Arbed	8 979	US steel	9 458
9	Kawasaki Steel	12 064	ThyssenKrupp	22 488
10	Sumitomo Metal	14 830	Nucor	6 266
A	Top ten total	126 831		165 317
B	World total	250 000		300 000
A/B (%)		50.7		55.1

Notes: (a) As Nippon and ThyssenKrupp have a relatively large proportion of sales revenue from non-steel sales, the figures in this table referred to the sales value of their steel and steel-products only.

(b) The data for Riva Group refers to that of 1997. The data of US Steel refers to 1996.

Sources: IISI, 2004; *Annual Reports* and press releases of each company in this table; *Fortune*, various years; *Steel Times*, 1998, 226 (12):435.

Enhanced Market Power and Intensified Consolidation Pressures

In 2003-04 the prices of many grades of steel increased by 50-100 per cent in most countries, and the share prices of the publicly quoted steel companies outperformed stock markets by almost 50 per cent (*FT*, 29 September 2004). In part this was caused by the boom in Chinese steel demand, but in part also it is thought to have been stimulated by the preceding period of intense consolidation, which permitted the bargaining power of large steel firms with their main customers to increase. A major motive for the steel industry's drive towards consolidation was the consolidation process in the surrounding value chain, especially in the auto and iron ore industries. In a symbiotic fashion, the subsequent consolidation process in the steel industry and the soaring steel price have helped to drive further consolidation in the surrounding industries.

In general, the more consolidated a particular sector is, the higher is the industry's bargaining power with the steel companies. For example, the household appliance sector is considered among the most exposed to higher steel prices 'since the industry is highly competitive, with few companies capable of passing on increases in raw material prices to consumers' (*FT*, 24 September 2004).

Spread of the Cascade Effect into Developing Countries

In order to meet their customers' needs, the global giant steel firms are rapidly expanding their production capabilities in fast-growing developing country markets, in order to supply their customers from a relatively short distance away and ensure just-in-time supply of high quality steel. Firms from developing countries find it relatively easy to enter the production of low technology, low value-added steels, but to compete with the global giants in high value-added segments of the market is a much deeper challenge.

4. The Challenge for Chinese Steel Firms

China is the world's largest steel market. The growth of global giant manufacturing firms' production systems in China has stimulated a rush of multinational steel firms to follow them to the country. The challenges facing Chinese steel firms have been accentuated by the impact of China's membership of the WTO, which has led to the reduction of tariffs, removal of subsidies, increased entry of international steel firms, and rapid growth of their direct production in China.

4.1 Global Steel Giants Target China

As we will see later, China already imports a large fraction of its high value-added steel from the world's leading steel firms. However, as Table 4 shows, each of the world's top ten steel companies has given high priority to expanding or starting their production operations in China. Posco's view is representative of the attitudes of these firms:

China is a formidable steel power, accounting for a fifth of the world's production and a quarter of its consumption. This, as well as close proximity to Korea and rapidly growing local demand for high-quality steel products, makes the Middle Kingdom a key market for us as we continue to shift our focus to value-added steel grades (Posco, 2003).

Table 4. The Formation of the Top Ten Firms and their Presence in China

Rank	Resulting firm	Merged or Acquired firm	M&A firms	Presence in China year
1	Mittal	LNM (MNCs), Ispat (MNCs), ISG (US)	2005 2004	Green-field project, JV with Valin, Wugang,etc
2	Arcelor	Unisor (France), Arbed (Luxembourg and Belgium), Aceralia (Spain)	2006 2001	JVs with Laigang, with Baosteel, and Nippon
3	Posco	Share-swap with Nippon	1999	15 JVs located all over China
4	Nippon	Share-swap with Posco	1999	JVs with Baosteel, and Arcelor
5	JFE	NKK (Japan) Kawasaki (Japan)	2003	JV with Guangzhou Iron & Steel
6	Nucor	BHP (Australia), Trico (US), Birmingham (US)	2002 2003	n.a
7	US Steel	US Steel (US), National Steel (US)	2003	Actively seeking partners to form JV
8	Baosteel	Shanghai Metallurgy Holdings (China), Meishan Group (China), etc	1998	JVs with Nippon, ThyssenKrupp, and Arcelor
9	Thyssen Krupp	Thyssen (Germany), Krupp (Germany)	1999	JVs with Baosteel, Angang, and plants in Wuhan, Dalian
10	Corus	British Steel (UK) Hoogovens (Netherlands)	1999	n.a

Note: All top ten firms have various cooperative relations with each other or with their value chain firms, which have not been demonstrated here due to limited space.

Sources: *Financial Times* and *Annual Reports* of these companies.

Comparatively, global steel firms have competitive advantages in one or more of a range of attributes, including product quality, product diversity, faster distribution channels, better and more reliable service, and a large spend on R&D. Consequently, the global steel giants place intense pressure on indigenous Chinese steel firms to improve their core competence, spend more on R&D and advanced equipment, and upgrade their management skills.

4.2 The Problems Facing the Chinese Steel Industry

China is the world's largest consumer of steel, reaching 376 Mt in 2005 (Figure 2). However, its per capita consumption is still below the global average, so there is still massive potential for further expansion of China's steel consumption as the country continues its surging industrialisation. China's steel output grew from 52 Mt in 1990 to over 371 Mt in 2005. However, this incredible growth masks deep problems, of which, diseconomies of small-scale production is the key problem.

Figure 2. China's Steel Consumption, Production, Import and Export 1990-2005 (Mt)

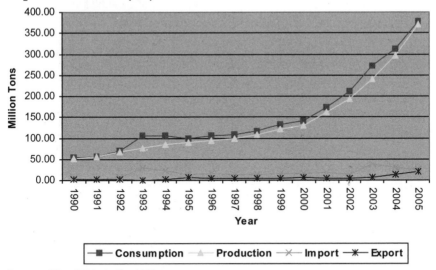

Sources: Yin, 2003: 4; Jia, 2006

In sharp contrast with the surge in industrial concentration among the world's leading steel firms, the share of China's top ten steel firms in total national steel output, fell from 49 per cent in 1999 to 37 per cent in 2003 (Table 5). By

2005 there were still 95 per cent of steel firms with an annual output below
500 000 tons. 'Small-scale has inevitably led to excessive segmentation and
excessive competition, irrational resource allocation, and low investment in
R&D' (Jia, 2004). As a result, most Chinese steel firms lack core competence.
In 2003 around nine-tenths of China's steel imports consisted of high value-
added products (Table 6). Indeed, the share of domestic supply in total supply
of high value-added steel products is declining, despite the surge in domestic
steel output (Table 7). The gap between the Chinese steel firms and their
foreign counterparts is shown in Table 8.

**Table 5. Change of Market Share of the Top Ten Chinese
Steel Firms 1999-2003 (Mt)**

Rank	Firm	Output	Rank	Firm	Output			
		2003			2002	2001	2000	1999
1	Baosteel	19.88	1	Baosteel	19.48	19.14	17.70	16.70
2	Angang	10.18	2	Angang	10.07	8.79	8.80	8.50
3	Wugang	8.43	3	Shougang	8.17	8.25	9.00	7.30
4	Shougang	8.17	4	Wugang	7.55	7.09	6.70	6.20
5	Bengang	7.20	5	Bengang	6.21	4.91	4.20	3.90
6	Tanggang	6.08	6	Magang	5.38	4.77	3.90	3.60
7	Hangang	6.06	7	Tanggang	5.07	4.60	3.20	3.20
8	Pangang	5.33	8	Pangang	5.00	4.70	3.60	3.30
9	Baogang	5.25	9	Hualing	4.91	4.10	2.80	3.00
10	Hualing	5.19	10	Baogang	4.80	4.20	3.90	3.90
Top ten total		81.77			76.64	70.55	63.80	59.60
National total		222.34			192.18	160.68	131.46	121.00
Top ten share(%)		36.78			39.88	43.91	48.53	49.25

Sources: CSIA, 2004; Yin, 2003; Jia, 2004.

Table 6. China's Imports of High Value Steel Products 2003 (Mt)

Items (high value products)	Quantity
Cold rolled sheets	9.65
Hot rolled sheets	6.98
Galvanized sheets/coated sheets	7.60
Cold rolled silicon sheets	1.58
Stainless sheets	2.75
Alloy steel sheets	0.75
Other high quality products	3.77
Sub-total (high value products)	33.08
Total import	37.17
Share of import by high value products	89%

Sources: Wu 2004: 5; Jia 2004.

Table 7. Change of Market Share in China's Steel Market by Home Products (%)

	All steels	Medium sheet	Hot-rolled sheet	Cold-rolled sheet	Galvanized sheet	Tin plate	Silicon sheet
2001	90.06	98.37 (a)	78.41	62.17	46.47	75.57	-
2002	88.41	95.2	74.16	59.55	37.88	71.72	64.59
2003	86.31	89.8	57.0	51.82	29.54	66.82	53.76

Note: (a) This was the figure of 2000.
Source: Wang, 2004:18-22.

Table 8. The Comparison of the China Top Five and the World Top Five Steel Firms (Rank by Revenue of 2003; Million US$, Million Tonnes)

	Firm	Revenue	Asset	Profit	Employee	Output
China Five						
1	Baosteel	14 561	20 809	947	102 039	19.88
2	Shougang	5 521	7 569	124	94 786	8.17
3	Angang	3 806	8 151	617	115 971	10.18
4	Bengang	3 565	5 393	72	95 458	7.20
5	Wugang	3 303	5 646	221	87 914	8.43
Total		30 756	47 568	1 981	496 168	53.86
Average		6 151	9 514	396	99 234	10.7
World Five						
1	Arcelor	29 339	31 039	291	98 264	42.8
2	Nippon	25 903	35 632	368	46 233	31.3
3	JFE	21 901	35 800	946	52 557	30.2
4	Posco	14 930	17 430	1 675	27 475	28.9
5	Corus	13 001	11 421	−499	49 400	19.1
Total		105 074	131 322	2 781	273 929	152.3
Average		21 015	26 264	556	54 786	30.5

Notes: (a) The China Five were the top five steel firms in the China 500 in 2004, the 500 largest firms in China ordered by revenue in 2003. The World Five were all the steel firms in the *Fortune* 500 in 2004 except Baosteel as it has been listed in the China top five.

(b) Figures for the China Five have been converted from RMB to US$ at the rate US$1 = 8.27 Yuan.

Sources: Liu, 2004: 21; *Annual Report* of each company.

4.3 China's Steel Industry Confronts the Challenges: The Case of Baosteel

China's steel industry policy-makers have, indeed, endeavoured to achieve industrial consolidation. The number of 'large-scale' steel companies, i.e. with over 500 000 tons annual output, fell from 1669 in 1994 to around 200 in 2005. The central government strongly encourages steel firms to expand their scale through both vertical and horizontal integration. Both Chinese and international analysts are agreed that Baoshan Iron and Steel Group Co. Ltd ('Baosteel') is by far the most competitive large Chinese steel firm, and the one with the greatest chance of competing with the global giants. It is, therefore, worthwhile giving special attention to this firm.

Baosteel's Competitiveness

Baosteel is a modern 'greenfield' plant, built in three stages between 1978 and 2001, with a total investment of 117 billion *yuan* (about US$ 14 billion). This greatly exceeded the annual total investment in China's steel industry, which amounted to 46 billion *yuan* in 1980 and 78 billion *yuan* in 1985 (CSIY, 2001: 133). The project was fiercely debated, with heavy criticism from those who favoured the allocation of the investment to existing large steel firms. By 2001 Baosteel had grown to be the only Chinese steel firm in the world's top ten steel giants by producing 19 Mt of crude steel. In 2003, Baosteel became the first Chinese steel firm to be listed in the *Fortune* 500.

Baosteel has important competitive advantages over its rivals, including both domestic firms and some international ones. It was the only large steel firm to be entirely equipped with advanced imported facilities, and permitted to use entirely imported high-grade iron ore. China's large steel firms all began life before 1976. This left them all with large 'legacy' problems in terms of old equipment and huge workforces, which was the case also for some of the leading international steel firms. Uniquely among large Chinese steel firms, the productivity of the listed Baosteel matches that of the world's leading steel companies. From the start, Baosteel was designed to focus on high technology, high value-added steel in order to substitute for imports. It has been the sole or the major domestic supplier of specialist steel for sectors such as automobiles, ship-building, pipelines and beverage cans. It has benefited greatly from the booming Chinese market. Baosteel has attracted outstanding management personnel, enthusiastic to work in China's leading indigenous steel company, with its serious intent to become a leading international firm.

Despite these advantages, even Baosteel faces large challenges from the internationalisation of China's steel industry in its efforts to secure a leading position in the high value-added segments of the steel industry. Over many years, it faced intense competition in high value-added steels from imports. For example, joint venture car-makers used mainly imported steel. However, as we have seen, alongside Baosteel's increased capability in supplying such steels, it faced a growing challenge both from rising imports (see Figure 2) and surging production within China by the multi-plant operations of the international steel giants, which is reflected in the consistent decline of market share by home products in all high value products (see Table 7). This threatens Baosteel. As its Chairwoman Xie (2004) acknowledged: 'There are obvious gaps between Baosteel and leading world steel firms, in terms of core competence, R&D capacity, new technology, human resources, and international management capability'.

Baosteel's Strategy: Struggle to Move Up the Global Value Chain

Acknowledging the gap with the global steel firms, Baosteel follows a strategy of pursuing alliances with both upstream and downstream global giants in order to secure its position within the global value chain, and has become the most active steel firm in China to strengthen itself by building up joint ventures and strategic alliances.

Following in the footsteps of global steel firms, Baosteel is seeking opportunities for overseas expansion, including not only increasing global procurement, but also setting up joint ventures to start overseas production. The reason is, once again, not that Baosteel cannot sell its products in China, but that it wants to link itself closely to global value chains: a joint venture in Brazil could allow Baosteel access not only to the Brazilian rich iron ore, but also to the massive American steel market.

Prospect of Baosteel

Baosteel has sufficient other reasons to be optimistic about its future success. One is the belief that Chinese firms can use the massive domestic market as a bargaining weapon to achieve rapid technological catch-up, 'exchanging markets for technology', or 'learning by doing'. Nippon and Posco are widely taken as the best examples of firms in late-developing countries that eventually surpassed their international rivals. However, research (e.g. Yonekura, 1994) has discovered that the most important factors in Japan steel's success were consistent focus on innovation, the monopoly position of the Big Five steel firms, and the constraints on cheap imports, which were all fuelled by the Japanese government.

China's top five steel firms, including Baosteel, in contrast to Japan's Big Five, in recent years have been unable to enjoy a monopoly position and prevent imports into China. While high investment in R&D was key to Japan steel's success, it is unclear how successful Baosteel has been in upgrading its technology through imports and building up joint ventures. Nor are there any data available to determine how much Baosteel spends on R&D.

The Failure of the Industrial Policy

When Deng Xiaoping approved the Baosteel project based mainly on imported equipment, he required that Baosteel should: 'Grasp control of new technology, and strive even more for innovation'. In 1983 the government even established the 'State Council Leading Group of vital technology and equipment', which aimed at obtaining key technology from imported equipment. However, 'after two decades of effort, despite considerable progress, the gap between China and the world in key technology and equipment, at least in the steel sector, has not been diminished, but has even widened' (anonymous official).

China's leading policy-makers now recognise explicitly the failure of the country's industrial policies. In his speech of September 2004, almost three years after China joined the WTO, Li Rongrong, Head of the National Assets Commission (*guoziwei*) acknowledged that 'there is still a huge gap between China's large enterprises and the world's leading multinational companies. ... Speeding up the process of nurturing a group of large enterprise groups with international competitive capability is a great strategic task for the country's economic and social development'. According to Li (2004), China is far from being a 'workshop of the world' in the sense that Britain was in the nineteenth century.

However, despite such awareness, consolidation among indigenous Chinese steel firms has been painfully slow. Multinational steel giants are making use of the advantage of forming JVs with leading Chinese firms to organise their own integrated production systems involving multi-plant operations across the whole of China. Some analysts have expressed the fear that top indigenous firms will be defeated one by one (*ge ge ji po*) by the global competitors. Local protectionism has prevented large-scale merger and acquisition of steel firms in different regions. The central government, meanwhile, does not have integrated government policies on M&A, trade, foreign investment, and R&D. It admits that in the market economy it can only play the role of an 'advisor' for a 'free marriage' but not act as the 'parent' for a 'forced loveless marriage'. There is the sharpest possible contrast between the painful progress of steel industry consolidation in China and the explosive process of consolidation globally.

Moreover, the Chinese government has also signalled its clear intention to gradually sell off the state's ownership in the country's leading firms. This raises the possibility of China's leading steel firm, Baosteel, being acquired by one of the global industry leaders. Mittal's takeover of Arcelor immediately raises the fear of the possibility of the acquisition of Baosteel by the new ArcelorMittal. Although Baosteel itself downplays the possibility, ArcelorMittal has identified China as a key market for its future growth and has called on the Chinese government to relax its controls over foreign ownership of steel companies in China (*FT*, 18 September 2006).

5. Conclusion

Mainstream economists believe that the basic tendency of capitalism is competition with strict limits to growth of firm size. They consider that, accordingly, developing economies should open up to global competition so that indigenous firms can take advantage of the broad opportunities to catch up with world leading firms (World Bank, 1997). However, they rarely distinguish between catch-up at the level of the country and catch-up at the level of the firm. International policy advisors to transitional and reforming developing countries typically pay little attention to the real structure or tendencies in international business systems within which indigenous firms must compete on the 'global level playing field'.

This chapter has shown that consolidation is the dominant feature of the international business system in the age of the 'global business revolution'. An unprecedented degree of industrial consolidation and concentration of business power at a global level has taken place since the 1990s. The most easily visible part of the structure of the industrial consolidation is the well-known firms with powerful, globally recognised brands and/or powerful technologies. In those industries that are heavy consumers of steel, this includes firms such as GM, Ford, Toyota, and Renault-Nissan in automobiles, Whirlpool, Electrolux, Bosch-Siemens, GE and Maytag in household appliances, Coca-Cola, Pepsico, Anheuser-Busch, Interbev and SABMiller in beverages. These constitute the 'systems integrators' at the apex of extended value chains. As they have consolidated their leading positions, they have exerted intense pressure across the whole value chain in order to minimise costs and stimulate technical progress. The 'cascade effect' across the global value chain has stimulated a period of unprecedented consolidation in the world's steel industry, resulting in the rapidly increasing size and power of leading steel firms such as Mittal, Arcelor, and Posco.

As this chapter has shown, the challenge that the global business revolution presents for firms from developing countries is much deeper than at first appears to be the case. Not only do firms from developing countries face immense difficulties in catching up with the leading systems integrators, the visible part of the 'iceberg'. They also face immense difficulties in catching up with the powerful firms that now dominate almost every segment of the upper reaches of the value chain, the invisible part of the 'iceberg' that lies hidden from view beneath the water. The steel industry is widely considered to be one in which the opportunities for 'catch-up' at the firm level for firms from developing countries are relatively high. However, even the world's largest steel producer, China, has produced only one firm that has any possibility of becoming established as a globally competitive firm over the long-term. Even for this firm, the prospect is uncertain, despite its considerable achievements. The reality of industrial concentration during the global business revolution presents immense challenges both for firms and for policy-makers in developing countries, even in the steel industry.

References

Arcelor, *Arcelor: A portrait* [www document]

ArcelorMittal, Company news [www document]

Boston Consulting Group, *Growing through acquisitions* (Boston: BCG Publishing, 2004)

Castells, M., *The rise of the network society*, 2nd edn. (Oxford: Blackwells, 2000)

Chandler, A., *Scale and Scope: the Dynamics of Industrial Capitalism* (Cambridge, Mass.: Harvard University Press, 1990)

Chandler, A., and T. Hikino., 'The large industrial enterprise and the dynamics of modern economic growth', in Chandler *et al*, (1997)

Chandler, A., F. Amatori and T. Hikino (eds), *Big Business and the Wealth of Nations* (Cambridge: Cambridge University Press, 1997)

Coase, R. H., *The Firm, the Market and the Law* (Chicago: University of Chicago Press, 1988) (originally published 1937)

CSIA, China Steel Industry Association, 'The rating of domestic steel firms among China Top 500 firms' [www document]

CSIY, *China Steel Industry Yearbook* (Beijing: CISY Editor Department, 2000)

Financial Times (*FT*), various issues

Fortune magazine, various issues

Friedman, M., *Capitalism and Freedom* (Chicago: University of Chicago Press, 1962)

Hymer, S., 'The multinational corporation and the law of uneven development' (1972) reprinted in Radice, H. (ed.) (1975)

IISI, International Iron and Steel Institute, *Steel Statistical Yearbook 2003* (Brussels: IISI, 2003)

IISI, International Iron and Steel Institute, *Steel ranks* [www document]

IISI, International Iron and Steel Institute, *World Steel in Figures* [www document]

Jia, Y., Interview, Beijing, 15 August 2004

Jia, Y., Interview, Beijing, 1 September 2006

Li, R., 'The potential danger of industrial chain can be seen. China's steel firms face life and death question', Xinhua News Net, quoted from [www document]

Liu, K., The analysis report of steel firms within Top 500 Chinese firms, *Metallurgy Management*, 9 (2004) 20-6

Malone, T. W. and R. L. Laubacher, 'The dawn of the e-Lance economy', *Harvard Business Review* (September-October 1998)

Marshall, A., *Principles of Economics* (London: Macmillan, 1920) (originally published 1890)

Marx, K., *Capital, Vol 1* (New York: International Publishers, 1967 edn.) (originally published 1867)

Meeks, G., *Disappointing marriage* (Cambridge: Cambridge University Press, 1977)

MEPS (International), 'Global stainless-steel output up by 4.4%' [www document]

Metallurgy Management, 'World steel industry needs super-large size of merger' 1 (2004) 51

Mittal, *Forging Ahead*, quarterly bulletin of LNM Group, Issue 1 [www document]

Mittal Group, News release [www document]

Morooka, Y., Presentation at the Association of Women in the Metal Industries on 13 March 2002 in Cleveland, OH.

Nolan, P., *China and the Global Business Revolution* (London: Palgrave Macmillan, 2001)

Osiris, Public companies worldwide [www document]

Penrose, E., *The Theory of the Growth of the Firm* (Oxford: Oxford University Press, 1995, 2nd edn.)

Piore, M., and C. Sabel, *The Second Industrial Divide: Possibilities for Progress* (New York: Basic Books, 1984)

Porter, M., *The competitive advantage of nations* (London: Macmillan, 1990)

Porter, M., *On competition* (Boston: Harvard Business School, 1998)

Posco, *Annual Reports* (2003 and 2004)

Radice, H. (ed.), *International firms and modern imperialism* (Harmondsworth: Penguin Books, 1975)

Smith, C. R, *Globalization of financial markets* [www document]

Steel Times 1998

SSS, Steel Success Strategies 18th Annual Conference, held in June 2003 by World Steel Dynamics and *American Metal Market*, in New York. Quoted from Mueller, H. 'Steel Success Strategies 18 Winners Emerging', *Steel Times International*, (July/ August 2003) 36-8

Stikova, J and Maug, E, 'Arcelor: Creation of a European Steel Company', memo (Berlin: Institute for Konzern management, Humboldt Universität zu Berlin, 2004)

Wang, J., 'Comments on supply and demand in domestic steel market in 2003', *China Steel*, 3 (2004) 18-22

Wheelan, S., 'British Steel and Hoogovens merge' [www document]

World Bank, *China 2020* (Washington D C: World Bank, 1997)

Wu, X., To develop steel industry in a comprehensive, coordinated and sustainable way, *Metallurgy Management*, 2 (2004) 4-7

Xie, Q., 'Ascend to *Fortune* 500 to compete with world giants: exclusive interview with Xie Qihua' [www document]

Yin, R., The achievement, issues, and prospects of China's steel industry, *Metallurgy Management*, 5 (2003) 4-11.

Yonekura, S., *The Japanese Iron and Steel Industry, 1850-1990.* (Basingstoke: Macmillan, 1994)

Chapter 5

CHINA IN
THE ASIAN FINANCIAL CRISIS:
'CUTTING THE TREES TO SAVE
THE FOREST'[1]
(*KAN SHU JIU LIN*)

Peter Nolan and Wang Xiaoqiang

Introduction

In December 1997, shortly after the onset of the Asian Financial Crisis (AFC), the Chinese Central government sent Wang Qishan, then president of the China Construction Bank, to become a member of the Guangdong provincial party committee. One month later, he was appointed executive vice-governor of the province. The Guangdong provincial party committee subsequently set up the 'Five-member team to deal with financial crisis'. Its main task was to deal with the intensifying payment crisis in Guangdong. Two of the flagship companies of Guangdong, Guangdong International Trust and Investment Corporation (GITIC) and Guangdong Enterprises (GDE), were insolvent and unable to survive. After intense debate, the Guangdong government decided to bankrupt GITIC and restructure GDE. These events caused an outcry in the international press. International creditors had wished to believe that regardless of the fate of the enterprises, the Chinese government would pay in full the international debts as it had normally done in the past.

In October 2000, after intense debate and tough negotiation, GITIC repaid US$ 85 million at the third creditors' meeting. In December 2001, the *International Financial Review* awarded GDE the title of 'Asia's best debt restructuring project'.[2] Subsequently, a much less-publicised event was the fact that by borrowing RMB 45 billion from the central government, the Guangdong provincial government had been able to restructure and close more than 800 local small and medium non-bank financial institutions. This was the third step to deal with the financial crisis by the Guangdong provincial government following the bankruptcy of GITIC and the restructuring of GDE.

On 7 December 2000, the Hong Kong newspapers reported that Wang Qishan would be returning to Beijing. This move was a promotion, since Wang Qishan would now be ranked a Minister rather than a Vice-Minister. Executive Vice-Governor Wang Qishan was regarded as having done a good job. He would become the head of the Office of Economic System Reform of the State Council – 'the leading minister in charge of economic reform'.

The AFC had passed. The debate on GITIC bankruptcy and GDE restructuring was no longer the focus of the press and the public. However, compared with the dramatic impact caused by the superficial story, the events had much deeper significance. They posed deep and critical challenges. They provided a terrifying warning of the dangers that lay in wait for the whole Chinese system of political economy as the country opened up further in the future. They showed the crucial importance of the financial sector in that process.

Until today, the widely-held view of the Asian Financial Crisis is that it had no substantial impact on China. This is attributed to the fact that China did not have capital account convertibility; that the capital inflows into China were mainly long-term FDI; and that the country had a strong trade and foreign exchange position. Since October 2000, we had been investigating and studying the 'three steps' to deal with the financial crisis by the Guangdong government. This study demonstrated that China's economic and financial system was far more vulnerable than most people realised, due to the high possibility of the AFC spreading into the heartland of the Chinese Mainland through Hong Kong and seriously affecting Guangdong Province, Hong Kong's 'backyard', the most highly developed province in the country, and the one most closely integrated with the international economy.

The impact of the AFC upon Guangdong was mediated through two channels. Firstly, it was channelled through international financial inflows into Guangdong, mainly from or through Hong Kong, especially through the international trust and investment companies (ITICs) at various levels and the red chip companies in Guangdong. The second, and apparently unrelated channel, was through the massive internal capital flows from elsewhere in China to Guangdong. The massive capital flows through the two channels flooded into Guangdong seeking for higher returns than the market average and were concentrated in a relatively limited part of the province, the Pearl River Delta. In 1997, the Pearl River Delta was one of the most dynamic in the world in terms of economy but also one of the most fragile in terms of the potential impact of the financial crisis. The strong impact of the AFC upon Hong Kong directly and indirectly led to a massive payments crisis not only in the red chips in Hong Kong and the ITICs on the Mainland but also in the local small and medium non-bank financial institutions including urban credit cooperatives (UCCs) and rural financial associations (RFAs). The red chips and ITICs had large international debts and local small and medium non-bank financial institutions had massive domestic debts. It was possible that the extensive payment crisis in Guangdong would not only spread into the ITICs, UCCs, and RFAs across the whole country, but also into the country's state-owned banks, which had massive debts and were themselves undergoing overall rectification. The crisis in Guangdong therefore threatened the security and stability of the whole country's financial system.

1. A Complex and Critical Challenge

The impact of the AFC on Guangdong produced one of the deepest challenges up until that point for China's reform strategy of 'groping for stones to cross the river'. Guangdong is the pioneer of China's gradualist reform and a successful model. The unprecedented payment pressure induced by the AFC exposed deep problems that had been accumulating over the years in Guangdong, and were exacerbated by the province's speculative bubbles: 'As the tide retreats the rocks begin to appear'.

The Vulnerability of Guangdong's Economy

In the late 1980s and the first half of the 1990s, Guangdong, with a population of over 70 million, achieved faster growth than any developing country. The province rose from low to middle-income level within a decade and a half. At the centre of the province's growth was the Pearl River Delta (PRD). The PRD's population (23 million) is as large as that of Taiwan or Malaysia. Real incomes of indigenous Guangdong residents had grown substantially during the high-speed growth process. Despite this super-normal high-speed growth, Guangdong was highly vulnerable to the impact of the AFC, due to its high degree of reliance on foreign capital and exports.

Since the 1980s, low value-added export processing industries from Hong Kong and East Asia had been transferred to the PRD on a large scale. Hong Kong and Guangdong province had formed a relationship of 'the shop at the front (Hong Kong) and the workshop at the back (Guangdong)' (*qian dian hou chang*).

Migrant workers from all over the country provided unlimited availability of low-cost labour for the rapid growth of Guangdong's export processing industry. From the 1980s to the 1990s, Guangdong province, and the PRD in particular, became the most important location for receiving FDI in China. By 1999, the province received around US$ 87 billion in 'actually used FDI', around 80 per cent of which went to the PRD, amounting to around US$ 3000 per person. This was probably the highest for any comparably-sized region in the world. The nine Pearl River Delta 'cities'[3] accounted for no less than 30 per cent of total Mainland FDI in 2001.

The Guangdong economy is highly integrated with the international economy. In 1997, the total value of Guangdong's imports and exports was equivalent to 150 per cent of the province's GDP, and the value of exports alone was equivalent to 86 per cent of the province's GDP. The bulk of the investments and manufacturing orders came directly from, or were channelled through, Hong Kong. In 1996, exports from foreign invested enterprises (*san zi qi ye*) and (*san lai yi bu*) enterprises accounted for 78 per cent of the province's total exports. In other words, 86 per cent of the Guangdong economy depended on exports, of which almost 80 per cent were contributed by foreign invested enterprises and '*san lai yi bu*'. This, to a large degree, depended on Hong Kong. In 1996, exports to Hong Kong and Macao accounted for 86 per cent of Guangdong's total exports while imports from Hong Kong and Macao accounted for 79 per cent of Guangdong's total imports. The majority of the investment and production in the province directly relied on Hong Kong. The AFC and the financial crisis in Hong Kong would definitely cause difficulties for Guangdong.

Guangdong's high-speed growth depended on foreign investment and exports. After the mid 1980s, with the progress in China's financial system reform, there were two flows of short-term 'hot money' flooding into Guangdong. A huge flow of capital poured into the province from international financial markets. On several occasions, GITIC and GDE issued bonds in the international capital market. More than 40 ITICs at various levels of the Guangdong government, the red chips listed in Hong Kong and up to one thousand 'window companies' in Hong Kong, borrowed heavily from international commercial banks through various channels. By the end of the 1990s, Guangdong's officially-registered borrowings totalled around US$ 18 billion. However, the official data does not include many of the borrowings by the TICs, which were not registered with the State Administration of Foreign Exchange (SAFE). Nor does it include the large sums borrowed by Guangdong's Hong Kong red chips and other window companies, which did not need to be registered with SAFE. The real extent of the overseas liabilities of Guangdong-based firms and institutions was far greater than the official figures suggested.

Even worse, the full extent of taking on new debts to pay for old debts would never be known until the firms became bankrupt.

Another flood of 'hot money' poured into the province. This flood came from other regions of China. A huge total of funds across the length and breadth of the country sought high returns outside the official banking system (*gao xi lan chu*) (high interest to pull in deposits), which was formally under tight control in terms both of the rates of interest offered and the allocation of funds. Guangdong's ITICs and the ITICs from other provinces in the country eagerly 'invested' (*tou zi*), or, more accurately, speculated (*tou ji*), in Guangdong. Guangdong was the first province to undergo financial reform. The province not only set up GITIC following the establishment of CITIC at the national level, but also had non-bank financial institutions such as various local ITICs, UCCs and RFAs developing vigorously 'like mushrooms springing up after the rain'. They made use of the high-speed growth story of Guangdong and created a variety of myths, giving depositors from all over the country promises of high returns from investing in Guangdong. Guangdong's official data estimates that funds up to at least RMB 100 billion flooded into the province through various local non-bank financial institutions.[4]

The two flows of 'hot money' appear to be unrelated. In fact, they were bound to have complex inter-relationships. Beginning from opium smuggling, Guangdong has always been the first to reform and open up during the historical process of China's modernisation. The majority of the 30 million overseas Chinese in South East Asia originated from Guangdong. In 1976, when China just began to reform and open up, the American historian J. K. Fairbank proposed the concept of 'China on the sea': 'Today, Guangdong is again leading China's international trade. "China on the sea" has fully developed, including the British colony of Hong Kong, Singapore, Taiwan, and tens of thousands of overseas Chinese in Kuala Lumpur, Penang, Bangkok, Manila, Colombo and other areas'.

Fairbank's insight helps us to understand the reality that in the area of developing export processing industries the widespread kinship relationships wove a complex network of 'the shop at the front and the workshop at the back' between Guangdong and Hong Kong, as well as Taiwan and Singapore, within a very short period of time. Dongguan City alone had over 40 000 Taiwanese business people resident in the city by the late 1990s, living in their own autonomously-run 'Taiwan village'.

The same logic applies to the opening-up of China's finance. Guangdong in particular, was the first to develop rapidly on the basis of such a network of 'China on the sea'. The two flows of 'hot money' both from home and abroad are definitely not simple textbook transactions consisting, as they do, of a myriad of anonymous agents. They interwove with each other, supplemented each other, and 'brought out the best in each other' using their own special channels of material flows, human flows and capital flows, and on the basis of an internal credit network. One can easily imagine that the participation of foreign business people with good credit would greatly enhance the credibility of investment projects and make fund-raising easier.

For example, Enping is well-known across the country for its skill in 'spinning'. It is a bleak place almost without any world class factories. However, it has large-scale and luxurious leisure facilities that are well up to international standards, invested in and managed by overseas Chinese, catering for foreign business people and high-ranking government officials. From this sharp contrast, one cannot help but suspect that these facilities provided 'special business functions' beyond the mere consumption of the services on offer at these facilities that were packed with people.

It is safe to hypothesise that against the background of high-speed growth of the export processing industry, there were countless cases of borrowing both domestically and internationally, nurtured by the intimate links between local people and their overseas relations, which promoted, directly and indirectly, the growth of a huge speculative bubble in Guangdong province.

After the mid 1990s, the large speculative bubbles in the property market in Guangdong, Macao and Hong Kong burst one after the other. One could say that the bubble in the Macao property market was created by the financial institutions and firms from Guangdong. The large speculative bubble in the Hong Kong stock market and property market reached a frenzied peak in 1997. This was closely related to the speculative activities by the firms with Mainland background operating in Hong Kong. The bursting of the bubble brought heavy financial pressure onto the various financial institutions engaged in property market speculation. Perhaps this was the direct force that drove these financial institutions to 'encircle money' (*quan qian*) both at home and abroad, promising ever higher returns?

Economics cannot explain what happened in Enping. The RCCs in Enping, followed by the local branch of China Construction Bank, talked about building local cement factories, promising interest rates of more than 30 per cent. They attracted up to RMB 10 billion in funds from all over the country. Similar fund-raising miracles took place in the non-bank financial institutions such as UCCs and RFAs on different scales and to different degrees. In 1991, the RFAs in Guangdong entered the cities, competing for residents' deposits by offering a 36 per cent interest rate. With the increasing difficulties in capital turnover, the return was increased to as much as 40 per cent. During the 1990s, the savings rate in Guangdong was already very high. In the mid-1990s, the investment rate in Guangdong was over 40 per cent. Indeed, Guangdong needed large amounts of capital investment in environment, education, medical care, infrastructure, research and development, housing for ordinary people and repairing a deeply damaged physical environment. However, the problem was that these badly-needed development projects that were desperate for investment could not produce such high private returns.

In fact, an annual investment return of over 30 per cent for cement plants in Enping was unrealistic, even if the demand for Enping's cement had been higher and the cement plants had been better managed. It was simply a matter of time before a payment crisis emerged. The only explanation for the offer of such high returns is that this was a form of gambling. Many depositors, having placed their 'bets', were able to exit safely having made enormous amounts of money. The widespread corruption and criminality that was revealed afterwards among the borrowing institutions show that these so-called '*gao xi lan chu*' are in essence 'Ponzi schemes'. For a short period of time and within a given area, the game could be played repeatedly, as long as the fresh supplies of money that were coming in were sufficient to pay the high returns that had been promised to the previous generations of depositors. The greater the amount of money sucked in, and the faster the speed at which it was pulled in, the greater the incentive for the institutions to speculate and take risks, and the greater the incentive to make even wilder promises of higher returns to attract potential depositors.

Unfortunately, for the financial authorities, the more money and the faster it was collected, the more serious the payment crisis that was eventually bound to erupt, and the greater the anger of the depositors cheated of their savings. Against the wild background of financial institutions 'springing up like mushrooms after the rain' and the 'Ponzi schemes' vying with each other to pull in funds, the gambling games played by the two flows of 'hot money' were bound to come to a halt at some point, independently of the impact of the AFC upon Hong Kong and the transmission of that impact to Guangdong. The phrase used by the local people '*shui luo shi chu*' (the rocks appear as the tide retreats) to describe the payment crisis across the whole of the province after 1998 is most appropriate. The '*gao xi lan chu*' that took place in Enping had a scale of up to ten billions of *renminbi*. It was exposed before the overall payments crisis in Guangdong emerged, due to the occurrence of large-scale runs on financial institutions and was dealt with during the 'three steps' to resolve Guangdong's financial crisis. Enping provided an advance warning of the precise meaning of 'the rocks appear as the tide retreats'.

Hong Kong's Financial Crisis

In 1983, the Hong Kong government pegged the Hong Kong dollar against the US dollar at the rate HK$ 7.8 per US dollar, establishing a form of currency board. In 1993, the Hong Kong Monetary Authority (HKMA) effectively assumed the function of 'lender of last resort' to the Hong Kong economy, and became the territory's *de facto* central bank. The AFC broke out only hours after the Special Administrative Region (SAR) had returned to the Mainland on 1 July 1997. During the AFC, Hong Kong's currency peg came under intense pressure from international speculators as contagion spread throughout the region. Following the collapse of currencies across the region, the speculators bet that the HKMA would at some point abandon the fixed peg. A dramatic battle took place over several months as the HKMA intervened to defend the exchange rate. Speculation against the Hong Kong dollar was closely linked with rumours that the Mainland would devalue the *renminbi*, which had been fixed at 8.3 to the US dollar for the previous three years. The fate of the two currencies was inextricably linked, especially through the deep inter-relationship between Hong Kong and Guangdong. During the crisis, the People's Bank of China (PBOC) officials even promised that in the last resort China would use its own foreign exchange reserves to assist the SAR. Defence of the Hong Kong dollar carried a high price in terms of the impact on the Hong Kong currency. The HKMA believed that this was a price worth paying, as it was the fixed currency peg that provided the ultimate source of security behind Hong Kong's role as an international financial centre.

The prolonged battle against the speculators began abruptly on 22 October 1997 and did not end until almost a year later, when it was revealed that Long-Term Capital Management was close to collapse. This forced the hedge funds to wind back their speculative activities and finally took the pressure off the Hong Kong dollar. To defend the currency, the HKMA sharply raised interest rates and used large amounts of its US dollar reserves to maintain the exchange rate. At one point, it mounted an unprecedented intervention in Hong Kong's stock market, buying an estimated US$ 13-14 billion in blue chip shares to thwart the speculators' ingenious 'double play' against the currency and the stock market simultaneously. In defending the Hong Kong dollar, Hong Kong's industrial interests were harmed seriously, since the Hong Kong dollar was effectively heavily revalued against the other currencies in the region,[5] reducing the competitiveness of its direct exports, and, especially, re-exports from the Mainland.

The effect on the Hong Kong economy was profound. The impact of the AFC upon Hong Kong marked the end of an epoch in the territory's development. Instead of 'communism' damaging the SAR's economic prospects, as so many had feared, Hong Kong's thriving capitalist culture had received a severe wound from capitalism itself. The free market in international finance, with the untrammelled 'right' to shift money wherever and whenever it wished, massively damaged the booming economy. If vibrant, powerful, confident Hong

Kong, regional 'home' to most of the global financial giants, could be so damaged, what were the chances of other less successful economies surviving against the massive force of global financial speculation?

The direct consequence of Hong Kong's 'financial crisis' was the collapse of the stock market and the property market. As the Hong Kong dollar appreciated against the other currencies in the region, speculation intensified about the impact on the Hong Kong economy. On 23 October, the same day as the speculation was launched against the Hong Kong dollar, the Hang Seng Index experienced its largest ever one-day decline. Over four days the market fell by 23 per cent. Between 30 September 1997 and 23 October 1997, in fewer than 20 days of trading, the Hang Seng Index dropped from 15 049 to 9767, a decrease of 35 per cent. The red chips in Hong Kong, with their Mainland backing, fell even more precipitously. Comparing the peak in 1997 with the situation on 14 August 1998, the Hang Seng Index fell 59 per cent, while the index for red chips fell 86 per cent. Among the 47 major red chips, the share price of forty dropped by over 80 per cent and twenty dropped by over 90 per cent. Thereafter, the market capitalisation of the red chips kept falling. In particular, after the bankruptcy of GITIC and during the restructuring of GDE, the two red chips under GITIC were themselves undergoing bankruptcy and liquidation proceedings, and the five red chips under GDE ceased trading. This further affected the continuing fall in the share price of the other red chips. Some of the red chips ended up totally worthless. In the words of one commentator: 'Objectively speaking, it is a miracle beyond imagination that any Western enterprise could manage to survive without the support from the government, after its share price dropped more than 90 per cent'.

The majority of Mainland companies in Hong Kong engaged in the property business through borrowing. Alongside the collapse in the stock market, Hong Kong's property market fell by over 50 per cent. The value of the red chips' assets, including shares and property, shrank by up to 80-90 per cent. Unfortunately, the companies' debts did not fall proportionately. Under these circumstances, even if any given red chip company had been well managed, it could not have escaped insolvency. Moreover, the pressure from creditors increased suddenly. During the financial crisis, Hong Kong enterprises with a Mainland background faced especially strong pressure to repay their debts.

In the financial crisis, the asset liquidity level became the basis for the survival of enterprises. 'Cash is the king' was the common wish of all the enterprises during the crisis. Even famous international firms based in Hong Kong, with a strong asset base, went bankrupt due liquidity failure. Peregrine, the so-called 'father of red chips', with assets of HK$ 24.6 billion, ranked in the *Fortune* 500, went bankrupt because of its inability to pay debts of US$ 60 million. The Zhengda Group, so-called 'prince of the princes', one of sixteen A-ranked

Hong Kong securities companies, went bankrupt because of an inability to pay debts of HK\$ 80 million.

During the financial crisis, many international banks based in Hong Kong had serious losses elsewhere in the region, and faced their own liquidity difficulties. As they stepped up their efforts to recover their debts from other 'Peregrines' and 'Zhengda Groups', they were faced with the reality that private companies in Hong Kong increasingly faced bankruptcy. In contrast, the Mainland-backed companies in Hong Kong not only had no record of bankruptcy, but also had 'the glorious tradition that the government would always step in to repay the debts in full'. Consequently, the red chips and H-share companies in Hong Kong suddenly became the targets for creditors, despite the fact that the fall in their share prices had been more severe than that of other Hong Kong companies.

Scholars estimated that the international debts of the Mainland companies in Hong Kong totalled over US\$ 80 billion. This estimation is not exorbitant, if we consider that GITIC and GDE alone had international debts of around US\$ 10 billion, and that they controlled a total of seven red chip companies. In addition, there were several tens of other red chip companies, as well as the H-share companies and countless 'window companies' backed by government institutions from all over the country. These companies all borrowed from each other, loaned to each other and acted as each others' guarantors in Hong Kong, weaving an open and gigantic network and forming a minefield of 'contingent liabilities'.

In January-April 2002, the 59 H-share companies and 69 red chips accounted for 32 per cent of the volume of equity transactions in the Hong Kong market. Nearly 21 per cent of the private enterprises from the Pearl River Delta had set up offices in Hong Kong. In addition, it was reported that of the more than 8000 Hong Kong companies that established plants in Dongguan, 130 had been listed in Hong Kong. Like the Mainland-backed companies in Hong Kong, these companies had complex relationships with each other. In the words of one commentator: 'If this "minefield" had exploded, and all the red chips, like Peregrine or Zhengda Group, had become bankrupt according to the principles of the market economy that companies are responsible for their own profit or loss, then Hong Kong's economy would have been finished'. The red chips, whose market capitalisation shrank by 90 per cent during the crisis, were the weak point of Hong Kong's financial system. They were the potential breaking-point threatening collapse of the whole Hong Kong economy. Hong Kong eventually managed to withstand the severe trial of the AFC after resisting the powerful attacks one after another from the international speculators. This was due partly to the HKMA's 'bayonet fight' with the international speculators. It was also due to the fact that the Mainland authorities adopted the correct approach to deal with the Mainland-backed enterprises in Hong Kong, particularly the ITICs and red chips in Hong Kong that had such gigantic international debts.

The Mainland government could not directly intervene in Hong Kong's economic affairs, but they had responsibility for the SAR now that it was back under Chinese sovereignty. Concern for the crisis in Hong Kong deeply influenced China's analysis of the policy options available to them in dealing with the crisis. In explaining why the Guangdong government decided to save GDE, but not GITIC, Wang Qishan said that the Chinese government regarded the issue as 'one beyond mere economic considerations'. He particularly pointed out: 'GDE is a group company registered in Hong Kong and includes five listed companies. We must consider the stability of the Hong Kong market'. He said he not only 'did not want to throw Hong Kong's stock market into turmoil', but that 'China should make a contribution to Hong Kong's stability'. Ultimately, among the 32 red chips whose share price dropped by more than 88 per cent, only GITIC's Guangxin Enterprise was liquidated, and this was due to the bankruptcy of GITIC. The Mainland government as well as the local governments and institutions from all over the country, used the GDE restructuring as the model, and contributed huge amounts of cash, injected a large number of high-quality assets and saved these giant companies on the brink of bankruptcy. Therefore, we can say that in real economic terms they did, indeed, save Hong Kong's economy from collapse.

Guangdong's Payment Crisis

The fall in trading and orders for export processing products in Hong Kong had a direct impact on the export processing industry in the Pearl River Delta – the pillar for the economic development in Guangdong – in three respects: FDI, trading, and orders for export processing products. Compared with the period from January to June 1997, between July to December 1997, export orders fell 4.9 per cent and price fell 5.3 per cent for the 73 export processing enterprises in Shenzhen and Baoan. In 1998, for the 92 enterprises mainly exporting to South East Asia in Shenzhen and Dongguan, export orders decreased by an average of 30 per cent and export orders from Japan decreased by 20 per cent. In the first quarter of 1998, exports to Thailand and Indonesia from Jiangmen declined 35.4 per cent and 11.2 per cent respectively. Exports to South East Asia and South Korea from Guangzhou declined 25 per cent and 78 per cent respectively. Along with the fall in exports, came a decrease in FDI. In 1997, Guangdong's growth rate of 'actually used FDI' was only 2.2 per cent and in Shenzhen was minus 1.9 per cent. Between January and February

1998, new foreign investment projects in Dongguan declined 50 per cent, compared with the same period in 1997. Under these circumstances, Guangdong's GDP growth rate fell from 22.3 per cent in 1993 to 10.6 per cent in 1997. This was the official data reported against the background that Premier Zhu Rongji required the national GDP growth rate to be maintained at 8 per cent.

Guangdong's export processing industry was propped up by migrant workers. The overall recession in the processing industry slowed down the pace of growth in the province, and caused social troubles due to problems such as overdue wage payments and unemployment. However, these difficulties were manageable and would not have had a disastrous impact upon the provincial economy.

What could not be digested was the fact that the significant worsening of the economic prospects for the region exposed as myths the promise of super-normal returns from financial games. The precise meaning of 'the rocks appear as the tide retreats' is that the 'high tide' of continuous high-speed economic growth had receded. Without the foundation of real growth over 20 per cent, people no longer believed the myth of high returns of 30 per cent, 40 per cent and even 50 per cent. Moreover, domestic and international creditors began to worry that their investment would never be recovered and demanded immediate repayment. The closure of the Hainan Development Bank in 1998 caused large-scale migration of deposits from local non-bank financial institutions (NBFIs) to the big four commercial banks. The large-scale migration of deposits during the financial crisis meant that Guangdong's NBFIs, big and small, struggled to survive, unable to continue the game of borrowing new debts to pay the old debts at an increasingly high rate of interest. Frequent runs took place on many institutions and projects. Once some institutions encountered a payment crisis and restricted deposit withdrawals, the contagion of the credit crisis grew in scale, and spread further afield, leading to more urgent runs across a wider area and on a larger scale. This then caused more serious payment difficulties and eventually evolved into a self-justifying and self-strengthening credit crisis.

Across Guangdong Province, especially in the Pearl River Delta, but also in some other areas, a deep crisis of runs on financial institutions developed. As early as 1996, serious runs took place on the Enping Branch of the China Construction Bank and the rural credit cooperatives (RCCs) in Enping. Following hard on the heels of these crises were runs on the UCC of Fukang Town in Zhongshan and the UCC of the High-tech Development District. In May 1997, RFAs in Zhanjiang, Jieyang, as well as other areas had payment crises. By 1998, not only RFAs in Zhanjiang, but also those in Maoming, Shantou and Shanwei had widespread payment crises. Trust and Investment Companies

(TICs) in various localities were in crisis, with problems including individual deposits, international debts, the securities business and enterprise bonds: 'First was the restriction on money withdrawal. The withdrawal permitted fell from thousands to hundreds of *yuan* per day. Later, it was even impossible to withdraw ten *yuan*. This caused large-scale runs. To a certain degree, systemic risks exploded.' In Shantou, large-scale runs spread to the state-owned commercial banks. In Huadu, a UCC was besieged by the masses. Water and food supplies were cut off if the UCC failed to provide money. Violent fighting even took place. The credit-payment crisis in the small and medium local financial institutions spread over the whole province. Over sixty large-scale runs took place. Many times runs developed into serious social riots. Angry depositors even camped outside the provincial government headquarters in Guangzhou, protesting in demonstration against the cessation of deposit payments.

An even more urgent matter was the pressure from international creditors in Hong Kong. On the first day that Wang Qishan walked into his office in the provincial government, the first affair for him to deal with was the urgent debt problems at GITIC and GDE. The debts of GITIC and GDE not only far exceeded the value of their respective assets, but also were beyond the payment capabilities of the Guangdong provincial government. How could the Guangdong government ask for help from the central government? The central government must consider not only the individual case of GITIC, but that of the 329 TICs across the whole country that had been borrowing from all over the world. The central government had also to consider not only the individual case of GDE, but also the fact that among the thirty-two red chips in Hong Kong whose share price had crashed by over 88 per cent, twenty-nine did not belong to the GDE Group. Could the central government save them all?

The Danger of the Crisis Spreading to the Mainland

After intense efforts to reduce their numbers and rectify their operations, by 1999, 329 TICs were still left across the country. The total value of their assets was US\$ 50 billion. It is estimated that the TICs' officially-registered international debts amounted to over US\$ 30 billion and their unregistered international debts also amounted to more than US\$ 30 billion. In addition, the international debts of the Hong Kong red chips were between US\$ 19-25 billion. That is to say, the international debts of the TICs and red chips amounted to over US\$ 80 billion, equivalent to over 60 per cent of China's foreign exchange reserves at the start of the AFC.

The problems were even more serious in the local NBFIs, including the RCCs, UCCs and RFAs. The *renminbi* debts of the local NBFIs in Guangdong

Province exceeded RMB 100 billion. In 1997, the total asset value of China's NBFIs (excluding TICs) was the equivalent of US$ 145 billion, accounting for 11 per cent of the total asset value of China's financial institutions. Before the AFC, the central government was painstakingly cleaning up the illiquid local NBFIs across the whole country. The central government was confronted with the international debts of the whole body of TICs and red chips from across the whole country, as well as the domestic debts of the local NBFIs from across the whole country. Obviously, it lacked the financial resources to repay all these debts at a stroke.

Over the years, China's big four commercial banks had accumulated astronomical sums of non-performing loans (NPLs). The four asset management companies (AMCs) established in 1999 removed RMB 1800 billion in bad debts from their balance sheets. Chinese officials estimated that in 1998 NPLs accounted for 25 per cent of the big four banks' total loans. International experts estimated that the level of NPLs was considerably higher than this figure. In 2001, in its preparation for listing in Hong Kong, the Bank of China revealed that its NPLs accounted for 28 per cent of its total assets. The Bank of China was widely regarded as by far the strongest and the best run of the top four banks. The announcement that it had NPLs as high as 28 per cent of its assets lent support to the likelihood that the level of NPLs at the other three 'big four' banks was much higher than had previously been acknowledged.

In 2002, Standard & Poor estimated that if the NPLs of the local NBFIs and the city commercial banks were added to the NPLs of the major commercial banks, then the bad debts of China's financial system were as high as US$ 518 billion, equivalent to 50 per cent of China's GDP in 2001. There were unofficial estimates in 2002 that county-level financial institutions had arrears totalling RMB 3000 billion. If these were added to the arrears in the township and village level financial institutions, as well as to the arrears in social security funds, China's total 'hidden bad debts' were estimated to amount to RMB 10 000 billion. This estimate was so widely circulated, and was so worrying, that the Minister of the Ministry of Finance, Xiang Huaicheng, came forward to issue an official denial of the figures.

George Soros was perfectly accurate when he stated: 'If the Chinese *renminbi* had been convertible, the Chinese banking system would have collapsed'. In fact, before and during the financial crisis, large national financial firms, such as the China Agricultural Trust and Investment Corporation, China Enterprise Investment Foundation, and Hainan Development Bank were closed down one after the other. The local branches of the major state-owned banks had many large-scale runs similar to that on the Enping Branch of the China Construction Bank.

The international creditors exerted intense pressure on the Mainland government to assume responsibility for the debts of the TICs and red chips. They were determined that the Chinese government should treat the debts as if they were sovereign debts. They intended to force the government to repay the debts in full as it had done in the past. Moreover, they wanted cash immediately.

The extent to which the central government, provincial government and the sub-provincial governments ought to take responsibility for the domestic and international debts of the insolvent red chips and TICs caused intense debate in the media and among scholars. For both the borrowing and lending parties, 'moral hazard' abounded on all sides.

The main borrowing parties in Guangdong, namely GITIC and GDE, were wholly owned by the provincial government, which was formally in direct control of their borrowing activities. GITIC and GDE had always had support, direct and indirect, from the provincial government. From the perspective of the international creditors, they were confident in the fact that large Chinese state-owned enterprises had no record of bankruptcy. The Mainland had always paid back the country's international debts. It is because they understood the close relationship between the enterprises and the Guangdong government that they competed with each other to lend to such 'ideal clients' as GITIC and GDE, with no repayment risks. A special advantage of lending to these entities had been that the interest rate had been appropriate for normal commercial debt rather than for sovereign debt. Consequently, over the course of two decades, the international creditors had benefited enormously from their lending to Guangdong-based large financial firms.

For the Chinese government decision-makers, the pressing question was whether they had enough money to pay back fully the international debts rather than whether they ought to take full responsibility to pay them back. As for the former question, the answer is simple: the Guangdong government did not have any foreign exchange. The only possibility was to seek help from the central government that uniformly manages the country's foreign exchange payments. The first action taken by the Guangdong government was to earnestly apply to the central government for emergency help. Indeed, in the previous cases of closing down financial institutions, the central government had stepped forward and paid in full the international debts of the enterprises that were closed down. This was the case in closing down the China Enterprise Investment Foundation, the China Agricultural Trust and Investment Corporation, and the Hainan Development Bank. But at the critical moment of the AFC, in order to support the Hong Kong dollar in its resistance to speculative attacks, the Chinese government undertook a grave promise that China would not devalue the *renminbi*. If China had devalued the *renminbi* it would have unleashed even more ferocious speculative attacks on the Hong Kong currency peg, and undermined Hong Kong's role as a global financial centre.

During the AFC, the decision not to devalue the *renminbi* against the US dollar was equivalent to a promise to maintain for China the disadvantageous position of a large appreciation of the *renminbi* relative to the hugely depreciated currencies across the neighbouring region. This risked a large negative impact upon China's exports, foreign exchange income, and the foreign exchange reserves which supported the credibility of the *renminbi*. It was impossible to control this process, or to predict the timing and extent of the impact. This would be determined by the duration of the ongoing Asian Financial Crisis, and the severity of its impact. Against this background, the central government's foreign exchange reserves were precious. If the central government had paid in full the international debts of GITIC and GDE as it had done for bankrupt enterprises in the past, it would have strongly encouraged the international creditors, who were desperate for cash for their own survival and prosperity, to continue to press urgently against the red chips in Hong Kong and the ITICs all over China (including CITIC) for debt repayment. During the AFC, paying international debts equivalent to over 60 per cent of China's foreign exchange reserves within a short period of time would have been disastrous for the government's pledge not to devalue the *renminbi*.[6] Failure to sustain this pledge would, in its turn, have had huge potential consequences for Hong Kong, and major implications for the whole surrounding region, possibly plunging it into further rounds of competitive devaluations.

An even more difficult issue for the Chinese government was the fact that the extent of the risks was unknown. At that time, the full extent of the international debts of the ITICs and red chips was unknown. Indeed, it is still unknown today. Moreover, another huge risk was that it was impossible to determine the *renminbi* payment risks. The ITICs all over China and the red chips also had a large amount of *renminbi* debt. Local branches of each of the major commercial banks all over China had competed for deposits through '*zhang wai zhang*' (off-balance-sheet accounts) and by pulling in funds through promising interest at above the official rate '*gao xi lan chu*'. The RCCs, UCCs, and RFAs all over the country and various kinds of non-bank financial institutions had accumulated huge debts through all kinds of means including 'Ponzi schemes', that they were unable to repay. No one knew or knows the size of these debts. The expectation of super-normal growth speed was shattered by the AFC: 'As the tides retreat, the rocks emerge'. This had dire implications not only for financial enterprises in Guangdong but also across the whole country. The full extent of both the internal and external debts on which high returns had been promised was impossible to estimate. But the financial institutions faced the probability that there would suddenly emerge an unprecedentedly large demand for cash from both domestic and international creditors. The government faced the reality of a massive payments crisis, both internal and external, of unknown dimensions.

The financial crisis entered Guangdong through Hong Kong and a widespread payments crisis immediately erupted in Guangdong. If the payment crisis in Guangdong was not dealt with properly, it was likely that the crisis would spread rapidly into the heartland of China. This 'fire' would have spread through the red chips in Hong Kong, various kinds of non-bank financial institutions in Guangdong, the ITICs all over China, the local branches of the state-owned commercial banks, and the dying local non-bank financial institutions all over the country as well as the hugely complex chain of borrowing, lending and payment among these financial institutions. Once started, this financial fire would have been extremely difficult to extinguish. In theory, as long as the *renminbi* was not convertible on the capital account, the financial crisis that took place in the other Asian countries could not happen in China. Under normal circumstances, even if the *renminbi* payment crisis within a limited area is extremely serious, it can be resolved by simply printing more money. But in the dangerous environment of the AFC, the payment crisis in Guangdong had shaken people's confidence. The Chinese financial authorities were forced into intensive action as 'firefighters'. There were constant reports of closure of financial institutions; media reports about *'gao xi lan chu'* and *'zhang wai zhang'*; numerous cases of illegal fund-raising; and the bad debts of the mushrooming UCCs and RFAs as well as the commercial banks. This was a special kind of crisis. Under these extreme circumstances, the central government's answer to the appeal for help from the Guangdong provincial government could only be: 'Whoever gives birth to the child must care for the child'.

2. The Response: the 'Three Steps' to Resolve the Financial Crisis

How was the 'child' of Guangdong's payments crisis to be cared for?

The Guangdong provincial government, supported by the central government, took two years to resolve the payment crisis across the province and prevent the AFC spreading into the heartland of the country. According to the sequence of events, the working team of the Guangdong provincial government summarised their intense day and night battle to deal with the crisis in the phrase the 'three steps': GITIC bankruptcy, GDE restructuring and the closure of over 800 small and medium financial institutions. These three steps were not designed beforehand. Wang Qishan termed the approach adopted to face the challenge, 'the choice of no choice'. The approach conformed perfectly to the basic principle of 'cutting the trees to save the forest' (*kan shu jiu lin*), namely, cutting trees to create a firebreak and preventing the giant conflagration from spreading into the rest of the forest.

The First Step: GITIC's Bankruptcy

The crucial first step was the decision that GITIC should be bankrupted. This decision was not taken lightly. GITIC was the second largest ITIC in China, next to CITIC. It had had a high reputation and a first-rate business credibility. GITIC's bankruptcy would be the biggest bankruptcy in Chinese history. In order to ensure that the bankruptcy was carried out in a professional fashion, acceptable to over 130 international creditors, the Guangdong provincial government appointed one of the 'Big Five' accounting firms, KPMG, as the nominal advisor to the Liquidation Committee and they acted, in fact, as the liquidator. This meant that GITIC had to be subjected to a deep investigation such as it had never experienced before. GITIC had to have exposed fully before the international public its ambiguous relationship with the Guangdong government, dubious mistakes in decision-making, serious corruption and embezzlement, rampant negligence of duties and criminal activities. At the same time, the two listed companies in Hong Kong (red chips) owned by GITIC were to undergo liquidation. This brought the Mainland's crude bankruptcy law aimed at small enterprises before the British law. An important by-product of the procedures in GITIC's bankruptcy was to provide a full and accurate case for rectifying China's bankruptcy law and for formulating a complete bankruptcy law in China.

The decision of 6 October 1998 to close GITIC caused deep consternation among international financial institutions. The decision to file for bankruptcy, announced on 10 January 1999 was a massive shock. It was revealed that GITIC's assets totalled only 60 per cent of its liabilities. Moreover, the recovery rate was then estimated to be only around 30 per cent of the value of the assets, and just 18 per cent of GITIC's liabilities. The long, protracted nature of the bankruptcy proceedings was deeply sobering. Creditors' meetings were told that 90 percent of GITIC's loans were overdue, and over 80 per cent of its equity investments were in companies that had either been liquidated or were 'in difficulties'. The first repayment did not occur until the third creditors' meeting on 31 October 2000. It amounted to just US$ 85 million, a mere 3.38 per cent of the amount of GITIC's liabilities admitted as proof. It was estimated that eventually, GITIC's recoverable assets would amount to just 34 per cent of the recognised debts. By this point most foreign creditors had already written off their exposure to GITIC.

The significance of GITIC's bankruptcy went far beyond the US$ 3 billion in losses for up to a hundred international creditors. The principal significance is that the Chinese government refused to acknowledge GITIC's international debts as sovereign debts. This was unprecedented in China. Through the bankruptcy of the second largest ITIC in the country, the Chinese government announced to the international creditors that it would not take direct responsibility for ITICs' and red chips' international debts which totalled between US$ 80-100 billion. This was also a 'choice of no choice'. Guangdong is the richest province in China. If the central government had taken responsibility for GITIC's international debts, it would have been impossible to avoid taking responsibility also for the international debts of ITICs and red chips from provinces such as Hainan, Fujian, and Guangxi, that were poorer than Guangdong and in deeper difficulties during the financial crisis. To shoulder the responsibility for the international debts of the whole country's ITICs as well as the red chips in Hong Kong, would have meant that the central government must 'appropriate' over 60 per cent of its total foreign exchange reserves during the financial crisis. Obviously, no state leaders who had a sense of responsibility could have considered such a policy choice, that would have brought disastrous consequences for the *renminbi*, which the government had promised not to devalue.

'The choice of no choice' has a simple basis in law. Since the enterprises are legal persons, they have the legal right to end their own lives by choosing to become bankrupt, just as large numbers of Western enterprises do every year. GITIC's bankruptcy conformed to standard international bankruptcy practice. The decision also conformed with the overall direction of China's SOE reform: state enterprises are responsible for their own profit and loss, and the government is no longer directly responsible for the enterprises' businesses. GITIC's bankruptcy sent a signal for further reform of China's SOEs: no matter how big they are, no matter how well-known in the outside world, no matter how glorious their history might be, no matter how badly they had performed or why, they would no longer be rescued by the government. It would no longer step in to pay their debts.

The signal was so powerful that up until today, the Mainland SOEs, particularly the leaders of many large enterprises, still hold strong reservations about the GITIC bankruptcy and the government's refusal to pay its international debts. It is not simply out of the emotion that they might share the same fate as GITIC. In reality, the government still does widely participate in the SOEs' business activities. Therefore, it is perfectly understandable that the enterprises are unwilling to take full responsibility when the enterprises encounter difficulties.

GITIC's bankruptcy sent a powerful signal to the international creditors who had business relationships with China's SOEs. According to the traditional definition, the owners of the ITICs and red chips are the respective Mainland state entities, no matter whether they are companies or government departments. The international creditors insisted that the international debts of ITICs and red chips should be treated as sovereign debts. Up until 30 June 1999, the international creditors refused to accept the Guangdong provincial government's proposal for restructuring GDE. The creditors' committee pointed out: 'It is the strongly held view of the financial creditors that lending to the Group (GDE) was extended on the clearly and mutually understood premise that the Guangdong provincial government would support the Group and ensure that it was able fully to meet its contractual obligations to the lenders'.

The creditors' argument deserves to be fully understood. Over the preceding two decades, based on such a view, the creditors competed with each other to lend large amounts of money to the ITICs and red chips. On the one hand, based on this understanding, the creditors felt it unnecessary to conduct a thorough investigation, or stringent monitoring, of the enterprises and projects to which they lent. This is normally a substantial part of the cost of a bank's commercial loan. On the other hand, the loans were arranged using normal business-to-business procedures and commercial interest rates. They were not loans between national governments or low-interest, developing country aid loans from the IMF, the World Bank, and the Asian Development Bank. A commercial interest rate normally includes a premium for risk. It was inconsistent for the creditors to now insist that loans to GITIC and other Mainland-based entities should be treated as if they were sovereign debt when they had benefited over many years from commercial rates of interest, including a premium for risk, in their lending to these same entities.

In May 1994 *Business Week*'s cover story was on GITIC, entitled: 'Inside the world of a red capitalist: Huang Yantian's financial powerhouse is helping to remake China'. The article reported that Huang's office was ' a revolving door of American, Japanese and other foreign bankers eager for a piece of lucrative financing or corporate deals in China's wealthiest province'. Just before GDE's restructuring, GDE had won the 'Annual Best Management Award' given by the Hong Kong government. Morgan Stanley had also included the Guangnan Group in its 'top 50 global small and medium enterprises'. It was later revealed that Guangnan had become almost a criminal group. It is obvious that the 'excellent business credibility' of these firms had been obtained to a large degree through reliably paying their debts over many years. The reality is that in the previous two decades, on the one hand, international creditors saved a large amount of money that would normally have been necessary to investigate and monitor commercial loans. On the other hand, they collected fees which included a risk premium, but had never had to shoulder the risks. In this sense, 'the big wok meal' (*da guo fan*) characteristic of China's SOEs had already been eaten by the international financial institutions during the years of China's reform and opening-up. GITIC's bankruptcy declared that the rules of the game of 'eating the big wok meal' in international lending and borrowing had changed.

From both the domestic and international aspects, GITIC's bankruptcy became a controversial historic milestone in the process of China's reform and opening-up. It marked a major change in the relationship of the Chinese government to the SOEs. It prevented the spread of the practice of eating the 'big wok meal' in international lending and borrowing. It made clear the fact that in the future, international lenders would have to undertake close risk evaluation of the Mainland firms to which they were lending as they do to enterprises in other market economies. They could not save this major cost and could not imagine that the Chinese state at any level would step in to assume the international liabilities of insolvent SOEs.

As well as considering the international creditors, China's policy-makers needed to give the closest attention to 'calming the tumult' among the individual Chinese depositors. This was the primary problem that needed to be resolved cautiously in the GITIC bankruptcy proceedings. GITIC had over 30 000 'natural persons' who had deposited around RMB 800 million with GITIC. There were numerous demonstrations across the province by people afraid they would not be repaid after GITIC was closed. There were also 500 employees who became unemployed due to the bankruptcy. The Bank of China (BOC) purchased the debts of the individual depositors to the extent of RMB 780 million, thereby becoming the largest single creditor of GITIC. The funds to make the purchase were provided by the provincial government. GITIC's employees were provided with their redundancy pay by the Guangdong Government in accordance with the provisions of the Chinese law. There were also 80 000 stock-owners who were buying and selling their shares through GITIC. These were dealt with by the transfer of the securities business to Guangfa Securities Company as a going concern. All these arrangements concerning the interests of maintaining social stability were combined with strict observation of the formal procedures of the bankruptcy law, without the interests of the other creditors being harmed. Therefore, much professional design work was needed, which would be much more complex than that of the government dealing with internal affairs in the past. The close cooperation between KPMG, well-known international law firms and well-known Mainland law firms played a special and active role in this respect.

The Second Step: Restructuring GDE

In late summer of 1998, pressure on GDE intensified. Creditors urgently sought the repayment of debts, and GDE's balance sheets quickly worsened. By September GDE was only able to meet its urgent debts through short-term assistance from the provincial government. Among the US$ 4.6 billion of international debts, US$ 680 million would be due in January 1999, US$ 1.17 billion would be due between January and April 1999. GDE's debt/asset ratio reached 74 per cent and the group was in a desperate situation and faced difficulties in simply surviving. On 8 October, the provincial government made the crucial decision to save GDE alongside the closure and eventual bankruptcy of GITIC. On 26 October, it was announced officially that GDE's insolvency was to be resolved through restructuring.[7] The two main flagship companies within the GDE group, GDI and Guangnan, were important companies in the Hong Kong stock market. By choosing to restructure GDE, the Chinese government avoided treating the debts of Mainland firms as if they were Chinese sovereign debt, but it also reassured the Hong Kong stock market that a way would be found to keep the insolvent red chips functioning.

Negotiations with creditors over restructuring GDE were protracted. After prolonged and tough bargaining, the international creditors finally accepted the restructuring scheme proposed by Goldman Sachs on 6 December 2000. The main reason that the negotiations were so protracted was that, despite GITIC's bankruptcy, the creditors still hoped that the Guangdong provincial government would pay back the whole of GDE's debts. The deadlock in negotiations lasted up until the end of July 1999 when the Chairman of the Bank of East Asia, Li Guobao (David Li), still insisted that the loans to GDE from the creditors were guaranteed by the Guangdong provincial government. He made it explicit in the media that he would not hesitate to 'die together' with GDE. Li Guobao was one of Guangnan's independent directors.

Of course, 'die together' was only an emotional expression of determination. It would not have commanded wide support among the international creditors. Even if some people wanted to see the Bank of East Asia die together with GDE, fewer people were prepared to see the whole Hong Kong financial sector 'die together' with the red chips whose market capitalisation accounted for one-third of the Hong Kong stock market and whose share price had fallen 90 per cent. The Guangdong provincial government demonstrated their uncompromising determination by ceasing to pay the interest on the loans. At the second creditors' meeting, a meeting 'without applause', Wang Qishan politely and sincerely threatened: 'I believe neither the Guangdong provincial government nor international creditors are willing to see GDE follow the steps of GITIC'. Who could refuse such a good wish? In fact, from the moment that it was announced that GITIC would be made bankrupt the fundamental terms of the negotiation changed. In the words of one commentator: 'The grim reality is that the bankers have little leverage against GDE short of winding up the company'. Moreover, the longer the GITIC bankruptcy process took, the less attractive the prospect of pushing GDE into bankruptcy appeared. KPMG estimated the debt write-down in the event of bankruptcy would be around 74 per cent on average for the international creditors. Eventually, international creditors had no choice but to accept to share their losses with the Guangdong provincial government. Otherwise, they would encounter even more serious losses if they forced GDE into bankruptcy.

At last, the GDE restructuring could be carried out smoothly. An important reason was that the Chinese government shared the 'pain'. On the Chinese side, the Guangdong government made a net injection into GDE of around US$ 2.01 billion, almost exactly the same as the 'haircut' for the creditors, around US$ 2.12 billion. This injection consisted almost entirely of the Dongshen Water Supply Project. This was the province's 'highest quality asset'. The project supplies 75 per cent of Hong Kong's water demand for businesses and households. According to the long-term water supply agreement between Guangdong and Hong Kong, the project has an annual income of HK $2 billion in cash. The asset injection into GDE and a large amount of stable cash income had the effect of cash collateral, which provided a solid and reliable guarantee for paying back international creditors' debts, the repayment of which was postponed in the restructuring plan.

Just as KPMG, one of the 'big five accountancy firms', was employed to take charge of the bankruptcy of GITIC, so Goldman Sachs, one of the giant 'bulge bracket investment banks', was employed for restructuring GDE. In the formal position of an advisor, Goldman Sachs proposed the restructuring plan and convened the international creditors' meetings. GITIC's bankruptcy and the GDE restructuring together involved more than 300 international creditors. The Japanese and Korean embassies in Beijing and consulates in Guangzhou respectively, presented formal notes, strongly expressing their respective government's grave concern over GITIC's bankruptcy and the GDE restructuring. Goldman Sachs and KPMG have rich professional experience. They provided important practical suggestions to the Guangdong government as to how to deal with complex international business affairs that it had never dealt with before. Moreover, as employees, Goldman Sachs and KPMG were obliged to transform the wishes of the Guangdong government into acceptable international practice by using their high international professional reputations. This was the prerequisite for smoothly undertaking the bankruptcy of GITIC and the restructuring of GDE that followed Hong Kong law and international practice, as well as for dealing with tough negotiations with international creditors and close monitoring by the international media. Of course, these two companies that sought profit maximisation would not refuse to make money. But without the participation of the world-class authoritative institutions, GITIC's bankruptcy and GDE restructuring would have been greatly protracted. It might even have involved unnecessary diplomatic, political, and ideological elements. These would have disrupted the urgent matter of dealing with Guangdong's payments crisis. This would in turn have diverted attention from the main target, namely, to prevent the financial crisis spreading into the heartland of Mainland China.

One can say in dealing with international creditors, that the Guangdong provincial government made full use of Mao Zedong's principle for diplomatic struggle: 'reasonable, beneficial and moderate'.

The Third Step: Closing Down 800 Small and Medium Financial Institutions

The cases of GITIC and GDE mainly involved international creditors. During the AFC and Hong Kong's financial crisis, the most urgent matter was to deal with the international debts that had fallen due. At the end of 1999, as soon as the bankruptcy of GITIC and restructuring of GDE were in motion, the Guangdong provincial government's working team immediately began the 'third step' to resolve the financial crisis, namely, dealing with the payments crisis in the other local ITICs, UCCs, RFAs and the local branches of the state-owned banks. This was a non-stop battle with no pause for breath or rest. The debts of local non-bank financial institutions were mainly from within the country. Speculative funds from enterprises and institutions all over the country were mixed with the deposits from local residents. Legal depositors following the official interest rate were mixed with the massive deposits promising higher interest rate. Normal deposit and loan business were mixed with illegally raised funds. Legal businesses were mixed with businesses outside the business range officially set in the business licenses. The profit and loss inside the accounts were mixed with debt rights and benefits outside the accounts. Mismanagement in businesses were mixed with corruption, embezzlement and criminal activities. All these intertwined and became 'like messy hemp' that could not be clarified. Although the 'third step' did not produce much response in the outside world, its level of complexity and its impact upon Guangdong's economic development and the daily life of ordinary people was no less than, and, in fact considerably greater than, that of the 'first step' and the 'second step'. The constant runs on financial institutions and mass protests caused 'serious and abominable impact upon social order'. This required the government to provide a clear and specific plan to resolve the problems at once.

The well-known Chinese saying, 'using sharp knife to cut the messy hemp', is a perfect description of the 'third step'. On 23 November 1999, Guangdong established the 'Working and coordinating team to deal with financial risks in local small and medium financial institutions and rural financial associations in Guangdong', headed by Wang Qishan.[8] By October 2000, less than one year later, Guangdong borrowed from the central government a package of RMB 45 billion and ordered the cessation of business to allow rectification at 1063 branches of 147 UCCs, sixteen ITICs and their fourteen offices, 48 securities businesses branches owned by ITICs and 843 RFAs. This was also 'the choice of no choice' at the moment of crisis. But this was a resolute decision and the best approach to resolve the crisis – boldly and resolutely 'using the sharp knife to cut the messy hemp'.

Borrowing *renminbi* would not affect the country's foreign exchange reserves and for this the central government need not revise the financial budget. In order to prevent the spread of the payment crisis, this time the central government gave a helping hand without hesitation. Within the package of loans provided to Guangdong by the central government, RMB 38 billion was directly from the central government, and RMB 7 billion from the People's Bank of China (PBOC) for dealing with the payment crisis in the local branches of state-owned banks (for example, the Enping Branch of the China Construction Bank). The loans were guaranteed by financial support from governments at each level in Guangdong. The annual interest rate for the loan was 2.25 per cent with no compound interest. The loans were supposed to be repaid within nine years beginning from 2001. The annual repayment was RMB 4.7 billion. This was feasible for Guangdong with an annual tax revenue of over RMB 110 billion.

Restructuring the TICs

By 11 March 2000, the seventeen city-level TICs stopped business and began rectification, including four ITICs in Guangzhou and one TIC in each of the following cities: Shanwei, Shaoguan, Meizhou, Chaozhou, Zhanjiang, Zhongshan, Zhaoqing, Shantou, Foshan, Zhuhai, Jiangmen, Maoming, Huizhou. Dongguan's ITIC ran its businesses well and became the only city-level ITIC that was allowed to be retained based on reaching the required standards (*gui fan bao liu*). Shenzhen ITIC was also '*gui fan bao liu*' since Shenzhen was at the vice-provincial level. Yuecai Trust was '*gui fan bao liu*' since it was backed by the Department of Finance of the Provincial Government. The provincial-level Huaqiao TIC had an excess of debts over assets totalling RMB 3 billion. After the provincial government injected RMB 2 billion and the international creditors had a 'haircut' of 30 per cent, Huaqiao TIC paid back all the residents' deposits. Its business licence was taken away and the company was restructured into an industrial company.[9]

GITIC's bankruptcy and GDE's restructuring provided models in both their internal and external aspects for 'stopping businesses and rectifying' (ting ye zheng dun) (actually, administrative closure) at the other ITICs and for debt restructuring. Internally, the 48 securities businesses' branches owned by ITICs in various locations transferred their securities business to Guangfa Securities Company as a going concern, following the GITIC example. The misused shareholders' guarantee funds were recovered and transferred with the support from the central government's loans. Externally, GITIC's bankruptcy changed the position of all the ITICs in negotiation with international creditors and GDE's restructuring provided a model of the implementation of 'haircut' through negotiation. The ITICs in Zhuhai, Jiangmen, Zhongshan, Foshan and Shantou had international debts of US$ 254.45 million. After respective negotiations that were much easier than those at GDE, all these debts were repaid after a 30 per cent 'haircut' and interest exemption.[10] It was completed smoothly without any serious disturbances or media stunts.

Closing Down 800 Small and Medium Financial Institutions

What really needed a huge amount of work was dealing with the 147 UCCs and 843 RFAs all over the province. They involved tens of thousands of ordinary households. They formed extremely complex debt and credit relationships with enterprises and institutions all over the country. The basic principles adopted sounded clear. In order to maintain social stability, before undertaking the closure of a local NBFI, the working team, under conditions of top secrecy, was supposed to carry out a general investigation of the financial institutions that needed rectification. Based on the result of the investigation, the coordinating team was to give first priority to residents' deposits and to international debts, and then proceed to deal with other depositors' interests. The residents' deposits were sub-divided into several categories depending on the size of their deposits. The majority of the depositors had a small amount of deposits and were to be paid out first. By doing so, social disturbances were lessened as far as possible. In addition, the employees who became unemployed due to the closure of their companies were to receive proper arrangements. In practice the implementation of these principles became more complex and colourful. They had eight distinctive characteristics.

First, large-scale comprehensive and unified leadership. The members of the coordinating team consisted of high-level provincial leaders from all the relevant institutions.[11] Closing down up to a thousand enterprises and institutions at one time needed the mobilisation of a large force of elite cadres from every government department at each level to form a working team. It was estimated that more than 2000 cadres participated in the battle.

Second, preventing the expansion of the extent of payment and the loss of state assets. The investigation of up to a thousand RFAs and UCCs before the closure provided the data needed for the forthcoming tasks. The policy that the government at each level was to provide a guarantee for the loans from the central government and to pay back the loans on time restrained the enthusiasm at the grass-roots level to expand the extent of payments. The Guangdong provincial government learned from the experience of GITIC's bankruptcy the working style of the Hong Kong liquidators: impartial and incorruptible, acting 'as swift and powerful as thunder and lightning'. All over the province, the working team carried out 'lightning attacks'. All of a sudden, they launched into the enterprises and institutions and took over and sealed off the accounts, forms, seals, certificates, licenses, guns and bullets, computers, archival statistics. The working team was set up on 23 November 1999. By 31 January 2000, within only two months including the Chinese New Year holiday, the UCCs across the province had paid out RMB 16 billion, accounting for 83.3 per cent of the total task. The result of this high-speed action across the whole province was that the extent of payments was not allowed time to expand. Also it meant that the possible loss of assets during the liquidation process, due to the complications involved in the process of handing over and taking over, was minimised.

Third, clear and in-depth policy propaganda to the general public to avoid a credit crisis beyond the extent of closure. During the payment crisis, with frequent runs on financial institutions, the massive and complete closure of RFAs and restructuring of UCCs was 'a bolt from the blue for the ordinary people', who were already extremely anxious. A large number of deposits was transferred to the major state-owned banks from the RCCs and the city commercial banks that were not scheduled for closure. The participation of certain government departments in this process aggravated the tense social atmosphere. In some places, panic runs affected the RCCs and city commercial banks. The government at each level fully mobilised all the available propaganda mechanisms. Local broadcasting and television stations broadcast information on various kinds of policies and regulations non-stop day and night. Leaders at each level made speeches, writing memorials, writing articles. Lu Ruihua and Wang Qishan 'spoke positively' ('*shuo hao*') about the RCCs in the *Nanfang Daily*, the newspaper with the largest circulation in Guangdong. Detailed information about the ongoing events, and surrounding policies and regulations, were made known to every household in the province, so that emotional and disastrous social disturbances were avoided.

Fourth, grasping the subtle policy boundary between illegal speculation and legal deposits. Numerous small depositors' legal deposits were given the first priority. This group contained a vast number of people, and their deposits were normally their lifetime savings. If their savings were diminished in value, they were bound to be angry. This large group of people more or less corresponded with the amount of legal deposits that needed to be paid out. Although the pay-outs did not include the high-return in excess of the official interest rate, people were sincerely convinced by this action. Once this part of the payment was completed smoothly, the victory of the third step in dealing with the financial crisis was in prospect.

During the process, the illegally-raised funds from enterprises and institutions were frozen. The most difficult group to identify and deal with was the individual big depositors. Guangdong's economic growth was mainly based on the individual economy. Where there were large deposits under individual names, it was almost impossible to decide the policy boundary between normal deposits and individual enterprises' funds for speculation. The term '*da hu shi*' originated from the special preferential treatment that securities trading branches gave to their big speculator clients, including an individual office, computers, and free drinks. During the process of liquidation and repayment, the preferential treatment to the big depositors had the same logic and form, but with different content. A great deal of the speculative funds seeking for high returns was 'immoral wealth' without legal income sources or paying official taxes. If the parties concerned did not have the courage to walk into the '*da hu shi*' within an officially specified time period, to register with, and to be approved by, the departments of industry and commerce, taxes and legislation, the debts were automatically written off.[12] The payment plans submitted by each level of government were, by and large, consistent with the principle that they should be 'either smaller than or equal to' the amount of payment that was identified in the investigation before the massive closure. This saved expenditures for the Guangdong provincial government in resolving the financial crisis.

Fifth, dealing with urgent payments in a timely and flexible fashion.
The policy that the private deposits were paid in categories and instalments,
and that the deposits of enterprises and institutions were temporarily frozen
caused inconveniences for some individuals, enterprises and institutions. For
example, in Shaoguan, many enterprises had no other source of income with
which to pay their debts other than that from their funds in the local financial
institutions, which were frozen. The Shaoguan government required that
public services such as electricity supply, water supply, telecommunications,
property administration, and road authority postpone sending out their bills
for three months and waive the fines for delay in payment of bills so that the
institutions that were affected could operate normally.

**Sixth, dealing in a timely fashion with the complex creditors' rights
and litigation outside Guangdong province.** Up to a thousand small
and medium financial institutions not only raised funds, invested, deposited,
and loaned in Guangdong, but also had massive credit and debt relationships
in financial institutions all over the country. This caused numerous cases
of litigation during the process of closure and restructuring. These
caused huge trouble for the Guangdong government in the process of
clarifying assets and debts.

**Seventh, adjusting measures to local conditions under the
precondition of maintaining the basic principles.** The advantages of
adjusting measures to local conditions were obvious. The development of UCCs
and RFAs was uneven in various areas and the extent and degree of their
impact upon social stability was correspondingly different. Since the local
governments at each level guaranteed and paid back the debts, it was not
necessary for the provincial government to formulate a unified plan. With the
same basic principles and actions of unified leadership, space was left for
adjusting measures in accordance with local conditions and governments at
each level shared the responsibility. Even if some parts of the masses were
dissatisfied with the specific solutions, they would not take it all the way to the
provincial government. This was where the wisdom of the local working team
was supposed to come into play.

**Eighth, striking as far as possible a balance between resolving the
crisis and avoiding moral hazard.** The fact that the central government
lent a massive amount of money to resolve the crisis presented a severe challenge
in terms of moral hazard. The central government could not afford the payment

crisis to remain unresolved. The non-stop runs and large-scale protests had a terrifying impact on social stability. Both the Guangdong government and local governments at sub-provincial level had to accept responsibility for their failure to monitor adequately the institutions under their control. Many hundreds of NBFIs were under the control of local city or township governments. Local cadres typically occupied the leading positions in the local NBFIs. Chaotic management often became the cover for criminal behaviour, for which there could be no amnesty. Moreover, the legal debts of the local small and medium financial institutions had to be recovered. If the debtors escaped the responsibility for repaying their debts, moral hazard would be worsened.

The Guangdong provincial government required the governments at each level to guarantee through the local budget and to repay the borrowings from the central government within eight years through local financial revenues. This increased the enthusiasm of governments at each level to sell the assets of the small and medium financial institutions that had been closed, and to recover debts owed to the institutions. To some degree, this formed a 'compensation for moral hazard'. In order to lessen the burden of debt repayment, local governments at each level were required to devise detailed plans to recover debts. Although it was impossible to totally avoid moral hazard, such measures were better than doing nothing.

All these grave decisions and complex policies were made public one after another. At the moment of crisis, the Guangdong provincial government's working team set up to deal with the financial crisis made great efforts to achieve a balance between these complicated and often conflicting objectives.

The Success of 'Cutting the Trees to Save the Forest'

Cutting trees in advance to save the forest is the most frequently-used approach to prevent the spread of forest fire. However, in intense bush fires, and sometimes in long-lasting tropical forest fires, fire-breaks are cut in the course of the fire. Often, fire-fighters 'back-burn' trees to create a fire-break during a large fire. In order to prevent fire spreading deep into the forest, people must fight against high temperatures, heavy smoke, work against time and often face strong winds, to create a firebreak. In medieval cities, fire-fighters fought to create fire-breaks by pulling down valuable buildings in the path of the onrushing fire. Creating fire-breaks in the course of a fire is dangerous and skilful work.

The contagion of the AFC reached Hong Kong in October 1997. At this critical moment, not only had a payment crisis broken out across Guangdong, but also there was a terrifying prospect that it would spread into the whole financial system with countless debts through the illiquid ITICs, red chips, UCCs, RFAs, other non-bank financial institutions and local branches of the state-owned banks all over the country. At this moment of crisis, the Guangdong provincial government's working team to resolve the financial crisis played a salvaging role in 'cutting the trees to save the forest', regardless of their own safety.

Under normal circumstances, cutting trees is illegal. Cutting trees damages the environment. GITIC was a 'big tree' which attracted attention far and wide. It could be widely seen. It had made a 'great constructive contribution' to Guangdong's reform, opening-up and economic development. In 2002, the 63-storey GITIC headquarters, Guangdong International Mansions, was auctioned for the third time. For many years, the skyscraper had been a symbol of Guangdong's opening-up and the prosperity of Guangzhou.

GDE was a 'window company' in Guangdong's opening-up. In 1994 and 1998, GDE Investment and Guangnan Holdings became constituent companies of the Hang Seng Index in Hong Kong. Each company made a large contribution not only to Guangdong but also to Hong Kong's prosperity. Up until June 1997, Guangnan supplied 98 per cent of Hong Kong's fresh water fish, 80 per cent of its poultry, 70 per cent of its vegetables, and 20 per cent of its live pigs. It was one of the largest trading companies in Hong Kong.

It was humiliating that GITIC and GDE had to face bankruptcy and restructuring. Therefore, scholars proposed a 'debt-equity swap' scheme to save face. In normal times, the approach of auctioning creditors' rights to deal with individual enterprise's liquidity crisis could kill two birds with one stone, by simultaneously facilitating financial restructuring and enterprise reform (diversifying ownership). However, during the financial crisis, people were in a state of anxiety and the enterprises' accumulated problems were hard to rectify. At the moment of heightened emergency, the only way to 'save the forest', and solve the onrushing 'fire' of the financial crisis, was through bold and resolute measures.

Prior to the onset of the AFC, the business situation of the country's 329 TICs was not fundamentally different from that of GITIC. For example, the Chairman of Hubei ITIC was executed for corruption and embezzlement. The leaders of Hunan ITIC were convicted.[13] Hainan ITIC lingered around and was liquidated in 2002. Its Chairman was sentenced to death.[14] During the AFC, the chaotic ITICs and red chips suddenly became the key targets for debt recovery by international creditors. The 'three steps' to deal with the financial crisis in Guangdong sent a clear signal. If the international creditors continued to exert great pressure upon the ITICs and red chips to recover their debts, greater even than they would normally exert upon enterprises in a normal market economy, then these enterprises, which had lost their market capitalisation in the financial crisis, were bound to go bankrupt and be liquidated due to lack of cash for debt repayment, just like Peregrine and the Zhengda Group.

GITIC served as the example. Before GITIC's bankruptcy, the offices of enterprises with Mainland capital in Hong Kong had been bombarded by telephone calls for debt repayment and were full of debt-collectors. Court summons, lawyers' letters, and letters for lawsuits flew to the office 'like snowflakes'. Various kinds of threatening measures were used.

On 10 January 1999, the Hong Kong newspapers announced GITIC's bankruptcy. Suddenly the offices were silent. Company leaders who every day had dealt with the creditors suddenly found themselves with nothing to do.

GITIC's bankruptcy fundamentally changed the situation that Mainland enterprises were passively under attack in international debt disputes. Up to the mid 1990s, CITIC's liabilities alone were equivalent to around 20 per cent of the central government's revenues. Those of GITIC were equivalent to around 30 per cent of Guangdong province's government revenues, rising to 40 per cent for Shandong, Shenzhen, and Fujian ITICs, and around 70 per cent for Shanghai and Tianjin ITICs. Premier Zhu Rongji was even more frank than Wang Qishan in warning the international creditors: 'If you press too hard, they [the TICs] will have no choice but to apply for bankruptcy'. During Premier Zhu's visit to Japan in October 2000, he was criticised in the Japanese press for his refusal to get the central government to play an active role in resolving the default on repayments at Hainan ITIC. However, after all the criticism and complaints one must face reality: as independent legal persons, each of the ITICs and red chips was entitled to have the same treatment as Peregrine and Zhengda Group, according to international practice. To deal with international debts during the financial crisis, enterprises either went bankrupt or were restructured. The final result was that the forty-seven major red chips had an average 86 per cent drop in their market capitalisation. Only Guangxin Enterprise was liquidated due to GITIC's bankruptcy. The other red chips' overdue international debts were re-arranged by restructuring.

In 1999, China had 329 ITICs and by 2002, there still were over 80 TICs in operation.[15] Apart from Hainan ITIC's bankruptcy, due perhaps to the uncompromising position of the Japanese creditors, the other ITICs' overdue international debts were arranged through restructuring. The basic principle of restructuring was the same as the 'international practice' proposed by Goldman Sachs in the GDE restructuring: a portfolio of asset injection by the owners, 'haircut' for the creditors, debt rescheduling, and partial debt-equity swap.

In 1998, the central government advanced the slogan of 'preventing financial risks'. In Guangdong, this was realised through the 'three steps' to resolve the financial crisis. The 'resolution' of the crisis in Guangdong realised the central government's objective of 'preventing financial risks'. This, in turn, enabled the Chinese government to stick to its promise that the *renminbi* would not be devalued. This provided support for the Hong Kong dollar in its crisis. Moreover, it provided a great and stabilising contribution to the 'passing' of the whole AFC, not just for China but for the whole region, and, indeed, for the whole world economy.

The 'three steps' to deal with the payment crisis created by the internal and external 'hot money', particularly the third step of borrowing from the central government and giving priority to residents' deposits and international debts, preserved overall social stability. Following the example of GDE's restructuring, international creditors took a 30 per cent 'haircut'. They had special preferential treatment from the Chinese government, compared with the total loss which seems to have been suffered by the domestic institutional creditors (or investment funds). In other words, while 'cutting the trees to save the forest', the Guangdong provincial government showed mercy to the ordinary people and foreign business people. Compared with the domestic creditors who had 'haircuts' as high as 100 per cent, the international creditors should be thankful that they only suffered a 'haircut' of 30 per cent.

A by-product of the 'three steps' to resolve the financial crisis in Guangdong was to expose massive financial corruption and financial crimes. Even if the objective was simply to clean up the enterprises' financial accounts, it had the result of directly exposing the activities of criminal groups and individual criminals. With the reality of conviction, prison, and death sentence awaiting the criminals, each step of the 'three steps' was a life and death struggle between evil and good. The Governor of the Guangdong provincial government, Lu Ruihua, required in public that the government leaders at each level should 'duly investigate and deal with cases that violate the law and regulations, and fight against financial crime'. As the Executive Vice-governor of Guangdong Province, Wang Qishan frequently appeared before the public and media. Behind Wang Qishan stood the 'five-member leading team of the provincial CCP Committee' that had never before been made public. The name list was ranked according to the member's position within the Party instead of their administrative position: Team-leader Lu Ruihua, Governor and Vice-secretary of the provincial CCP Committee; Chen Shaoji, Vice-secretary of the Provincial CCP Committee and Secretary of the Political and Legislative Committee; Liu Fengyi, Vice-secretary of the provincial CCP Committee and Director of the Department of Organisation; Wang Qishan, member of the Standing Committee of the provincial CCP Committee and Executive Vice-governor; and Wang Huayuan, member of the Standing Committee of the provincial CCP Committee and Secretary of the provincial Disciplinary and Supervisory Committee.[16] If there had not been such a politically powerful leading team, none of the 'three steps' could have been taken. It was because the 'three steps' were under the direct leadership of the Political and Legislative Committee, the Department of Organisation, and the Disciplinary and Supervisory Committee, that massive cleaning-up of the corrupt criminals could be accomplished within the framework of the 'three steps'.

In July 2000 Huang Yantian, the President and Vice-Chairman of GITIC for most of the 1990s, was arrested. Two other senior GITIC managers were arrested, as well as the general manager of Shenzhen GITIC. Warrants were issued for the arrest of two senior managers of GITIC Hong Kong in connection with fraudulent letters of credit to the value of one billion Hong Kong dollars: 'If the people are caught and the case is proven, it will be the biggest case of fraud in the history of Hong Kong'. In the 1990s, GITIC was visited by six different government investigation groups. They unearthed extensive evidence of corruption. GITIC's overseas operations turned out to be thoroughly corrupted, with extensive cooperation with networks of Overseas Chinese criminals and with the collaboration of senior officials in GITIC's headquarters.

At GDE, during the investigations conducted by KMPG for the restructuring, it was revealed that the Group headquarters had 'serious problems with falsification of accounts', which, under Hong Kong law would have constituted criminal fraud. A total of thirty-five people from GDE had warrants issued for their arrest. The most serious criminal activities exposed were in Guangnan Holdings under GDE. A total of eighteen arrest warrants was issued by Hong Kong's ICAC for Guangan's employees. These included Sun Guan, the former chairman, as well as six other former directors of the company, including the financial manageress and the assistant financial controller. Three of these were brought to trial in late 2000, but the rest fled to safe hiding in the Mainland. Guangnan was described by one insider as 'a collective, large-scale fraud company'. Another described it as 'a criminal enterprise to generate private wealth for those who ran it'.[17]

Investigations into the Enping case resulted in the arrest of numerous government officials and senior officers of financial firms. Zheng Rongfang, the head of the local branch of the China Construction Bank was so successful in bringing capital into Enping that he was elected deputy mayor of Enping. He was arrested and sentenced to death, commuted to fifteen years' imprisonment. Other local officials arrested for their roles in the Enping case included Li Guanghua, former mayor of Enping, and Kuang Ren, the former Deputy Party Secretary of Enping. Kuang had been promoted to be deputy mayor of Jiangmen City (which included Enping).

The significance of the 'three steps' to deal with the financial crisis in Guangdong for the overall situation is clear. There are many aspects of the crisis that deserve further exploration. However, the fundamental contribution of the 'three steps' in terms of resolving the financial crisis was that of 'cutting the trees to save the forest'. By 'cutting the tall tree' of GITIC, with all the pain, humiliation and anger this engendered, the 'forest' of the Guangdong financial system, and, ultimately, the Chinese financial system, was saved.

3. The Problems Remaining

The 'three steps' to deal with the financial crisis in Guangdong courageously and resolutely created a firebreak among 'the chaotic hemp' and prevented the AFC spreading into China's heartland. However, resolving the crisis of the contagion from the fire does not mean that the ecological system full of wild weeds has been changed. After the crisis, what could grow on this rich soil? Is it possible that 'the wild fire burnt out the grass, but the grass will grow again when spring comes?' Is it possible that, before long, the massive steps again become 'the choice of no choice'? The 'three steps' exposed a series of deeper problems that are cause for serious reflection by China's decision-makers.

Business Practices and Structure

GITIC and GDE

The GITIC bankruptcy and restructuring of GDE both took place in the full glare of international publicity, and under the scrutiny of international accountants. Both cases revealed a catalogue of unbelievably chaotic management. As the owner, the Guangdong provincial government had full responsibility for the failure in monitoring the two companies.

Both GITIC and GDE developed a hugely complex and opaque business organisation. Each was characterised by a multi-tiered structure with hundreds of child, grandchild and great-grandchild companies. Up until the bankruptcy and restructuring, the leaders in the headquarters of GITIC and GDE did not even know how many subordinate companies the two companies had, let alone exert effective control and management over them. Each allowed lower level companies to pursue their own interests. Most of them were independent legal persons and had business licences covering a wide range of business activities. They raised capital using the name of GITIC or GDE, and made investment decisions without consulting higher levels. In each case, large amounts of capital were gambled in speculative real estate investment, and, eventually, in speculation in the stock market and derivative markets. Behind countless suspicious investment mistakes were the 'mad transfer and embezzlement of state assets', corruption and crimes. In these activities people in the companies had extensive cooperation from Mainland Chinese and Overseas Chinese as well as the top leaders of the companies.

It is thought-provoking that deep failures in the management of both firms were known about at both the provincial and the central government level long before the AFC erupted. Despite numerous efforts to improve their operational mechanisms, nothing fundamental was achieved. Based on previous experience, we can hypothesise that without the AFC it is likely that little would have changed. Why were the efforts made before GITIC's bankruptcy and GDE's restructuring ineffective? Can the bankruptcy and restructuring resolve the accumulated serious problems? If not, what does this mean for the 329 TICs, for the growing number of red chips, for the RCCs participating in illegal fund-raising activities as well as for the local branches of the major commercial banks?

The attitudes of international lenders and investors played a role in the management and monitoring of shortcomings at GITIC and GDE. International capital was attracted by the growth prospects of Guangdong, and the intimate relationship of the firms to the Guangdong Government. This appeared to guarantee insider access to high return investment opportunities, and to offer an implicit guarantee of debt repayment. International investors were pleased to lend to companies that were non-transparent, as long as that appeared to offer the path to high and secure returns. There were few complaints from international lenders and investors about lack of transparency in Guangdong's NBFIs and red chips before the AFC. Investors prided themselves on the relative strength of their 'insider relationships', which constituted a form of competitive advantage. The international capital that poured into GITIC and GDE in search of high returns parallels that which poured into the local NBFIs from across China.

Alongside the restructuring of GDE's debt, the company underwent comprehensive business restructuring, employing McKinsey to guide the process. In 2001, Wu Jiesi published his book entitled *Chinese Phoenix*, a record of the GDE restructuring including all the technical details. The book predicts that the New GDE will rise 'like a phoenix' to become a powerful Hong Kong conglomerate. Governor Li Changchun pointed out: 'Not only Guangdong province, but also China as a whole and the international financial markets are watching closely to find out whether the restructured GDE will become merely a debt-repayment machine, or whether it will, instead, continue to grow and expand to become a vital modern corporation operated and managed according to international practice'.

New GDE merged 50-60 second-tier companies into seven companies, making 650 employees redundant and saving management costs of Hong Kong $130 million. From the first half of 2001, business improved and assets were auctioned. New GDE became a profit-making enterprise again. The main force within New GDE for making profits was GDE Investment, a constituent of the Hang Seng Index. The newly injected assets of Dongshen water project and electricity plant accounted for 78 per cent of the total profits.[18] However, New GDE was still directly owned by, and directly responsible to, the Guangdong provincial government.[19] Its managers were still appointed by the Guangdong government. They were paid far below international standards of remuneration. For the core of new GDE, GDI, around one half of its revenues were provided by a single monopoly project supplying water to Hong Kong.

In the Spring Festival of 2001, the former Chairman Zhong Guangchao, who had directly participated in the whole process of restructuring, was attacked by a massive stroke brought on by the intense psychological and work pressure. He was transformed into a 'human vegetable'. Kang Dian accepted the order to become the Vice-Chairman at a critical moment during the restructuring crisis. He promised through the media that he would be the last person to leave GDE, like the captain of the Titanic. After the successful restructuring of GDE, he suddenly resigned, giving the unconvincing reason of 'wishing to reunite with his family'.[20]

The Chairman of New GDE is Wu Jiesi, former assistant to the Governor of Guangdong, and the General Manager of New GDE is Li Wenyue, Vice-Secretary to the Guangdong provincial government. The Board of Directors representing the shareholders' interests and the executive managers continue to be inseparable. Their salary is still far below the level in a similar Hong Kong enterprise. The old problem of the reward not corresponding to the responsibilities still exists. The 'seventeen regulations' to transform the internal behaviour of New GDE's employees were reported to be 'not taken seriously by the staff in Hong Kong'. When asked what fundamental institutional change could guarantee that GDE 'rose from the hell of restructuring' and became a 'phoenix', a fabled animal that did not in fact exist, Wu Jiesi could only answer: 'The "ideological consciousness" of the new leaders will determine whether or not the effort to build New GDE will be successful'. Undoubtedly, in the 1950s and 1960s, the intangible factor of 'ideological consciousness' could resolve many difficult problems that could not be solved by institutional arrangement. It is open to question whether that is so today.

TICs

Despite the bankruptcy of GITIC and the passage of a new trust law and the extensive restructuring of the whole trust and investment company (TIC) sector, the door was left open for renewed growth of the TICs. An important aspect of China's economic system reform was the financial separation between the central and local governments. The local government set up TICs to provide them with an independent source of finance and profits under their local control. At the peak period in the 1980s, the whole country had up to a thousand TICs. Xiao Gang, Deputy Governor of the People's Bank of China acknowledged: 'There may be another wave of growth of the TICs'. The final number of TICs is likely to be significantly larger than was originally planned. Guangdong alone has four. Even Hainan had more than half a dozen TICs at the end of 2001. By the end of 2001, 'poor little Hainan Province' still had more than six ITICs. As long as a TIC has RMB 300 million in assets it can keep operating legally. The local governments still have a strong interest in supporting the TICs as a mechanism for them to collect funds outside the official banking system. In the view of Hu Shuli (*Caijing* editor): 'The ITIC game is not over'.

Red Chips

As an institutional arrangement, the red chip firm backed by local government is a unique and innovative form. There is no comparable type of firm elsewhere in the world. The red chips register as a legal person in Hong Kong. They have a close relationship with Mainland governments and they have developed the unique concept of 'asset injections': governments can use administrative measures to 'inject' assets into enterprises whenever necessary. In law, red chips are firms. In fact, red chips do not have core businesses. Moreover, the boundary of their assets is open. In theory, local governments can inject any assets into enterprises. This characteristic became a powerful attraction for investors during the peak of the red 'frenzy' in 1997. The red chips' IPOs were oversubscribed. Through further 'asset injections', the red chips could in principle continue their expansion indefinitely in the future. In this sense, the red chip is an imaginative and extremely attractive fund-raising tool. From 1993 when the first Mainland SOE listed in Hong Kong, to the end of April 2002, there were fifty-nine SOEs listed in Hong Kong, and sixty-nine red chips. These 128 enterprises raised a total of Hong Kong $651 billion from the Hong Kong stock market.[21]

However, once the market and investors treat the red chips as normal firms instead of an 'investment concept', serious problems appear. Absence of transparency is the attraction for raising funds but is the enemy of effective enterprise management. An absence of core business is directly determined by the fact that the local governments inject assets across a wide range of industries. GDE not only has real estate businesses and plants in various industries, but also owns ports, road, bridges, transportation, and the Dongshen water supply project. The headquarters of the red chips in Hong Kong only have a few people. Where does the professional knowledge come from to exercise effective operation and management? Chaotic enterprise management and investment mistakes are unavoidable. After the AFC, red chips backed by local governments continue to exist. Although some of the red chips were restructured, such as the China Travel Agency (Hong Kong), few went through such a comprehensive business restructuring as GDE. Despite thorough restructuring of GDE, as an independent enterprise, the company's internal self-contradiction still has not been changed.

A handful of red chips, such as China Telecom (Hong Kong) and China National Petroleum Corporation (Hong Kong), do have a specialised business focus, but these are exceptions to the rule for the whole sector. Although the possibility exists that the Mainland headquarters continue with 'asset injection' into such companies, the nature of these companies is similar to the H-share companies with clear business scope. It is hard to imagine that unrelated businesses such as road and water would be injected into these companies. They have a relatively high transparency. Because of this, the headquarters of the Mainland parent company can exert clearer and more powerful leadership over this small group of red chips. The frenzy of speculation did not generally affect this group of red chips, and they rarely encountered the deep liquidity problems that were widespread across the rest of the red chip sector.

Local NBFIs

The massive closure of RFAs and restructuring of UCCs resolved the immediate payment crisis and the threat to social order. However, this did not eliminate fundamentally the rich soil for the growth of local non-bank financial institutions. Small cities and, especially, the townships still had a powerful incentive to establish their own locally-controlled financial institutions to serve local development needs. Despite the closure of RFAs, restructuring of UCCs and improved regulations where little or no regulation had existed before, 'new forms of illegal disguised forms of fund-raising are constantly appearing'. Although some of the bad loans were absorbed by higher levels, this harmed the balance sheets of the RCCs. Guangdong provincial officials recognise that the level of risk in the RCC is still 'high'. Little has changed in the corporate credit culture in which loans from the local NBFIs are treated as 'dad's money' (*aiye de qian*) that doesn't need to be repaid. The RCCs' bad loans are officially estimated to be 'well over 50 per cent'. It cannot be forgotten that the mad '*gao xi lan chu*' in Enping began with the RCCs. The institution that most actively engaged in '*gao xi lan chu*' was the Enping Branch of China Construction Bank, not the UCCS or the RFAs.

The Financial Relationship Between Central and Local Government

The more general question is how to establish an appropriate financial relationship between central and local government. Hu Shuli, Chief Editor of *Finance*, pointed out: 'if this problem is not resolved, Guangdong's tragedy will happen again'. In fact, all the issues analysed in this study involved this problem. The relationship between central and local government is an old problem that troubled China for thousands of years. Today, in the time of integration and liberalisation of global finance, this problem again poses a critical life and death challenge to the nation.

In the 1980s, a fundamental aspect of reform has been financial separation between central and local governments. From macro development and planning, to resource allocation, system reform, and introducing foreign capital, each provincial government, to a greater or lesser degree, has assumed all kinds of functions to serve local economic development. The only function they lack is independent financial resources. Therefore, in his one-week visit to China, Paul Volker, former Chairman of the US Federal Reserve, made the acute observation: 'Each of China's provinces wants to have its own central bank.'[22] What makes the problem more complicated is that the provincial government has delegated the same power to the city and regional level and following this sequence, right through to the bottom unit of social life, the towns and villages.

The initial idea in cleaning up the TICs was to retain one for each province. With its mighty economic power, Guangdong had an unanswerable case for retaining three TICs. If a similar logic were applied to the whole country, the number of ITICs could not be lower than eighty. The final number has still not been decided and seems certain to be at least sixty. Despite the fact that the number of red chips listed in Hong Kong was under strict central government control, the logical prospect was for an increase in their numbers, not for a decrease. Various kinds of specialised companies compete with each other for flotation. In addition, each of the coastal provinces owns more than one red chip. With the western development truly progressing, the western provinces have for long complained that government policy is biased towards the eastern provinces in terms of approving red chips.

The government was unable to prevent all kinds of legal and illegal financial institutions and fund-raising activities springing up at the grass-roots level. In Enping, we saw not only UCCs and RFAs, but also the local branch of China Construction Bank and RCCs become major forces for illegal fund-raising. After the closure of these financial institutions (including the RCCs engaging in illegal fund-raising), the normal credit demand from ordinary people could not be met and the local economy was depressed. Of course, this 'bitter fruit' was brought about by the misdeeds of the former governments at each level in Enping. The problem is that the requirements of economic development urgently demand the establishment of a healthy local credit system. Because the fate of their cadres and families is ultimately determined by the local governments in numerous aspects, even the local branches under the direct leadership of state-owned commercial banks, sooner or later, cannot resist the local governments' demands that these institutions undertake different kinds of financial activities for developing the local economy. There are countless examples of local branches of the main state-owned banks all over the country losing control.

It is a cause for deep reflection that among the forty cases in Xiao Chong's *The Financial Crimes of CCP High-ranking Officials* (2002), thirty-eight of them are cases of state-owned commercial banks and their local branches, with only Hunan GITIC and Hubei GITIC standing apart from the banks.

Financial System and Financial Reform

We have seen that the theoretical framework governing the relationship within the financial system between central and local government lacks a clear line of thought. Now we turn to consider the logic governing the current reform path for the state-owned commercial banks.

Since China joined the WTO, China's commercial banks immediately faced powerful competitive pressure from the global giant financial firms. According to China's commitments on joining the WTO, after five years, foreign banks could compete with the local banks without any restrictions. [23] The global giants have already begun an intense remorseless struggle to penetrate the Chinese market. In order to stand up to the competitive challenge, Dai Xianglong, Governor of PBOC, promised to step up financial reform. He proposed the plan of 'three steps' to reform the big four state-owned commercial banks: 'The first step, under the precondition of wholly state-ownership, allows the banks to undertake commercialised businesses; the second step transforms the banks into joint share-holding companies with the state controlling the majority of shares; the third step involves listing the banks on the domestic and international markets.'[24]

The basic logic of the 'three steps' to reform the state-owned banks continues to follow the theory of private property rights that 'one cares for the assets one owns', just as the reform of SOEs has done over the past twenty years. This deserves careful thought and evaluation. Despite the fact that the reform of SOEs has not been successful, few people doubted that the only way to enhance the standard of enterprise governance was to place the management under the scrutiny of the shareholders. Therefore, the restructuring and flotation of banks, big and small, is seen as progress. Taking away massive NPLs and getting rid of the burden of redundant employees become the major content of the reform of state-owned banks.[25] It is dangerous to believe that the fundamental difference between financial enterprises and physical production enterprises is the fact that financial enterprises specialise in managing other people's assets. If the logic of property rights that 'one cares for the assets one owns' failed to solve the problems in physical production enterprises, it is even more irrelevant if it is applied to financial enterprises that specialise in managing other people's assets.

During the process of the 'three steps' to deal with the financial crisis in Guangdong, 'massive shocking sickness, chaos and misdeeds' were exposed in the province's financial enterprises. Problems on such a scale are unimaginable for firms engaged in physical production. To find similar examples in the advanced capitalist countries, we have to look to firms such as Enron, Arthur Anderson and Barings.

If we take the example of *'gao xi lan chu'* at the Enping Branch of the China Construction Bank, the participants also included the county's many financial institutions such as branches of the Industrial and Commercial Bank of China, the Bank of China, the China Agricultural Bank, the RCCs, UCCs, and RFAS. From February 1994 to November 1995, within just one year and a half, single specialised bank branches at the county level, through high *'agio'* and off-balance-sheet daily lending, sucked in RMB 3.2 billion, and granted working capital and off-balance-sheet loans worth RMB 2.5 billion plus HK$ 2.4 million. It caused economic losses to the state of RMB 3.6 billion plus HK$ 3.68 million. Moreover, it caused large-scale runs, mass demonstrations and riots. Two hundreds employees lost their jobs after the branch of China Construction Bank was closed. This speed of sucking in money and destructive energy is unimaginable for any of Enping's cement plants. In 2001, the Director of Enping's CCB branch, Hou Chunxing, was arrested, having been on the run for three years. He was sentenced to three and a half years imprisonment.[26] This experience suggests that applying the reform principles that failed in the cement plants, to the reform of large state-owned commercial banks and to the whole financial system, has indescribable dangers.

One cannot help questioning the theoretical prediction that transforming China's main commercial banks into joint stock companies and floating them on international stock markets will improve their management and performance. Great doubt is cast on these confident predictions by the harsh reality of the huge payment crisis that erupted in Guangdong's financial enterprises; by the huge accumulated stock of NPLs in China's banking system; by the flow of NPLs that kept being produced; and by the financial scandal and financial crimes that were exposed by the media before and during the financial crisis. In reality, the history of the red chips has already demonstrated that the belief that introducing private property rights will improve enterprise management is unrealistic. All the H-share companies and red chips are internationally listed companies following the law in Hong Kong and international practice. They each have a board of directors, a supervisory committee, and the financial accounts are audited by respected institutions that are employed at a high price. For many years, the red chips under GDE had distinguished social personages as independent directors and employed local general managers with salaries to match those of senior managers in local financial firms. Moreover, they had the Big Five accounting firms to undertake their audits. During the AFC, 'massive shocking sham, chaos and crimes' were exposed.[27]

In fact, listing overseas, diversifying property rights, operating under Hong Kong law, the system of enterprises freely conducting businesses and different systems of accounting and bookkeeping, often became important reasons for these enterprises to distance themselves from, and resist and escape the monitoring from, their owners in China according to the domestic practices. The result of going overseas to 'clarify property rights' based on theories of property rights, often led to the fact that the Mainland's governments at each level had less and less power, and fewer and fewer means of scrutinising the overseas enterprises, while the overseas enterprises had more and more freedom to act wildly against the law and flout public opinion. The problem became more serious when these enterprises were financial enterprises rather than physical production enterprises.

The relationship between China's big four commercial banks and the government, their enterprise system as well as the loss of control over '*zhang wai zhang*', and corruption and crimes widely existing in the subordinate branches, are in many respects, and to a large degree, of the 'same basic nature' as the problems exposed at GITIC and GDE. The only major difference is that they have not yet had financial businesses which allowed the domestic and overseas parts of the business to work closely without direct control from the government. The Bank of China has been responsible for foreign exchange businesses for a long time. The recent exposure of corruption, crimes, and loss of control in management at BOC is terrifying. If one of the big four banks is reformed into an overseas financial enterprise similar to GDE through getting rid of the NPLs, flotation, strengthening enterprise autonomy, and weakening government monitoring, it would be possible to cause destructive disaster once the 'ideological consciousness' of the leadership has problems. This cannot be easily resolved by 'a few steps'.

Financial Corruption and Criminality

In the case study on the 'three steps' to resolve Guangdong's financial crisis, we found the corruption and criminality in financial institutions – ITICs, red chips and local non-bank financial institutions – to be more serious than that in government departments and manufacturing sectors. It is misleading to treat the degree of corruption in financial institutions as the same as that in government departments and in manufacturing activity. The boundary between mistakes and intentional crimes in financial transactions is most unclear in terms of techniques, law and morality. There is a subtle boundary between 'crime' and negligence of duties. Moreover, financial transactions are highly complex and volatile. What are traded are not materials, but intangible numbers and 'bytes' rushing at the speed of light in the labyrinth networks of computers. These are extremely difficult to monitor, investigate, obtain evidence about, and control. In the real world, financial services provide more chances for illegal profiteering activities than other sectors. The accountants at KPMG acknowledge the greater difficulty in monitoring the accounts of financial service firms compared to firms based on physical production.

A wide variety of well-known methods were used to steal from the state, from the company, from the local community, and from shareholders. Much the most widespread methods were those that did not involve immediate benefit to individuals or groups but made use of third parties. The individuals and groups concerned could then claim that there was no immediate benefit for themselves. The funds did not go directly into their pocket. Typical methods included insider lending, and failure to pursue loans made, to entities owned by or controlled by insiders. Associated with this was frequent failure to issue demands for repayment of loans in accordance with the law, rendering the loan invalid. They then either waited for the bankruptcy and restructuring of the enterprise or hastily packaged the enterprise for flotation in order to get rid of the bad debts.

Among numerous other methods were false accounting to present a misleading view of the firm's performance in order to attract investors; buying enterprises or projects directly or indirectly owned by themselves at above market prices; selling assets at below market prices to companies owned by or controlled by insiders; use of political connections to re-allocate land from one development category to another, in order to benefit from the consequential inflation in land prices; false letters of credit used to obtain bank loans illegally; even embezzling public funds and then running away. In early 2002, in Kaiping, next to Enping, five officials of BOC stole US$ 483 million and escaped to North America. The amount of money stolen is equivalent to half of the GDP of the whole of Kaiping. In addition, there were numerous methods of 'borrowing' funds (with no intention of repayment) from the financial institutions and red chips in order to make private speculative investments in land, property, stocks and futures. Across the whole banking system, there was widespread use of 'off-balance sheet accounts' (*zhang wai zhang*), which was outside the scope of official reporting mechanisms, to undertake '*gao xi lan chu*'. With this situation, a major source of corruption was the process of appointment of officials to leading positions in financial institutions. The appointment amounted to a licence to make large personal gains if the people concerned wished to do so.

In financial transactions, there are too many methods that can be used to embezzle public assets. In almost all of the incredible mistakes in investment, one can see the clear logic of the collusion between insiders and outsiders to steal state assets. For no reason, massive funds were invested in ordinary local individuals without any commercial background in Guangdong. Many of these individuals became 'foreign businessmen' with Hong Kong or foreign passport. Even today, they continue to closely 'cooperate' with other ITICs, red chips and even banks. However, despite the clear logic, it is very difficult to obtain legally effective sound evidence. This becomes almost impossible in the chaotic accounts made up intentionally by the enterprises. The special nature of financial transactions becomes the blanket screen covering corruption and criminality. It is very difficult to monitor the enterprises either for the government or the shareholders. Barings Bank, with over a hundred years experience, went bankrupt due to the speculation in financial derivatives by a young man in its Singapore branch. This is a very good illustration. The investigative media that are gradually becoming independent, such as *Caijing*, reported some significant cases. But these reports, after serious losses have been made, are far from the formal monitoring mechanisms in the process of operation.

Although corruption and criminality in financial circles occur at the local level, the possible loss is often at the overall system level. The 'three steps' to deal with the financial crisis in Guangdong itself demonstrated how serious the dangers could be. Moreover, financial corruption and criminality can easily penetrate other sectors, including the state apparatus. In the late 1990s numerous cases were investigated involving Party officials, members of the

People's Bank of China, the police force, and the judiciary. Between 1997 and 1998, within a year, the Guangdong government sent 4258 inspection and audit teams to visit 9913 enterprises. Over 1000 people investigated in this campaign lost their jobs or were demoted. Among the substantial number who were arrested were two deputy chairmen of the Standing Committee of the Provincial People's Congress. Also arrested were the head and deputy head of the executive division of the Shenzhen People's Court, the head of the Public Security Bureau of Huizhou, and the head of the Armed Police Force in Huilai County. In the notorious case of Zhanjiang's smuggling ring, the 'collective corruption' involved over 200 government officials, with twelve cadres at the office or bureau level, and four at the division level. The head of the Zhanjiang Customs Administration was sentenced to death, and a further twenty-five people were punished, including the city's Party Secretary.

4. Conclusion

The 'three steps' to resolve Guangdong's financial crisis achieved huge success. The critical step was the decision to 'cut the trees to save the forest'. The deep issues involved in and exposed by the 'three steps' deserve close study. The widespread payment crisis in Guangdong demonstrated that China's economy is far more fragile than most people imagined. The financial system is at the heart of this fragility. The payment crises in Guangdong and the AFC are of deep significance for understanding the stability of China's whole system of political economy. The collapse of the former Soviet Union enhanced people's level of understanding of the extreme dangers of comprehensive political and economic reform represented by shock therapy. If the 'June 4th' disturbances had not been suppressed, China might have disintegrated even before the former Soviet Union. A Chinese financial crisis would threaten the stability of the entire system of political economy.

Guangdong's economy is heavily dependent on exports and foreign capital. These account for a high percentage of those of the whole country. This means that Guangdong's economic growth path is fragile. This is also the fragility of China's economy. In 2000, China's imports and exports were equivalent to 44 per cent of its GDP (less than 20 per cent in the United States and Japan) and China's exports were equivalent to 23 per cent of its GDP. Foreign-invested enterprises accounted for 30 per cent of the country's industrial profits and 50 per cent of its exports. Based upon this foundation of dependency on foreign capital and exports, George Soros's warning that China's financial system could collapse if the *renminbi* was convertible, was not an exaggeration. In this regard we should consider the fact of the weakness of China's whole financial system, including the TICs, red chips, RCCs, and UCCs, that have been restructured into city commercial banks; the astronomical 'triangular debt' between enterprises that the central government had made great efforts to clean up, but eventually had to give up the efforts; the *'zhang wai zhang'* that is everywhere in the state major banking system; the constant occurrence of illegal fund-raising; the shocking financial corruption and financial crimes, and their penetration into the state apparatus. Even though the *renminbi* was not convertible, the payment crisis, with runs on financial institutions and mass protests, meant that the government was extremely busy.

The speed with which crises can happen, develop and spread is a unique characteristic of this sector, far removed from the cyclical ups and downs in the physical production sector. The 'fire' of financial contagion has the capability of transferring the international financial crisis to the domestic payment crisis, from there to the credit crisis in the whole society, and finally, of endangering the social and political stability. It was Guangdong's 'three steps' that contained the severe danger of contagion from the crisis. Other Asian countries and regions with heavy losses paid a very high price for their close integration with, and the liberalisation of, global finance.

The path of China's reform and opening-up has been extremely fortunate. After the 'June 4th' disturbance, the disintegration of the former Soviet Union made China extremely cautious in its political and economic reform. Less than ten years later, the heavy price that other Asian countries paid for their financial liberalisation provided an invaluable lesson for China. Only through the 'three steps' to resolve Guangdong's financial crisis was China able to suppress the possible contagion from the payment crisis. Everyone involved was deeply affected by this searing experience.

Just as the suppression of 'June 4th' did not mean that China stopped the exploration of political reform, so Guangdong's 'three steps' to resolve the financial crisis has not stopped the reform of China's financial system. By joining the WTO the path of opening-up China to trade and FDI has been set. The increasingly open economy inevitably and increasingly brings the focus of further reform and opening-up onto the service sector, led by financial services, in both the international and domestic aspects. The difficult economic situation of Hong Kong encourages strengthened financial cooperation between the Mainland and Hong Kong.

In June 2002, the policy of opening up foreign securities investment was announced. This is only one step away from the convertibility of the *renminbi* on China's capital account. The tide for the further integration of China's financial system into the global financial system is irreversible. Liberalisation cannot be reversed. At this historic moment, it is of special and urgent significance to review the great efforts made and the price paid to resolve Guangdong's financial crisis, and fully understand both the rich meaning and the warning contained in the 'three steps'.

Notes

1. This paper was published in Chinese in *Hong Kong Fax (Xianggag chuanzhen)* CITIC Pacific Research Advance, 2006, No. 4, 7 February.
2. The *International Financial Review* commented that the GDE restructuring 'fully demonstrated the promise made by the Guangdong provincial government that the restructuring must be transparent and fair, which had never happened before in China'.
3. The term 'city' is purely administrative in this context, including both urban and rural areas within the given boundaries.
4. The debts of the UCCs and RFAs alone amounted to more than RMB 100 billion. The total debts could be around (perhaps even exceeding) RMB 200 billion if the debts of the whole country's TICs, RCCs, and local branches of the state-owned banks are included.
5. Between January 1997 and January 1998, the local exchange rate against the dollar fell by 56.2 per cent in Thailand, 84.8 per cent in Indonesia, 43.4 per cent in the Philippines, 48.3 per cent in Malaysia, and 12.3 per cent in Singapore.
6. In the first half of 1998, China's foreign exchange reserves were US$ 145 billion and the total international debts were US$ 138 billion.
7. According to KPMG's auditing report, by 30 September 1998, GDE Group's total debts were HK$ 30.3 billion and assets on balance sheet were HK$ 21.2 billion. GDE was seriously insolvent.
8. The Vice Head were Wu Jiesi, Assistant to the Governor, Jiang Chaoliang, Director of PBOC Guangzhou Branch (current Assistant to the Director of PBOC), and Liu Xingqiang, Director of Guangzhou Securities Administration Office.
9. Another one was Zhongye TIC, originally owned by CCB and registered in Guangdong.
10. For example, Zhuhai ITIC agreed with five international creditors a 30 per cent 'haircut' with exemption of interest. Zhuhai Special Economic Zone ITIC and another two international creditors reached agreement for a 30 per cent 'haircut'. Shantou Huaqiao TIC and Shenzhen Branch of Bank of East Asia, and the Hong Kong Branch of the Netherlands Commercial Bank agreed to a 30 per cent 'haircut'. Shantou ITIC and Nanyang Commercial Bank agreed to a 35 per cent 'haircut'. The international debts in Zhongshan were largely with individuals. The result of the negotiations was as follows: paying the principle of domestic individuals' foreign exchange deposits but with no interest payment; 30 per cent 'haircut' for the principle of the overseas individuals' deposits with no interest payment; 30 per cent 'haircut' for overseas institutions with no interest payment.
11. The members of the coordinating team consisted of leaders from the General Office of the Provincial Government, Provincial Court, Provincial Procurator, Department of Propaganda of the Provincial CCP Committee, Provincial Department of Agriculture, Provincial Department of Finance, Provincial Department of Auditing, Provincial Department of Public Security, Provincial Department of Supervision, Provincial Department of Labour, Provincial State

Assets Administration Bureau, Provincial Development Research Centre, Guangfa Securities, Provincial ICBC, Guangzhou Foreign Exchange Administration Bureau, Provincial PBOC, Provincial Agriculture Bank of China.

12. This procedure had first been adopted in early 1990s by Wang Qishan, then governor of the China Construction Bank, when he had received orders to take charge of and close down the China Agricultural Trust and Investment Corporation which he had established. Some large sum debts that no-one came to claim had been written off. This experience was promoted on a wider basis in Guangdong.

13. Xiao Chong, 2002: 351-70, 382-8.

14. At the same time, Hainan GITIC's General Manager was sentenced to fifteen years in prison. Each of the other two Vice-Chairmen was sentenced to thirteen years (Li Yaoqi was sentenced to death for 'stealing massive amounts of state assets', *People's Daily*, 26 March 2002: 2)

15. 'Dai Xianglong: eighty TICs were retained', *Xin Bao*, 18 March, 2002: 6.

16. Under the system of government structure led by the CCP, the CCP Political and Legislative Committee is responsible for guiding all the government departments including public security, prosecution, and court. The Department of Organisation is in charge of the appointment of cadres for all the government departments and CCP. The Discipline and Supervision Committee is responsible for supervising and disciplining leaders and cadres at each level within the CCP.

17. Eight out of ten directors from Guangnan's Board of Directors were suspects, including Chairman Sun Guan. On 12 October 1998, Assistant General Manager Li Ruihua was arrested by ICAC. On 20 January 1999, Li Ruihua escaped and ICAC issued orders for arrest. On 8 June 1999, ICAC issued warrants for search and arrest under the code name '*Da Guan Yuan*' for arresting eight top cadres at Guangnan including Director and General Manager Huang Xiaojiang. On 15 January 2000, ICAC took search action under the code name 'torpedo' and arrested nine persons. On 25 January, Ye Xiaosui hanged himself using a bed sheet in the detention centre. On 5 April, the conspirator, the accountant of the Ji Jie International Company and Ning Yangfeng, Director of Hong Kong Industrial and Commercial Development were sentenced to four years in prison. 17 August, ICAC sued nine top cadres of Guangnan and issued orders for the arrest of twelve at large, including Chairman Sun Guan and six Executive Directors. On 7 December, Huang Xiaojiang was convicted of fraud using false license of credit and was sentenced to six years in prison. Two other accessory criminals were sentenced to four years (Gu Liang, ed., 'Three non-executive directors of Guangnan, Li Guobao, Wen Jiaxuan, and Zeng Wenqiang should not shirk their responsibilities': 292-311). By 2002, in the case of Guangnan falsifying license of credit involving HK $1.8 billion, there were fourteen people sentenced to 2-9 years by the Hong Kong court ('More directors were sentenced in Guangnan case', *Xin Bao*, 4 April 2002: 4).

18. 'GDE benefited from restructuring and turned into profit', *Dongfang Daily*, 24 September 2001: B1.

19. New GDE is still owned by the Guangdong provincial government except that Goldman Sachs honoured its promise at the restructuring and bought symbolically 5 per cent shares.

20. Xu Jingyi, *et al.*, 2002.

21. 'SOEs and red chips raised HK $651 billion in Hong Kong', *International Financial Times*, 29 May 2002: 1.

22. Paul Volker and Xing Tian Feng Xiong (1996), Changes of Times: the Challenges of International Currency to American Leadership Position, China Finance Press, p. 334.

23. Lan Hai, 2001: A3; and 'Renminbi business will be opened up gradually', Xin Bao, 10 December 2001: 2.

24. The famous Chinese economist Wu Jinglian thought the reform of commercial banks should be further stepped up, combining the first step with the second step into one step (Wu Jinglian, 2002).

25. Shenzhen Development Bank was floated at the beginning of 1990. Pudong Development Bank was floated in 1999. China's first private bank, Minsheng Bank, was listed in 2000. In 2001, Huaxia Bank and Merchant Bank announced they were to be listed in the domestic market. In May 2001, Bank of China announced it was to be floated 'within a few months'. During the preparation for flotation, BOC announced a merger with ten 'sister banks' in Hong Kong. BOC became the second largest financial institution in Hong Kong next to HSBC.

26. 'The former director of CCB Enping Branch was convicted', Hong Kong Commercial Daily, 25 July 2001.

27. For example, GDE Investment, the red chip under GDE Group, employed Xu Haoming as General Manager, at an annual salary of HK$ 4 million. The Chairman of the Bank of East Asia, Li Guobao was the independent director of Guangnan Holdings, the leadership of which was a criminal group. One of the big five accountancy firms, De Loitte Tomatsu, was responsible for Guangnan's financial auditing.

Chapter 6

CHINA AT THE CROSSROADS

Peter Nolan

[T]he disparity between our technology and our ethics is greater than it has ever been. [This] is mortally dangerous…[I]n spite of his scientific and technological prowess, modern man, like primitive man, is not the master of the situation in which he finds himself. He has failed to master it because he has failed to master himself…The individual self is alienated from the universal self by greed. This greed is a desire to exploit the universal for the individual self's purposes. The converse of greed is compassion. By practising compassion, the individual self can become the universal self actually…If mankind is not to destroy itself, it must now cleanse the pollution it has produced and must refrain from producing any more. [T]his can only be by co-operation on a world-wide scale…Unrestrained greed is self-destructive because it takes suicidally short views…[I]n all industrial countries in which maximum private profit is the motive for production, the competitive economic system will become unworkable. [T]he survival of mankind is more precarious today than it has been at any time since mankind established its ascendancy over non-human nature…[T]he human race will be unable to survive unless it achieves political unification quickly. It is conceivable that the future unifier of the world will not be a Western or a Westernised country but will be China…[F]or most of the time since the third century BC, [China] has been the centre of the world. Within the last five hundred years, the whole world has been knitted together by Western enterprise all except on the political plane. Perhaps it is China's destiny now to give political unity and peace not just to half but to all the world…East Asia preserves a number of historical assets that may enable it to become the geographical and cultural axis for the unification of the whole world…Do we expect China to meet the world's life and death demands? Will China make this attempt? If it attempts, will it succeed? We cannot predict the future, but it is already obvious that if China tries and fails, the prospect for mankind will be dim…The world's unification is a way for mankind to escape suicide.

(Arnold Toynbee in Toynbee and Ikeda,
1976: 41, 120, 133, 232, 245-6, 307-08, 316, and 342)

Introduction

Since the late 1970s, China has enjoyed one of the most remarkable periods of economic growth ever seen. However, the country faces deep economic, political and social challenges as it moves into the next period in its development. These challenges include the vast extent of poverty and rapidly growing inequality; the challenge for Chinese businesses from the global business revolution; a deeply degraded natural environment; declining capabilities of the state; a comprehensive challenge in international relations; widespread corruption; and extreme dangers in engaging closely with the global financial system, which were vividly exposed during the Asian Financial Crisis. The Chinese leadership is trying to deal simultaneously with the challenges of globalisation, transition and development. No other country has ever faced such a set of challenges. There are no textbooks to guide China along this path. The responsibilities for the leadership are massive, because the price of failure is so huge. The possibility of social and political disintegration is real. Every effort of policy has to be directed towards avoiding this potentially catastrophic outcome. In their search for a way forward, China's leaders are looking to the lessons from the country's own past, as well as to those from other countries, in order to find a way to build a stable, cohesive and prosperous society. This effort is of vital importance, not only for China, but also for the whole world.

This chapter examines the following question: is it possible for China to build a civilised, socially cohesive society over the next few decades, during what is still the early phase of China's industrialisation, and during which time there will still be a huge rural reserve army of labour?

1. The Challenges to China's Economic and Political Stability

Poverty and Inequality

Behind almost every aspect of China's development process in the early twenty-first century lies the harsh reality of the 'Lewis model' of economic development with unlimited supplies of labour (Lewis, 1954).

China has a huge population of almost 1.3 billion, increasing by around 15-16 million people each year (SSB, ZTN, 2002). Almost 70 per cent of the Chinese population still lives in the countryside. There are as many as 150 million 'surplus' farm workers. Rural incomes stagnated from the mid-1990s to the early 2000s, and may even have declined.[1] Rural income distribution has become much more unequal: the Gini coefficient of rural income distribution rose from 0.21 in 1978 to 0.40 in 1998 (Yao Shujie, 2002). There was a massive decline in absolute poverty in the early years of China's rural reforms post-Mao (Nolan, 1988). However, Chinese official data show that there are approximately 580 million rural dwellers (73 per cent of rural households) with less than US$ 360 per year (SSB, ZTN, 2002: 343).[2]

The massive extent of rural underemployment provides intense incentives for rural-urban migration, and great downward pressure on non-farm wages in unskilled and low-skilled occupations. There are as many as 150 million rural residents working in the urban areas without permanent urban residence qualifications. They are predominantly unskilled labour, earning US$ 1-2 per day. As well as the poor rural migrants, as many as 40-50 million people lost their jobs due to reform in state-owned enterprises.

Alongside these disadvantaged social groups, a new 'middle class' is fast emerging. Large amounts of FDI by multinational firms is producing clusters of modern businesses within China's major cities, inhabited by Chinese and foreign employees, isolated and protected from the surrounding mass of poor people. Chinese privatisation has been characterised by widespread insider dealing and corruption. Central to this process is the 'triangular' relationship between the local Communist Party, the banks and the allocation of publicly owned land for 'development'. The Gini coefficient of the urban distribution of income rose from 0.25 in 1992 to 0.34 in 2001 (SSB, ZTN, 1993 and 2002). However, these official data exclude most rural migrants and foreign employees. They also underestimate the income of the highest segments of the native Chinese urban population. If all these factors are considered, then China's urban income distribution is among the most unequal in the world.

The early years of the twenty-first century witnessed a level of strikes and protests that has not been seen in China since the 1920s, and a significant increase in the number of rural protests. China's policy-makers are trying to ensure that during this tense period, the country is sustained as a 'steady and harmonious society'. China's leaders have a declared vision of an 'everlasting and peaceful nation', building a dynamic economy, while 'laying the groundwork for a market that is moral and fair'.

The Global Business Revolution

Since the 1980s, China has implemented industrial policies intended to nurture a group of globally competitive large firms. In a fundamental sense these industrial policies have failed. China is becoming the workshop *for* the world, rather than the 'workshop *of* the world'. Over 60 per cent of its industrial exports are from foreign invested enterprises. A substantial fraction of the remainder of the country's exports consists of industrial products that are either OEM manufactures, or low value-added, low technology, non-branded goods for global giant firms (e.g. garments, footwear, furniture, toys). While the world's giant firms are rapidly building their research and development bases in China, employing relatively cheap, highly-skilled Chinese researchers, indigenous Chinese firms spend negligible amounts on research and development. China does not have a single one of the world's top 100 brands. China's leading firms are almost unknown outside the country. Among the fourteen Chinese firms in the *Fortune* 500, none has become a truly globally competitive company that could compete without government protection.[3] All of these firms are state-owned and subject to systematic state interference in their operation. There is not a single Chinese firm in the world's top 700 firms by research and development expenditure (DTI, 2003).

On the internal front, China's industrial policy encountered numerous problems. These included policy inconsistency; misguided pursuit of 'enterprise autonomy' rather than multi-plant large firm; an impoverished mass of consumers within the protected domestic market; institutional constraints on cross-regional mergers and acquisitions; pursuit of firm size through diversified operations, leading to an 'illusion of scale'; persistent intervention in enterprise decisions by Party and Government officials; and vast 'legacy costs' deriving from the huge numbers employed in the former large-scale SOEs.

On the international front, China's large firms face severe challenges. China's attempt to build large globally competitive firms has coincided with one of the most revolutionary epochs in world business history. Since the 1980s, there has been a period of unique intensity of merger and acquisition. An unprecedented degree of industrial concentration has been established, with a veritable 'law' coming into play. Within the high value-added, high technology, and/or strongly branded segments of global markets, which serve mainly the middle and upper income earners who control the bulk of the world's purchasing power, a handful of giant firms, the 'systems integrators', occupied upwards of 50 per cent of the whole global market (Nolan, 2001a and 2001b).

The process of concentration is rippling across the value chain at high speed. The leading firms in each sector select the most capable among their suppliers, in a form of 'industrial planning', adopting 'aligned partners' who can work with them across the world. A 'cascade effect' is at work in which intense pressures have developed for first tier suppliers of goods and services to the global giants to themselves merge and acquire, and develop leading global positions, achieved through necessary research and development, and investment in global production networks. The result is a fast-developing process of concentration at a global level in numerous industries supplying goods and services to the systems integrators.

The full flowering of capitalism's inbuilt tendency towards industrial concentration presents a comprehensive challenge for large firms in developing countries, not least China. At the dawn of the twenty-first century, the reality of the intense industrial concentration among both systems integrators and their entire supply chain, brought about through pressure from the 'cascade effect', presents a comprehensive challenge for both Chinese firms and policy-makers. Not only do they face immense difficulties in catching up with the leading systems integrators, the visible part of the 'iceberg', but they also face immense difficulties in catching up with the powerful firms that now dominate almost every segment of the supply chain, the invisible part of the 'iceberg' that lies hidden from view beneath the water.

In September 2004, almost three years after China joined the WTO, Li Rongrong, Head of the National Assets Commission (SASAC, or *'guoziwei'*) acknowledged:

There is still a huge gap between China's large enterprises and the world's leading multinational companies, whether one looks at the comparison in terms of their number, scale or efficiency, or from the angle of strength of profits and innovative capability, or internationalization (*People's Daily* website).

Successful late-comer industrialising countries, from the United States in the late nineteenth century to South Korea in the late twentieth century, each produced a group of globally competitive firms. China is the first successful latecomer not to have done so. It is remarkable that China has reached a position in which it is the world's sixth largest economy (China is the second largest in PPP terms) (World Bank, 2004) without having a group of internationally competitive large firms. This is highly significant in the history of economic development.

The Environment

China's environmental deterioration presents a further deep challenge for the Chinese state. This reflects the intense pressure of a huge and growing population upon China's already fragile natural environment, with the impact hugely reinforced by high-speed industrial growth.

The area affected by serious soil erosion has increased to include around 38 per cent of the entire country (UNDP, 2000: 70). The area of desert is increasing at the rate of around 2,500 square kilometres per year, equivalent to the area of a medium-sized country. In the past four decades, almost one half of China's forests have been destroyed, so that China now has one of the sparsest forest covers in the world. There is 'rampant water pollution', and a serious and worsening shortage of fresh water.

China explosive industrial growth has led to high-speed expansion of energy-intensive industries. By the mid-1990s, China had overtaken the United States as the world's biggest coal producer, accounting for almost 30 per cent of global output. Coal provides a low-cost way to meet a large fraction of China's booming demands for energy to meet the needs of the country's 'industrial revolution'. China will soon overtake the United States as the world's largest producer of carbon dioxide (the United States' share currently stands at 23.4 per cent) (World Bank, WDR, 2000: 248-9). If China follows the US path allowing complete dominance for the automobile, then the prospects for the world are terrifying. If China's 1.4 billion people were to sustain their current growth path and at some point catch up with today's US level of per capita income, and were to use similar technologies, China's use of commercial energy and emission of carbon dioxide would be one-fifth greater than those of the entire world today.

Recent Chinese provincial-level studies of 'Green National Product' estimate that 'real output growth' reduces to negligible levels when destruction of the natural environment is taken into account. Whatever combination of measures is adopted, involving more or less use of the price mechanism to achieve the hoped-for results, the Chinese state will be central to the country's ability to achieve environmentally sustainable development, not just for China, but for the whole world.

The Capability and Role of the State

The professional capability of the Chinese state has greatly increased since the early 1980s. However, the Chinese state needs comprehensive reinvigoration that goes far beyond improved technical competence. It needs to substantially expand its scope in order to undertake activities that the market is unable to provide and to re-establish its ethical foundations (*zai zao guo jia*). Reinvigorating a state apparatus that has atrophied may present even greater challenges than constructing from scratch a strong, effective apparatus to serve the needs of development.

Government. China is a vast, poor country with urgent development needs, which can only be met by state action. The Chinese state attempted to increase its fiscal strength after the mid-1990s, with a series of important reforms. However, even in 1999 the share of budget revenue still stood at only 14 of GDP (SSB, ZTN, 2001: 256). The share of government revenue in GDP is not only below that of many developing countries, but also of Russia. One can say that 'state desertion' during the 'transition' period in China outstripped even that in Russia.

The state's reduced fiscal strength has forced it to look for drastically increased contributions from fees paid by people when they use health and education services. By the end of the 1990s, budgetary allocations covered just 46 per cent of actual expenditures on education (World Bank, 2002: 85). A wide variety of other sources of funding have been mobilised to finance education, including surcharges, fees collected from students, revenues from school-run enterprises, work study programmes, donations and gifts. Between the late 1980s and mid-1990s, there was 'a substantial deterioration in the educational status of the poor' (World Bank, 2002: 42).

Over the past five decades, China has built an impressive rural health system, and overall health achievements are impressive, with a life expectancy of 70 and an infant mortality rate of 31 per 1000 live births. At the peak of the rural people's communes before 1976, around 85 per cent of villages had a cooperative medical system, albeit often rudimentary (World Bank, 2002: 116). When the agricultural collectives were disbanded in the early 1980s, the financial basis for risk-sharing was largely eliminated. The World Bank estimates that at the end of the 1990s, more than 90 per cent of the rural population, or 700 million people, were without any coverage from collective risk-pooling schemes (World Bank, 2002: 116). In 1999, the government budget funded just 11 per cent of total health expenditure, while 59 per cent came from out-of-pocket payments (World Bank, 2002: 43). These changes have resulted in a system that provides highly unequal access to health services. The World Health Report, 2000, ranked China 61st out of 191 countries in overall quality of health, but 188th in terms of fairness in financial contribution (quoted in World Bank, 2002: iv).

Party. The Chinese Communist Party, with 64 million members, faces immense ideological and organisational challenges. Leadership by the Communist Party is the foundation of the Chinese modernisation drive. The Party is deeply intertwined with every aspect of economic, social and political life in China. In the late 1980s and early 1990s, Deng Xiaoping had repeatedly warned of the dangers of China collapsing into chaos if the wrong decisions were taken. In his 2001 speech to celebrate the 80th anniversary of the founding of the Chinese Communist Party, Jiang Zemin stated: '[The Party] must address the two major historic subjects of enhancing the Party's ability of exercising state power

and art of leadership, and resisting corruption and warding off risks...
[W]e must be strict in Party discipline. We should have a deeper understanding
of the loss of political power by some Communist Parties in the world that
had long been ruling parties and learn a lesson from them' (Jiang, 2001).

The level at which Party members were investigated and brought to trial for
corruption has risen to include many in high positions. A succession of
high-level government officials were forced out of office, arrested and in several
cases, were even sentenced to death, for corruption. These included a former
deputy governor and former mayor of Shijiazhuang, Hebei's largest city
(*FT*, 22 January 2001); the mayor of one of China's largest cities, Shenyang
(*FT*, 27 December 2000, and 2 June 2001); a former vice-minister of public
security; a former chief of military intelligence (*NYT*, 23 December 2000); and
a deputy chairman of the National People's Congress (*IHT*, 1 August 2000).
Official reports to the National People's Congress in early 2003 declared that
in the previous five years, the war against graft had been substantially stepped
up, with a total of almost 13 000 prosecutions of government officials
(*SCMP*, 11 March 2003).

The very reason that so many cases of corruption have come to light, and
been written about in the Chinese press, is precisely the fact that the Chinese
leadership is fully aware of the deep threat that it poses, and is trying hard to
do something about it. The task they face is enormous.

International Relations

The United States fears that China's rise will transform fundamentally the
balance of world economic and military power. After September 11, President
Bush warned China: 'In pursuing advanced military capabilities that can
threaten its neighbors in the Asia Pacific region, China is following an outdated
path that, in the end, will hamper its own pursuit of greatness. It is time to
reaffirm the essential role of American military strength. We must build and
maintain our defences beyond challenge...Our forces will be strong enough to
dissuade potential adversaries from pursuing a military build-up in hopes of
surpassing, or equalling, the power of the US' (quoted in *Financial Times*, 21
September 2002). Following September 11, the consensus among the inner
core of the Bush administration shifted to the view that 'in the long-term the
US would only find security in a world in which US values were widely held
and spread' (*FT*, 6 March 2003). There is a powerful set of interests that
believes serious conflict with China is unavoidable. Henry Kissinger warned
that the US foreign policy hawks see China 'as a morally flawed inevitable
adversary'. Brent Scowcroft warned: 'If there is a real division within this

[Bush Junior] administration, it is probably on China. There is a division between those who see China as inexorably developing into the primary security threat to the US, and those who feel China is transforming rapidly but…that its been overwhelmingly positive' (*FT*, 20 August 2001).

In 1999, the United States' military budget stood at US$ 253 billion, compared with just US$ 135 billion for NATO Europe (IISS, 1999: 37). In the wake of September 11, the United States announced that the military budget would rise to US$ 379 billion by 2006, while there are no plans to increase real military expenditure by NATO Europe countries (*FT*, 18 February 2002). Europe trails far behind the world's military superpower. As the war against Iraq demonstrated, today's friends in international relations can be tomorrow's enemies. China's military strategists cannot rule out the possibility that at some point, the object of 'regime change' may even include China.

However, the final shape of the United States' view of how best to 'engage' with China is still unclear. In the 1980s, the prime goal of American foreign policy was the overthrow of the 'evil empire' in the Soviet Union. This goal was pursued through acceleration of the arms race and numerous channels of influence upon Soviet policy-makers. US policies played a significant role in the collapse of Soviet communism and the disintegration of the USSR. 'Regime change' resulted in the collapse of the state, which had disastrous consequences for the Russian economy and for the welfare of most Russians. The Soviet economy had only negligible linkages to the US economy. The USSR accounted for a tiny fraction of American exports and there was no investment in Russia by US multinationals. Soviet exports to the United States were trivial in scale. The collapse of the Soviet economy had a negligible impact on the US economy other than the short-term fall in military expenditure.

The Chinese and US economies have become deeply inter-twined. US consumers benefit from the explosive growth of low-priced Chinese exports. US companies and shareholders benefit from China's absorption of booming American investments and from access to the low-cost manufacturing supply-chain in China. US primary product producers (including food, oil and mining companies) benefit from exports to China, both directly from the United States and, increasingly, from production bases in other countries. The US government benefits from Chinese government purchase of its debt, which, ultimately, helps to underpin the growth of US personal consumption. 'System disintegration' in China, such as the US helped bring about in the USSR, Afghanistan and Iraq, would be a disaster for China, but would also have severe economic consequences for the United States. One can only guess at the military consequences. From this perspective it is in the interests of US business and the mass of US citizens, not to speak of the rest of the world, to support the efforts of China's Communist Party leadership to sustain the country's 'peaceful rise'.

Financial institutions. The Asian Financial Crisis provided China's leaders with a shocking insight into the fragility of the country's financial institutions. China appeared to escape any effects of the crisis, due to the fact that the *renminbi* was not fully convertible. In fact, the crisis had a deep impact through the medium of Hong Kong and Guangdong province.

The Guangdong government established two flagship firms during the reform period. One was GITIC (Guangdong Trust and Investment Company), a non-bank financial firm based in Guangdong, but with extensive interests in Hong Kong. The other was GDE (Guangdong Enterprises), whose main activities were in Hong Kong, including five floated 'red chip' companies. During the Asian Financial Crisis, GITIC went into bankruptcy and GDE was insolvent, and was comprehensively restructured. Immediately prior to the crisis, they each had been regarded as outstanding institutions by international lenders. In May 1994 *Business Week* magazine described GITIC as 'a financial powerhouse that is helping to remake China'. The Hong Kong government awarded GDE the Territory's annual 'Best Management' award. Morgan Stanley selected Guangnan, one of GDE's red chip companies floated in Hong Kong, as one of the world's 'top fifty small and medium-sized companies'.

The bankruptcy of GITIC and the restructuring of GDE allowed the outside world to look closely inside large Chinese companies for the first time. The investigations showed that they each had huge failures in corporate governance. Both were shown to have followed disastrous lending policies: a large fraction of their loans and investments were made to firms and institutions that were unable or unwilling to repay their debts. A substantial part of their 'investments' were highly speculative, including heavy participation in the property boom in Guangdong and Hong Kong. Investigations into Guangnan, one of GDE's 'red chip' companies, concluded that it was basically a 'criminal company': a total of thirty-five people from Guangnan were either arrested or had warrants for their arrest issued by the Independent Commission Against Corruption (ICAC) in Hong Kong. Guangnan was a Hong Kong-listed company, a 'red chip', operating in Hong Kong's environment of high quality rules on corporate governance; over 40 per cent of its shares were owned by public investors; its accounts were audited by a famous international accountancy firm; it had two independent directors, both prominent businessmen from Hong Kong.

China's four main banks are in the process of comprehensive restructuring. The cases of GITIC and GDE demonstrate how long and complex will be the process of changing China's financial institutions into well-governed, modern financial institutions. They demonstrate that 'privatisation' and stock market flotation, operating according to global rules and regulations on corporate governance, and with close scrutiny from investigative financial journalists, are not sufficient to ensure that China's financial institutions operate in a way that eliminates risk for China's financial system. They show that for Chinese financial firms to go out into the 'high seas' of global finance before their corporate governance structures have been fully transformed would be incredibly dangerous.

In the late 1990s, especially after the Asian Financial Crisis, the central government began a massive attempt to 'cleanup' the country's financial institutions. These revealed shocking evidence about the state of corporate governance in China's main banks. In early 2002, it was revealed that five bank officials at the Bank of China (BOC) branch in Kaiping city (Guangdong) had stolen the equivalent of 'nearly US$ 500 million' (*FT*, 16 March 2002, and *FEER*, 30 May 2002). The problems penetrated to the apex of the country's banking system, Zhu Xiaohua, Li Fuxiang and Wang Xuebing were members of Premier Zhu Rongji's team of four 'can-do-commanders' (*gan jiang*). From 1993 to 1996, Zhu Xiaohua was deputy governor of the People's Bank of China (PBOC) and then head of China's foreign exchange reserves. In 1996 he was appointed head of China Everbright Bank (CEB). In 1999, he was arrested, and subsequently sentenced to fifteen years imprisonment. Li Fuxiang was formerly the head of the Bank of China's foreign exchange dealings in New York, and subsequently was placed in charge of the national foreign exchange reserves. In May 2000 he committed suicide. Wang Xuebing, formerly head of the China Construction Bank (CCB) and then of the Bank of China, was arrested in 2002 and subsequently sentenced to twelve years imprisonment.

Under the terms of the WTO Agreement, China's financial firms will face steadily escalating competition from global financial institutions. Since the 1980s leading financial services firms, all from the high-income economies, have been through a period of unprecedented merger and acquisition, to take advantage of global markets, and to benefit from economies of scale and scope in respect to research and development, branding, human resource acquisition, and central procurement (especially IT systems). The period saw the emergence of super-giant financial services firms, such as Citigroup, JP Morgan Chase, and HSBC. The explicit objective of the global giants is to penetrate the financial markets of developing countries. They have at high speed acquired dominant positions in the financial markets of most of Latin America and Eastern Europe. When Citigroup acquired Banamex, Mexico's 'national champion' in financial services, the *Financial Times* commented: 'The acquisition of Banamex underscored the rapacious appetite of Citigroup for assets in the developing world'. Citigroup itself said: 'China is top of our radar screen'.

If China's indigenous large financial firms cannot achieve their own self-reform, then the global giants are likely to be given an increasing role in running the country's financial sector. Citigroup argues that the big four banks in China should be 'torn apart into small units in order to avoid a financial crisis'. Undoubtedly this would make it far easier for the global giants to 'rout the enemy one by one' (gege jipo).

Conclusion

As China enters the twenty-first century it faces a wide-ranging series of deep challenges that threaten the entire social, economic and political systems. Due to the number and intensity of the challenges that China faces, there is a high possibility that at some point a 'fire' will break out. It cannot be predicted where, when, or how. It is highly likely that it will be connected with the financial system. During the Asian Financial Crisis, China came close to a major financial crisis. The country was able to survive only by adopting bold and effective policies. If China were to face a financial crisis of the dimensions of those that have regularly attacked developing countries since the 1980s, it would be difficult to maintain overall system stability. The relationship of political instability with financial crisis is long-standing: 'Since the commencement of the eighteenth century there has been no serious revolution in Europe which has not been preceded by a commercial and financial crisis' (Marx, 1969: 9).

2. China at the Crossroads: Which Direction?

China's political economy has reached a crossroads. The path taken will be the result of complex social, economic and political forces, both internal and external. The development possibilities in the decades ahead may be analysed under four stylised types.

2.1 Harsh 'Primitive Capitalist Accumulation'?

Many people believe that China has no choice but to follow the harsh logic of 'primitive capitalist accumulation', as outlined in Marx's *Capital, Vol. 1* (Marx, 1967). They argue that China will become a 'normal' capitalist economy. Indeed, it is already well-advanced on this path, with the state-owned sector occupying well under one-half of national output. They argue that the brutal nature of the accumulation process during the 'Lewis' phase of industrialisation, with its foundation in 'economic development with unlimited supplies of labour' at a constant real, subsistence wage, demanded an authoritarian political structure, with voting rights confined to the narrow ruling class.

In Britain during the take-off into capitalist industrialisation after the mid-eighteenth century, it took around one hundred years before the large rural reserve army of labour was absorbed into the modern sector. This provided strong downward pressure on urban real wage rates, with no significant improvement in urban real wages between 1750 and the 1820s at the earliest. There was a prolonged phase of early capitalist accumulation during which there was a sharp widening of income disparities, and no diminution of absolute poverty. Capitalist accumulation was accompanied by harsh measures of social control to maintain political order. In the late eighteenth and early nineteenth century the predominant political philosophy in Britain considered that the wide divergence of interests between socio-economic groups made it impossible to obtain a democratically worked-out compromise consistent with advancement of the national economy (Hirschman, 1977).

Advocates of the primitive capitalist accumulation approach in China draw comfort from the wider lessons of the history of early capitalist industrialisation. Democratic institutions were introduced in almost all cases only after the harsh phase of early capitalist accumulation had been accomplished (Therborn 1977: 33-4). The examples of Japan in the Meijii Period (1868-1912), as well as Taiwan and Korea in recent times are invoked to provide support for the necessity of China passing through a prolonged phase of primitive capitalist accumulation during the prolonged 'Lewis Phase' of development. In each case there was an initial phase of harsh political rule, with rapid absorption of rural surplus labour into the urban workforce at a constant real wage. Once the supply of rural surplus labour dried up, real wages for ordinary workers started to grow in the urban areas. It was at this point that demands for political democratisation began to develop.[4]

It will be many decades before China's rural surplus labour supply is exhausted. If the main rationale for political authoritarianism is the existence of a 'Lewis-type' process of capital accumulation, then China would face the prospect of a long period under such a structure. It is questionable whether this structure would be stable over such a long period, given the prospects for growing inequality in the midst of accelerated integration of China into the global economy. In the event that such a structure did survive, it would constitute a prolonged and oppressive form of late industrialisation.

2.2 Regime Change?

Regime Change in Chinese History

Many people, including many Chinese intellectuals, especially economists, as well as international advisors, believe that the fundamental condition for continued successful Chinese development is a drastic downgrading of the role of the state. A major reason that they advocated China joining the WTO was precisely in order to reduce radically the role of the state. Within China, but especially among international politicians and intellectuals, influential thinkers and policy makers believe that the Chinese Communist Party should give up its monopoly control of political power.

At international meetings and in their writings, leading US government advisors on China policy under George Bush have promoted the desirability of 'regime change' in China. No idea was more pervasive in the early years of 'transition' in the former USSR and Eastern Europe than that which argued that the state should first be destroyed before it could be reconstructed. In China at the end of the 1980s, before and during the occupation of Tiananmen Square, a consensus among international opinion developed which believed that the overthrow of the Chinese Communist Party would lead to a great improvement in welfare for the Chinese people. It was given added impetus by the development of *'perestroika'* and *'glasnost'* in the former USSR, which quickly led to the downfall of the Communist Party of the Soviet Union. The blunt reality is that the overthrow of the Chinese Communist Party would plunge the country into social and political chaos. China has experienced long periods of system disintegration. The 'dynastic cycle' was a regular phenomenon, with high levels of bureaucratic efficiency at the start of each dynasty, followed by a gradual disintegration of the morality and effectiveness of the central government. The dynastic cycle was so regular and so devastating when it entered a downward path at the end of each dynasty, that the theme of avoidance of 'great turmoil' *(da luan)* was the focus of all Chinese political thought from the earliest times right through to the present day. At the core of the Chinese reform programme after the death of Chairman Mao was a belief in the need to prevent China's political economy from disintegrating and the country descending into 'big turbulence', which would 'deprive the Chinese people of all hope'.

It is perfectly possible that the entire Chinese system of political economy could disintegrate, notwithstanding US$ 500 billion-worth of FDI. In the late 1980s, few people could imagine that the USSR would disintegrate, yet this hugely sophisticated country, with massive human and technological resources, which had huge potential for high-speed advance in economic performance and living standards, has been sent spinning backwards (Nolan, 1995). It has been 'de-developed' in a way never witnessed before in peacetime. China is still a poor country. Comparable 'de-development' for China would cause immense suffering. It was unimaginable beforehand to most people that there could be system meltdown in the USSR, in the sophisticated European state, formerly known as Yugoslavia, in the IMF's favourite pupil in Latin America, Argentina, or in the exemplar of the East Asian model, Indonesia. Yet there was just such a comprehensive meltdown, with disastrous consequences for the people of those countries. The reasons were easy to understand with hindsight. The central task of Chinese political economy is to learn from those experiences and avoid such an outcome in China.

The 'Freedom' of Free Market Capitalism?

A widespread view among those who wish for 'regime change' in China is the belief that China can 'follow the American path'. American foreign policy is based on the premise that the whole world, including China, should, and will, follow this 'natural' path of development. Intense external pressure is exerted already through innumerable channels upon Chinese internal ideology to promote this view of the desirable future political economic structure for China. The same populist illusion was fostered among the population of the former USSR in the late 1980s and early 1990s. Such views will become ever more influential as the US-dominated global mass media increasingly penetrates the Mainland following the 'opening-up' of the mass media in accordance with the WTO Agreement.

President Bush's national security strategy document of September 2002 (Bush, 2002) was entitled 'How the US will lead "freedom's triumph"'. The Report states: 'Freedom is the non-negotiable demand of human dignity; the birthright of every person - in every civilisation...Today, humanity holds in its hands the opportunity to further freedom's triumph over all [its] foes. The US welcomes our responsibility to lead in this great mission'. It commits the United States to 'defend liberty and justice because these principles are right and true for all people everywhere'. It commits the United States to 'stand firmly for the non-negotiable demands of human dignity: the rule of law; limits on the absolute power of the state; free speech; freedom of worship; equal justice; respect for women; religious and ethnic tolerance; and respect for private property'.

In fact, the interpretation of the word 'freedom' has been the object of intense debate within the history of the United States (Foner, 1998). At the heart of the struggle for the meaning of 'freedom' in the United States was the battle over the role of the state, and its function in the achievement of 'negative' and 'positive' freedoms. Was the US state to serve purely as the guardian of individual liberties or 'negative freedoms', or was the state to serve as the instrument for the achievement of positive freedoms of all citizens to enable them to be fulfilled human beings? These struggles over the interpretation of 'freedom' have existed in America since the eighteenth century.

The idea that 'freedom' essentially meant freedom of contract became the bedrock of 'liberal' thinking at the end of the nineteenth century. In this view, the true realm of freedom, was 'the liberty to buy and sell, and mend and make, where and how we please, without interference from the state' (Foner, 1998: 120). The period saw the rise of Social Darwinism, which strongly opposed any form of state interference with the 'natural' workings of society. Laws regulating labour conditions were seen as a form of slavery, since they interfered in the rights of free agents to dispose of their property as they saw fit.

The 1890s saw deep class struggle in the United States. Powerful critiques of free market fundamentalism emerged, deeply opposed to the idea that meaningful 'freedom' could exist in circumstances of extreme inequality, both economic and racial, such as those of the United States. In the academic sphere, the American Economics Association was founded in 1885 with the express purpose of combating both Social Darwinism and 'laissez-faire orthodoxy'. The founder of the AEA, Richard T. Ely, wrote: 'We regard the state as an educational and ethical agency whose positive assistance is one of the indispensable conditions of human progress (quoted in Foner, 1998: 130).[5] Many younger economists believed that private property had become a 'means of depriving others of their freedom', and that 'poverty posed a far graver danger to the republic than an activist state' (Foner, 1998: 130). During the Progressive Era leading up to the First World War, T. H. Green, the British philosopher, made a profound impact with his lecture in the United States in which he argued that freedom was a 'positive concept'.[6]

The Great Depression had a major impact on the struggle over the interpretation of 'freedom' in the United States. When he assumed the Presidency in 1933, Franklin D. Roosevelt proclaimed: 'For too many Americans, life is no longer free; liberty no longer real; men can no longer follow the pursuit of happiness' (quoted in Foner, 1998: 196). Under Roosevelt's guidance, the Democratic Party led the country towards large-scale state intervention to reconstruct the economy and provide citizens with social security. These ideas remained as the mainstream of US political thought for long into the post-war world, reinforced by the massive task of economic and social reconstruction in war-ravaged Europe.

In the 1950s, a group of conservative thinkers set out to 'reclaim the idea of freedom'. For them, freedom meant de-centralised political power, limited government, and a free market economy. The immediate intellectual origins of the movement can be traced back to the publication in 1944 of Friedrich Hayek's book, *The Road to Serfdom*. Hayek's ideas were a 'clarion call for conservatives to reclaim the word "freedom", which, he charged, had been usurped and distorted by socialists' (Foner, 1998: 236). By the 1980s, and even more forcefully in the 1990s, the dominant view of 'freedom' in the United States came to be the equation of 'freedom' with individual choice in the market place with minimal interference from the state. As the US business system became increasingly powerful globally, the idea gained force that the United States should lead the world towards a single universal free market. The collapse of the USSR deeply reinforced Americans' confidence in the free market, and in the country's duty to lead the world towards this as a universal form of socio-economic organisation. By the 1990s, in the United States there was no serious intellectual challenge to the economic philosophy of the free market.

The idea that the free market is a moral concept stands at the centre of political discourse in the United States at the start of the twenty-first century. President Bush's Security Strategy declaration of September 2002 states: 'The concept of "free trade" arose as a moral principle even before it became a pillar of economics. If you can make something that others value, you should be able to sell it to them. If others make something that you value you should be able to buy it. This is real freedom, the freedom for a person - or nation - to make a living' (Bush, 21 September 2002). In his speech to West Point military academy in 2002, President Bush said: 'Moral truth is the same in every culture, in every time, in every place' (quoted in *Financial Times*, 7 February 2003). In his state of the union address to Congress in 2003, he said: 'The liberty we prize is not America's gift to the world, it is God's gift to humanity' (quoted in *Financial Times*, 7 February 2003).

In the wake of September 11, the US government is even more firmly convinced of its historic function to spread the moral principle of the free market across the whole world: 'The great struggles of the twentieth century between liberty and totalitarianism ended with a decisive victory for the forces of freedom - and a single sustainable model for national success: freedom, democracy and free enterprise. Today, the US enjoys a position of unparalleled military strength, and great economic and political influence...We seek to create a balance of power that favours human freedom...The US will use this opportunity to spread the benefits of freedom across the globe...We will make freedom and the development of democratic institutions key themes in our bilateral relations' (Bush, 21 September 2002).

When China tries to 'learn from the United States', which tradition should it turn to: that which argues for a powerful role for the state to ensure positive freedoms for all citizens, or 'free market fundamentalism', whose current intellectual and political ascendancy may turn out to be a relatively brief intermission in the long sweep of US history?

2.3 The Left Wing: Backwards to Maoism?

Chairman Mao led the Chinese Communist Party in an attempt to drastically attack social inequality. This amounted to nothing less than an attempt to transform people's work motivation, to overcome the classic 'principal-agent' problem, by liberating human productive energies from the link with material reward. 'Serve the people' (*wei renmin fuwu*) was the foundation of Maoist ideology. Chairman Mao hoped to build a non-capitalist, humane society, which provided the opportunity for the whole population to fulfil their human potential. It was a philosophy that was powerfully driven by the intention to restrict drastically the population's 'negative' freedoms to act in accordance with their individual wishes free of external restriction, while providing the maximum equality of opportunity for citizens to achieve their 'positive freedoms'. 'In a socialist society, it is necessary to acknowledge the differences in the rewards for labour, but the differences ought not to be too great. We must actively create the conditions for communist society's stage "from each according to their abilities, to each according to their needs", and should constantly strive to lessen the three great differences and increasingly extirpate the influence of the bourgeois right' (Comrades, 1974: 597).

From the mid-1950s, through to the mid-1970s, China made enormous progress in many key aspects of social and economic development. The growth rate of national product was faster than in most developing countries. In normal times, the mass of the people enjoyed a high degree of livelihood security. The country achieved enormous advances in health and education. Life expectancy at birth rose from 36 years pre-1949 to 71 years in 1981 (Nolan, 1995: 49). These achievements were applauded by numerous Western scholars as evidence that redistributive policies could enable low income countries to achieve high levels of 'basic needs' long before average per capita incomes had risen to high levels.[7]

However, China paid a high price for the attempt to suppress market forces completely, to cut the country off from the global economy and society, to drastically constrain the dimensions of inequality, to eliminate material incentives, to radically limit cultural freedom and to lead the society in wild, nation-wide mass movements: 'The decade of the Cultural Revolution brought catastrophe upon us and caused profound suffering...Had it not been for "Left" interference, and the reversals of 1958, significant progress would certainly have been achieved in our industrial and agricultural production and in science and education, and the people's standard of living would certainly have improved to a fair extent' (Deng Xiaoping, 1980: 234).

Diversity of thought was crushed. Large numbers of people were imprisoned for their political views. Freedom of cultural expression was dramatically narrowed, causing large-scale damage to people's welfare. The intense political struggles to limit social differentiation caused immense suffering to innumerable participants. Although growth rates were high, they were achieved in a highly inefficient way, with slow technical progress, a long-run fall in capital productivity, and stagnation in average per capita incomes after the mid-1950s. Apart from improvements in consumption of a narrow range of consumer durables (the 'four big goods' - watches, bicycles, radios and sewing machines), per capita consumption of most other items either stagnated or declined (Nolan, 1995: 49). The proportion of the population in absolute poverty remained at around 30 per cent in the mid-1970s, totalling around 270 million people, compared with around 190 million in 1957 (Nolan, 1995: 50). The utopian attempt to leap into a communist society during the Great Leap Forward resulted in a colossal man-made disaster. The collapse in farm output caused the biggest famine of the twentieth century, with as many as 30 million 'excess deaths' (Nolan, 1995: 48).

The Maoist development path is not one to which many Chinese people would wish to return. China cannot go back. It must find a path between a development philosophy which steers a course between extreme individual 'negative' freedoms and extreme collective 'positive' freedoms.

2.4. China at the Crossroads: 'Use The Past to Serve the Present'? (Gu Wei Jin Yong)

In its search for a way forward amidst the immense challenges that it confronts, China's leaders can turn to the country's own past for a source of inspiration. They can use this rich history to provide intellectual nourishment for the attempt to persist in the non-ideological approach of trying to 'grope for a way forwards', an approach that 'seeks truth from facts' devising policies in a pragmatic, experimental fashion to solve concrete problems as they emerge.

China's Long-Run Economic Dynamism

The monumental work of Joseph Needham (Needham, 1954-) demonstrated that China made great technical advances before the West in many important fields. For many years the question that scholars asked was: 'Why did China not experience an 'Industrial Revolution', despite having made much early technical progress?' The answer that most scholars have provided is that the 'totalitarian' traditional Chinese state crushed the development of the market economy (e.g. Balazs, 1964; Huang, 1990; Wittfogel, 1957). A widely-held corollary of this perspective is that China today should 'learn from the past' by substantially removing the state from an active role in the economy if it wishes the Chinese economy to grow rapidly and achieve prosperity for the Chinese people.

The recent research of numerous Chinese economic historians has shown that the traditional Chinese economy was far more dynamic over the long-term than had formerly been thought. [8] Increasingly, the key question has become: 'What factors permitted the Chinese economy to make sustained progress over more than 1000 years?' To answer this question, we need to probe more deeply into the structure of traditional Chinese political economy, especially the relationship of state and market. By analysing this rich tradition we can see key aspects of China's traditional system of political economy that can form the inspiration for understanding the possible solutions to the challenges that face the Chinese leadership today. They can provide a source of confidence to the leadership in resisting the strong pressures of free market economics that are proposed both within China and from the outside, especially from the United States, as the solution to these challenges.

The foundation of Chinese civilisation was, and still is, agriculture. Between the fourteenth and the mid-twentieth century Chinese rice-based agriculture responded to huge long-term population growth and absorbed productively the huge long-term increase in the farm labour force (Perkins, 1968). From the tenth to the thirteenth century, China set out along the path of the 'Second Industrial Revolution' well before Europe (Needham, 1954-). A steady stream of significant technical advances was made thereafter through until the nineteenth century (Xu Dixin and Wu Chengming, 2000), without China making the leap to a full-fledged modern 'Industrial Revolution'.

China's technological developments were stimulated by powerful long-term growth of both domestic and international trade. For long periods, the Chinese state united the vast territory of China into a single integrated market. For most of the last two thousand years, international trade operated free of government controls, other than the levying of import duties. The textile industry was much the most important in traditional China, as it was in early modern Europe. Towards the end of the Ming dynasty (1368-1644), cotton replaced hemp and silk as the principal fabric for daily wear. The spinning and weaving of cloth became the largest handicraft industry. By the early nineteenth century, there were around 60-70 million peasant households engaged in the occupation as a subsidiary activity to farming (Xu Dixin and Wu Chengming, 2000: 217). Around one-half of the cloth was for self-consumption and one-half for sale on the market. Of the marketed cloth, it is estimated that around 15 per cent entered long-distance trade. By the early Qing dynasty (1644-1911), in the late seventeenth and early eighteenth century, there were many examples of large-scale businesses (Xu Dixin and Wu Chengming, 2000: 250- 298). Many of these were in the metallurgical industries, in both iron manufacture and mining. However, there were numerous examples of large-scale businesses in industries such as salt-making and trading, in porcelain and in the manufacture of iron products.

Late Imperial China had a high level of urbanisation for a pre-industrial society. In the nineteenth century there were estimated to have been a total of 35 000 'standard' and 'intermediate' market towns. Above this dense local trading structure were a further 2300 'central market towns', 932 'cities' and 26 huge 'metropolitan trading systems', which in turn formed eight 'great economic systems'. Among these were cities of a size and level of sophistication that far exceeded those of contemporary Europe until late in the latter's development.

Paul Bairoch (1982) estimates that in 1750, China's share of global manufacturing output stood at 33 per cent, compared with 25 per cent in India/Pakistan and just 18 per cent in the 'West'. In 1800, China's per capita GNP was US$ 228 (at 1960 prices) compared with US$ 150- 200 for England and France (Bairoch, 1981). As late as 1798, Malthus declared China was the richest country in the world (Dawson, 1964: 7). In his description of McCartney's mission to China in 1793, Sir George Staunton says that 'in respect to its natural and artificial productions, the policy and uniformity of its government, the language, manners, and opinions of the people, the moral maxims, and civil institutions, and the general economy and tranquillity of the state, it is the grandest collective object that can be presented for human contemplation or research' (quoted in Dawson, 1964: 7).

State and Market in Chinese Development

The bureaucracy. The key feature of the traditional Chinese state was a combination of a hereditary emperor with a large professional civil service, selected mostly by competitive examination.[9] In addition, there was a much larger number of members of the local 'gentry' (*shenshi*), 'who dealt with many interests of their local communities for which the official government had no time' (Michael, 1964: 60). The dominant ideology of bureaucratic rule was conveyed continuously through the examination system. Confucian ideology, the foundation of the examination system, was the key to the system's long-term stability and cohesion. The over-riding values were those of 'the primacy of order and stability, of cooperative human harmony, of accepting one's place in the social hierarchy, of social integration (Feuerwerker, 1976: 15).China's long tradition of political philosophy emphasised that the sole test of a good ruler is 'whether he succeeds in promoting the welfare of the common people...This is the most basic principle in Confucianism and has remained unchanged throughout the ages' (Lau, 1979: 32 and 37). In order to serve the interests of the mass of the people, the bureaucracy must gain the trust of the masses: 'Only after he has gained the trust of the common people does the gentleman work them hard, for otherwise they would feel ill-used' (Confucius, 1979: 154). If the bureaucracy becomes corrupt, losing its moral foundation, the result is disaster for social order: 'Those in authority have lost the Way and the common people have for long been rootless' (Confucius, 1979: 155).

China's merchants occupied a subordinate ideological and political role. Merchants were placed at the bottom of the bureaucracy's official ranking of social strata, behind the scholars, farmers and artisans. There was no official representation of the merchants' interests in either the local or the central government. However, the fact that the merchant's political standing was degraded, did not mean that trade itself was regarded as undesirable. The successful merchant's wealth 'had always drawn covetous awe if not respect' (Faure, 2001). If merchants wished their families to enter the ruling bureaucratic class, their children needed to go through the laborious and highly competitive examination system. The consequence was thorough absorption of the ideology of the ruling scholar-bureaucrat elite. The merchants were allowed to perform their essential function of stimulating economic interaction through expanding the division of labour, facilitated by trade, but were firmly kept in their place in terms of the political power structure and the ideology that underpinned that structure.

The law. During the long periods in which it functioned relatively effectively, the Chinese state provided a framework of law and order and protection for property rights within which powerful long-term economic development took place and was matched by corresponding technical progress. Chinese merchants were never able to develop the independence from the state that began to develop in increasingly autonomous towns in late medieval Europe (Balazs, 1964). However, the control exercised by the state ensured that in periods when the central government functioned well, the cities provided a secure environment in which to conduct business, not only due to the peaceful environment, but also due to an environment in which their property rights were protected by the state. It is unimaginable that such huge quantities of merchandise could have been stored and traded without security that the corresponding contracts were legally enforceable, or that robbery of the merchants' property was illegal. Rowe's meticulous research on late Imperial Hankow (Rowe, 1984) has shown that before 1850 there were all manner of written commercial agreements, including shipping orders, bills of lading, promissory notes and contracts of sale, all of which were routinely circulated and enforceable in Hankow. Without them the bulk trade of the port would hardly have been conceivable. Local officials in late imperial Hankow played a key role in guaranteeing debt repayment.

The army. The most important function of the imperial state was to provide long periods of relative peace and stability over the vast territory under its rule. Although there were terrible periods of state disintegration, for long periods China was distinguished from the rest of the world by the fact that the central authorities were able to establish peaceful conditions over vast territories. Even in the midst of long dynasties, such as the Ming, China had the world's largest army (Huang, 1981: 160). Most importantly, the presence of so many troops also provided a source of security for economic activities during the long periods in which they were under effective control from the civilian authorities. They provided merchants with the confidence to undertake trade that far exceeded that in other parts of the world until modern times. The normally peaceful environment over wide areas provided a powerful incentive to those with capital to undertake long-term investments. It also enabled the entire territory of China to form a single unified free trade area. The degree of state interference in trade was small, in normal times confined mainly to taxation of a small number of key items. Estimates for the eighteenth century show that only around 7 per cent of national income went into the central government budget, of which the vast bulk, 74 per cent, came from the land tax and just 14 per cent came from the domestic and international customs revenue (Nolan, 1993: 17). Therefore, long before any other comparable region of the world, China was able to enjoy for long periods the powerful 'Smithian' stimulus of specialisation, the division of labour, the rapid spread of best practice techniques, and powerful incentives to accumulate capital.

Money. In the traditional Chinese economy exchange was almost always a monetary transaction (King, 1965: 42). Marco Polo was fascinated by the control exercised by the central authorities over the supply of money. During the Yuan dynasty, the Mongol rulers were the first economy in the world to have paper money. He was amazed that 'all the peoples and populations who are subject to [the Great Khan's] rule are perfectly willing to accept these papers in payment, since wherever they go they pay in the same currency, whether for goods or for pearls or precious stones or gold or silver. With these pieces of paper they can buy anything and pay for anything' (Marco Polo, 1974: 148). For over two thousand years, the Chinese government was aware of the importance of money to a sound economy. One of its ongoing struggles was to ensure that the money supply was not debased and that the quantity of money corresponded to the current economic needs. The central government tried persistently to maintain central control over the amount and nature of currency in circulation. Detailed accounts from the early Qing dynasty show the way in which the central government closely monitored the money supply, frequently changing the specified weight and composition of coins in response to changing economic conditions, and attempting to maintain a constant exchange rate between copper cash and silver coinage (King, 1965: 133-143).

Water control. The most important single function of the state in traditional China was water control, both for drainage and irrigation, as well as for transport. Large water control projects were almost exclusively public, organised either directly by the central government, or by lower levels of the bureaucracy. Water control activities carried a grave moral imperative for government officials, with a similar responsibility to that of national defence: '[B]uilding embankments on the Yellow River is like constructing defences on the frontier, and to keep watch on the dike is like maintaining vigilance on the frontier' (a high official of the Ming dynasty, quoted in Ch'ao-ting Chi, 1936: 73). The central administration had important functions in inter-district water projects or projects with large expenses. In the Ming and Qing dynasties, the construction of the embankment of the Yellow River was in the charge of a special official ranking high in the bureaucratic hierarchy. The Grand Canal was by far the greatest transport infrastructure achievement of the traditional Chinese state. It played a significant part in providing a transport system linking the productive south with the political north, engaging the attention of the best minds of China for more than ten centuries. It demanded countless millions of lives and a large portion of the wealth of the country for its improvement and maintenance.

Local government officials had an important role in water control. For almost any local water works beyond the capacity of the peasants of a single village, the magistrate intervened with the delegation of the duty of mobilising forced labour, supervising the construction of local works, and regulating the use of water by rival villages. There was a heavy moral burden upon local officials to ensure that the innumerable local water control activities were provided at an adequate level. The ideal magistrate 'is an official close to the people, and flood and drought should be of as much concern to him as pain or sickness of his person' (Ku Shih-lien, an early Qing dynasty scholar and official, quoted in

Ch'ao-ting Chi, 1936: 72). The ideal magistrate should make extensive visits to the countryside during the slack season: 'He should survey the topography of the region, ask about conditions of drainage, and investigate sluices and locks...All these affect the conditions of the public treasury and the welfare of the people and must be carefully considered by the magistrate' (Ku Shih-lien, quoted in Ch'ao-ting Chi, 1936: 72).

Famine relief. Famine relief in the Chinese empire included famine investigation, providing relief funds, supplying relief grain, controlling price, strengthening and rebuilding production (Will, 1990).[10] Many of the measures demonstrated subtle strategies by the State in providing relief to the poor and the capability of the State in using the market to combat famine problems. Many of the measures adopted anticipate the analysis of famine made by modern writers such as A. K. Sen. The 'detailed and formalised procedures for combating famine' were permitted by 'the sophistication, centralisation, and stability of the (Chinese) bureaucratic system' (Will, 1990: 4).

The local gentry had a prominent part in fighting famine and distributing relief. Collective action at the local level was 'to the advantage of both the bureaucrats and the holders of local power, headed by the great landowners and the gentry, that appropriate measures be taken to prevent the ruin of the economy and social disorder, and this was certainly a powerful factor for cohesion within the global power system' (Will, 1990: 5). Official famine prevention measures had been formulated as early as the Song period. Many of the recommended procedures - surveys of the disaster and its victims, the regular distribution of grain, public soup kitchens, and so forth - had been practised for centuries, albeit on a smaller scale, by the local notables and landlords in cooperation with the bureaucracy (Will, 1990: 74).

Commodity price stabilisation. From early in Chinese history, the Chinese state was deeply interested in ways to stabilise the prices of basic commodities. From very early on, China's bureaucrats were aware of the dangers of speculation for the ordinary people's livelihood. This anticipates the modern interest in 'commodity price stabilisation'. As early as in the Warring States Period, Fan Li's price policy held that fluctuations in the price of grain should be kept within a certain range so that it could benefit both production and distribution. (Hu Jichuang, 1984: 17). Marco Polo described the provision of grain in the Yuan Dynasty (1271-1368). When the harvests were plentiful and the price of crops was low, 'the Great Khan accumulates vast quantities of corn and every kind of grain and stores them in huge granaries'. When some crops failed and there was dearth of grain, he drew on these stocks: 'If the price is running at a *bezant* for a measure of wheat, ... he supplies four measures for the same sum. And he releases enough for all, … and this he does throughout all parts of his empire' (Marco Polo, 1974: 157).

Will (1990) provides a meticulous account of the way in which in the Qing Dynasty in the eighteenth century the bureaucracy intervened in the rice market to protect the livelihood of the masses from price fluctuations and speculation. The government established a vast network of 'evernormal granaries' (*changpingcang*) across the country in order to stabilise grain prices. In addition to maintaining emergency reserves, the purpose of the *changpingcang* was 'to cushion the impact of seasonal price fluctuations by buying up grain immediately after the harvest, when prices were low, and reselling it at a low price during the lean period before the new harvest came in'. The 'evernormal granaries' spring sales and autumn purchases were supposed to even out prices by compensating for the weakness of the private sector or by competing with it when it tended to take advantage of, and speculate on, seasonal and/or regional price differentials (Will, 1990: 182). The sale of public grain became 'one of several strategies available to the State to combat a subsistence crisis' (Will, 1990: 186).

Conclusion. Even economists who have been powerful advocates of the dynamic power of the market in promoting economic development, have sometimes acknowledged the frequency with which market failure necessitates state intervention. The more subtle have distinguished between the different ways and levels of market failure in different countries, at different stages of development, and confronting different challenges in the international economy. Criticism of market failure needs also to be tempered by sharp awareness of the potentialities for state failure. There is nothing intrinsically good or bad about either the state or the market.

The Chinese state strongly encouraged the development of the traditional market economy. The state stepped in where markets failed, not only in respect of immediate growth issues, but also in relation to the wider issues of social stability and cohesion. It nurtured and stimulated commerce, but refused to allow commerce, financial interests and speculation to dominate society. Behind the edifice of authoritarian Imperial rule was a pervasive morality based on the necessity all strata of society observing their duties in order to sustain social cohesion, to achieve social and political stability and to ensure social sustainability. When these functions were operating effectively, there was 'great harmony' (*da tong*), a prosperous economy and a stable society. When they were operating poorly, there was 'great turmoil' (*da luan*), economic retrogression and social disorder.

3. Conclusion

If by the 'Third Way', we mean a creative symbiotic inter-relationship between state and market, then we can say that China practised its own 'Third Way' for two thousand years. This was the foundation of its hugely impressive long-run economic and social development. The Chinese 'Third Way' was not simply an abstract set of rules about intervening with the market, but was a complete philosophy that combined comprehensive thought about concrete ways of both stimulating and controlling the market, with a deeply thought out system of morality for rulers, bureaucrats and ordinary people. When the system worked well, the philosophical foundation was supplemented by non-ideological state actions to try to solve practical problems that the market could not solve. It is a complete misunderstanding (not least, by Karl Marx) to view the traditional Chinese state as a stagnant 'Oriental Despotism'. Confucianism produced a highly developed concept of 'duty' which was the foundation of social prosperity and collective action. The fact that the system went through regular cycles when these principles were poorly observed, rulers and bureaucrats were corrupt and the economy and society foundered should not blind us to the underlying coherence and lasting benefit from this integrated system.

China today is groping for its own Third Way in totally different circumstances from those in Europe in recent decades. Europe was already industrialised, militarily strong, contained a mass of powerful, globally competitive firms and was able to assert strong controls over international capital movements until the 1970s without incurring international pressure to do otherwise. China today is painfully weak militarily compared with the United States. The vast mass of the population are still poor farmers and will remain so for a long period ahead. It is still firmly locked into the 'Lewis phase' of development. The 'global middle class' constitutes a tiny fraction of the population. The economy is increasingly 'dependent' in the classic sense used by Latin American economists in the past. The high value-added modern sector of the economy is increasingly dominated by international capital, with close to US$ 400 billion in accumulated investments, forming complete productions systems within China, and accounting for over one-half of the country's export earnings. China faces intense pressure comprehensively to liberalise its financial system as the price for participation in the international economy.

Europe tried to pursue a 'Third Way' in order to build a civilised society after it had already industrialised and developed. China is trying to construct a 'Third Way', while it is still in the midst of economic development and industrialisation, with a huge rural surplus labour force, amidst a turbulent international environment, and with a surging flow of foreign capital into the country. China's leaders are trying to construct a civilised society in this uniquely challenging setting.

In the early twenty-first century, China cannot step outside the mainstream of world history. It cannot close itself off from the main trend in international economics and politics. It cannot turn round and go back to the Maoist period. However, system survival necessitates that it use the market as the servant of the development process, not the master, as if the market possesses an intrinsic moral value, which the current US leadership and Western propagandists for the unfettered free market believe to be the case. In this effort China's leaders can make common cause with powerful streams in international thought that have gone against the current mainstream. They have at certain periods been highly influential both in the West, including even in the United States, and in the Far East outside the Chinese mainland.

Writers such as Fukuyama (1992) and Ohmae (1990) argue that the collapse of communism and the rise of the global corporation have produced an end of ideological conflict. Yergin and Stanislav (1998) have chronicled the 'withdrawal of the state from the commanding heights, leaving it more and more to the realm of the free market', across a wide swathe of countries. However, they conclude their book with a prescient warning about the market: '[I]f its benefits are regarded as exclusive rather than as inclusive, if it is seen to nurture the abuse of private power and the specter of raw greed, then surely there will be a backlash – a return to greater state intervention, management and control' (Yergin and Stanislav, 1998: 398).

Can free market fundamentalism prevent a 'China Financial Crisis'? Can it solve the problem of the rapid rise in social inequality within China? Can it solve the problems of the Chinese farm economy? Can it enable China's large firms to compete on the 'global level playing field'? Can it help China to deal with the massive international relations challenge? Can it solve the Chinese environmental crisis? Can it provide China with an ethical foundation for building a socially cohesive society? Anglo-Saxon free market fundamentalism, which reached its modern apogee in the 1990s, offers no hope for sustainable global development, at the level either of ecology, society, or international relations. China's numerous deep socio-economic challenges each requires creative, non-ideological state intervention with the market, to solve the innumerable practical problems that the market alone cannot solve. The biggest challenge of all is in the relationship between China's financial system and that of the global economy, since this has the greatest potential in the near future to trigger system disintegration.

In groping for its own system survival, China can make a powerful contribution to global system survival. In tackling these problems China can look to its own long history of nurturing market forces while simultaneously placing them under control, in the service of the whole society, in order to achieve a socially cohesive overall political economy. It must creatively adapt these traditions to the particular challenges facing the country today, namely dealing with the challenges of globalisation in the context of a huge and still poor developing country, firmly rooted in the 'Lewis phase' of 'economic development with unlimited supplies of labour'.

If China is able to marry the 'snake' of the global market economy with the 'hedgehog' of China's ancient history, as well as its recent history, especially that of the Chinese Communist Party, it will be able to offer a way forward for a stable, socially cohesive society within the country. If it fails to do so, the entire Chinese system of political economy may collapse. This would be devastating, not only for China, but for the whole global political economy. At the very least, China may be condemned to a long period of harsh social control to contain the surging tensions of the country's high-speed growth. During the Asian Financial Crisis, China had to take a 'choice of no choice' (*mei you xuanze de xuanze*) to survive by 'cutting the trees to save the forest' (i.e. making GITIC bankrupt). If it wishes the system to survive today it must also take the 'choice of no choice' to re-establish social cohesiveness, confidently using its own past traditions and the best traditions from outside the country.

If China were to 'choose' the path of 'state desertion' and free market fundamentalism, it would lead to uncontrollable tensions and social disintegration. Full liberalisation of international financial firm competition inside China and full liberalisation of international financial flows is the most dangerous area through which this disintegration might occur. A crisis in the financial system would fan the flames amidst the 'combustible material' in all other sectors of society, into which the long tentacles of the financial system extend. The 'choice' to increase and make more effective the role of the state to solve the intensifying socio-economic challenges facing the country can only succeed if the Chinese state today, with the Communist Party at its core, as in periods of greatest prosperity in the past, can radically improve its level of effectiveness, and eliminate rampant corruption. State improvement, not state desertion, is the only rational goal for Chinese system reform. This is the 'choice of no choice' for China's system survival.

By taking the 'choice of no choice', China's own survival can contribute to global survival and sustainable development, by offering a beacon as an alternative to the US-dominated drive towards global free market fundamentalism. This is a crossroads not only for China, but for the whole world.

Notes

1.   e.g. Chen Xiwen, deputy director of the State Development Research Centre, (quoted in *Financial Times*, 31 October 2002).

2. The World Bank estimates that in 1995 there were 716 million people (58 per cent of the population) who had less than US$ 2 per day, and around 280 million who lived on less than US$ 1 per day (World Bank, 2001: 236).

3. Baosteel is a possible exception.

4. See Nolan (1995) and Chang (2002) for summaries of the evidence on this point.

5. It is an extreme irony that one hundred years later, the AEA should have become the vehicle for conveying the most stultifying form of orthodoxy, which eliminated from the subject of 'economics' anything other than formal mathematical modelling, largely based on free market models, leaving the subject far removed from the open-minded analysis of the real world from which the AEA originally derived its inspiration.

6. Green's ideas on 'positive freedom' far precede similar notions propounded by such late twentieth century philosophers as Isiah Berlin (Berlin, 1969) or A. K. Sen (e.g. Dreze and Sen, 1989).

7. See, especially, the numerous writings of A. K. Sen on this topic.

8. See especially Li Bozhong, 1986, 1998 and 2000; and Xu Dixin and Wu Chengming eds, 2000.

9. At the end of the Qing Dynasty, there was a substantial increase in the number of lower level positions in the Civil Service that were sold in order to meet the state's pressing budgetary needs.

10. Will (1990) provides a meticulous account of famine relief in late Imperial China.

References

Aveneri, S. (ed.), *Karl Marx on Colonialism and Modernisation* (New York: Anchor Books, 1969)

Bairoch, P., 'International industrialisation levels from 1750 to 1980', *Journal of European Economic History* (Fall, 1982) 269-334

Bairoch, P. and M.Levy-Leboyer (eds), *Disparities in economic development since the Industrial Revolution* (London: Macmillan, 1981)

Balazs, E., *Chinese civilisation and bureaucracy* (London: Yale University, 1964)

Berlin, I., *Four essays in liberty* (Oxford: Oxford University Press, 1969)

Bush, G.W., 'America's Security Strategy' (Washington DC: The White House, 2002)

Chang, H-J., *Kicking away the ladder* (London: Anthem Press, 2002)

Chi, Ch'ao-ting, *Key economic areas in Chinese history* (New York: Paragon Reprint, 1936)

Comrades from the Shanghai Hutong Shipyards, and the Sixth Economic Group of the Shanghai Municipal May Seventh Cadre School (1974), 'Two kinds of society, two kinds of wages', in Selden, (1979)

Confucius, *The Analects (Lun Yu)*, translated, with an Introduction by D.C.Lau (Harmondsworth: Penguin Books, 1979)

Dawson, R., 'Western conceptions of Chinese civilisation', in Dawson (ed.), *The Legacy of China* (Oxford: Oxford University Press, 1964)

Deng, Xiaoping, 'The necessity of upholding the four cardinal principles in the drive for the four modernisations'(1979), in Major Documents (1991)

Deng Xiaoping, 'The present situation and the tasks before us', (1980), in Deng Xiaoping, *Selected Works of Deng Xiaoping* (Beijing: Foreign Languages Press, 1984)

Department of Trade and Industry (DTI), *The UK R&D Scoreboard 2003* (Edinburgh: DTI, 2003)

Dreze, J. and A. K. Sen, *Hunger and public action* (Oxford: Clarendon Press, 1989)

Far Eastern Economic Review (FEER), (20 May 2002)

Faure, D., 'Beyond networking: an institutional view of Chinese business', mimeo (2001)

Feuerwerker, A., *State and society in eighteenth century China: the Ch'ing Empire in all its glory* (Ann Arbor, Michigan: Center for Chinese Studies, 1976)

Feuerwerker, A. (ed.), *Modern China* (Englewood Cliffs, NJ: Prentice-Hall, 1964)

Financial Times (FT), various issues

Foner, E., *The Story of American Freedom* (New York: W.W.Norton, 1998)

Fukuyama, F., *The end of history and the last man* (Harmondsworth: Penguin Books, 1992)

Hayek, F. A., *The Road to Serfdom* (London: Routledge, 2004) (originally published 1944)

Hirschman, A.O., *The Passions and the Interests* (Princeton: Princeton University Press, 1977)

Hu, Jichuang, *Chinese Economic Thought before the Seventeenth Century* (Beijing: Foreign Language Press, 1984)

Huang, R., *1587, A Year of No Significance (Wanli shiwu nian)* (New Haven and London: Yale University Press, 1981)

Huang. R., *China: A Macro-History* (New York: M.E.Sharpe, 1990)

International Institute for Strategic Studies, *The Military Balance, 1998-99* (London: IISS, 1999)

Jiang, Zemin, 'Speech to celebrate the eightieth anniversary of the founding of the Chinese Communist Party' (Beijing, 1 July 2001)

King, F.H., *Money and Monetary Policy in China* (Cambridge, Mass.: Harvard University Press, 1965)

Lau, D.C., 'Introduction', to Confucius, 1979

Lewis, A., 'Economic development with unlimited supplies of labour' *The Manchester School* (May, 1954)

Li, Bozhong, *The development of agriculture and industry in Jiangnan, 1644-1850: trends and prospects* (Hangzhou: Zhenjiang Academy of Social Sciences, 1986)

Li, Bozhong, *Agricultural Development in Jiangnan, 1620-1850* (Basingstoke: Macmillan, 1998)

Li, Bozhong, *The early industrialisation of Jiangnan, 1550-1850* (in Chinese) (Beijing: Shehui kexue wenjian Publishing House, 2000)

Mao Zedong (Mao Tsetung), (1944), 'Serve the people', in Mao Zedong, *Selected Works of Mao Tsetung, Vol. 3* (Peking: Foreign Languages Press, 1965)

Mao Zedong (Mao Tsetung), (1949), 'Report to the Second Plenary Session of the Seventh Central Committee of the Communist Party of China', 5 March, in Mao Zedong, *Selected Works of Mao Tsetung, Vol. 4* (Peking: Foreign Languages Press, 1969)

Marx, K., *Capital, Vol. 1* (New York: International Publishers Edition, 1967) (originally published 1867)

Marx, K., 'The British Rule in India' in Aveneri (ed.) (1969) (originally published 1853)

Needham, J., *Science and Civilisation in China* (Cambridge: Cambridge University Press, 1954 -)

Nolan, P., *The Political Economy of Collective Farms* (Cambridge: Polity Press, 1988)

Nolan, P., *State and Market in the Chinese Economy* (Basingstoke: Macmillan, 1993)

Nolan, P., *China's Rise, Russia's Fall* (Basingstoke: Macmillan, 1995)

Nolan, P., *China and the Global Business Revolution* (Basingstoke: Palgrave Macmillan, 2001a)

Nolan, P., *China and the Global Economy* (Basingstoke: Palgrave Macmillan, 2001b)

Ohmae, K., The *Borderless World* (London: Collins, 1990)

Perkins, D.H., *Agricultural Development in China, 1368-1968* (Edinburgh: Edinburgh University Press, 1968)

Polo, Marco, *The Travels* (Harmondsworth: Penguin Books, 1974)

Rowe, W.T., *Hankow: Commerce and Society in a Chinese City, 1796-1889* (Stanford: Stanford University Press, 1984)

Selden, M., *The People's Republic of China* (New York: Monthly Review Press, 1979)

State Statistical Bureau (SSB), *Chinese Statistical Yearbook (Zhongguo tongji nianjian)*, (ZTN) (Beijing: Zhongguo tongji chubanshe, various years)

Therborn, G., 'The rule of capital and the rise of democracy', *New Left Review*, No. 104 (May-June 1977)

Toynbee, A., *Man himself must choose - conversations with Daisaku Ikeda* (London: Oxford University Press, 1976)

UNDP, *China: Human Development Report 1999* (New York: Oxford University Press, 2000)

Will, Pierre-Etienne, *Bureaucracy and Famine in Eighteenth-Century China* (Stanford: Stanford University Press, 1990)

Wittfogel, K.A., *Oriental Despotism* (London: Yale University Press, 1957)

World Bank, *World Development Report* (WDR) (Washington, DC: Oxford University Press, various years)

World Bank, *China: National development and sub-national finances* (Washington DC: World Bank, 2002)

Xu Dixin, and Wu Chengming, *Chinese Capitalism, 1522-1840*, (edited and annotated by Charles Curwen) (Basingstoke: Macmillan, 2000)

Yao, Shujie, 'Prospects for Chinese agriculture' mimeo (2002)

Yergin, D. and J. Stanislav, *The Commanding Heights* (New York: Touchstone Books, 1998)

Chapter 7

CAPITALISM AND FREEDOM: THE CONTRADICTORY CHARACTER OF GLOBALISATION

Peter Nolan

It was the best of times, it was the worst of times, it was the age of wisdom, it was the age of foolishness, it was the epoch of belief, it was the epoch of incredulity, it was the season of Light, it was the season of Darkness, it was the spring of hope, it was the winter of despair, we had everything before us, we had nothing before us...

(Charles Dickens, *A Tale of Two Cities*)

Introduction: Humanity at the Crossroads

Since ancient times the exercise of individual freedoms has been inseparable from the expansion of the market, driven by the search for profit. This force, namely capitalism, has stimulated human creativity and aggression in ways that have produced immense benefits. As capitalism has broadened its scope in the epoch of globalisation, so these benefits have become even greater. Human beings have been liberated to an even greater degree than hitherto from the tyranny of nature, from control by others over their lives, from poverty, and from war. The advances achieved by the globalisation of capitalism have appeared all the more striking, when set against the failure of non-capitalist systems of economic organisation.

However, capitalist freedom is a two-edged sword. In an epoch of capitalist globalisation, its contradictions have intensified. They comprehensively threaten the natural environment. They have intensified global inequality within both rich and poor countries, and between the internationalised global power elite and the mass of citizens rooted within their respective nations. They have produced a world of extreme potential financial instability. The world's dominant economic, political and cultural power refuses to dismantle its vast stock of nuclear arms, sufficient to obliterate the entire global civilisation. It benefits in numerous ways from global capitalism. It also feels under intense threat, both internally and externally from those same forces.

Since ancient times, philosophers have debated about the essential features of human nature, and the relationship of these features to the market economy. It has long been recognised that human beings are inherently contradictory. Within themselves they have the capacity for selfish, aggressive and warlike behaviour (the 'death instinct'), alongside a capacity for cooperative, loving and benevolent behaviour (the 'love instinct').

The challenges that are faced by human beings are the product of people's own purposive activities, expressed mainly through the economic system. It is within their collective power to resolve these contradictions. The very depth of the challenges they now face may shock them into the action necessary to ensure the survival of the species. Alongside human beings' competitive and destructive instincts are their instincts for species survival through cooperation. However great the challenge may be, human beings are capable of solving the contradictions that are of their own making. It may only be the approaching 'final hour' which finally forces human beings to grope their way towards globally cooperative solutions.

1. Capitalist Globalisation in Historical Perspective

1.1 Pre-modern Capitalism

Capitalism, in the sense of production for market-place profits by private entrepreneurs, is an ancient phenomenon. Large parts of the world outside Europe contained significant pockets of capitalism within overall non-capitalist socio-economic structures. It is estimated that in 1750, China accounted for around one-third of total world manufacturing output, and South Asia for around one-quarter, while 'the West' still accounted for only around 18 per cent (Bairoch, 1982). Most of this output was manufactured in profit-seeking privately-owned firms producing for the market. Many of the key technical innovations of the late Middle Ages in Europe either originated in Asia, or were independently invented there.[1] Typically, technical progress occurred through innovations sought by profit-seeking entrepreneurs who responded to commercial opportunities. Commercial growth interacted with institutional change, stimulating the evolution of urban-based legal and financial mechanisms to facilitate commerce.

1.2 Capitalism, 1750-1914

The technical advances that had slowly evolved within the capitalist segments of the non-European world made their way to Europe in the Middle Ages. These interacted with indigenously evolving technical progress and with the fast-evolving capitalist institutions to produce the European Industrial Revolution. By 1900, the share of 'The West' in global manufacturing output had risen to over three-quarters, from less than one-fifth a mere 150 years previously. Large parts of the 'non-Western' world were integrated through military conquest into global industrial capitalism. By the end of the nineteenth century, industrial capitalism had enjoyed over a century of high-speed growth, with large parts of the world integrated by relatively open trade systems and free movement of capital. The world appeared to be on the threshold of limitless expansion of global capitalism.

1.3 Capitalism, 1914-1970s

The advance of global capitalism was interrupted violently in 1914. A succession of phenomena stifled its growth for much of the twentieth century. These included the impact of violent international conflicts; [2] protectionism in high-income countries following the Great Depression; inward-looking policies in communist planned economies as well as in most developing countries; and widespread nationalisation.

1.4 Capitalism Since the Mid-1970s

From the mid-1970s onwards far-reaching changes set the scene for the renewed spread of global capitalism. The high-income countries moved decisively towards floating exchange rates and freedom of international capital movements. Europe's vast structure of state-owned enterprises was privatised. In the communist world, there began a period of comprehensive system reform. Non-communist developing countries implemented sweeping privatisation of state assets, dismantled protectionist barriers and opened their economies to international investment.

From the 1970s onwards, the global economy took up where it had left off before the First World War. Once again, private enterprise dominated, international trade was relatively unregulated and capital could flow freely across national borders. Leading global firms increasingly were international in terms of their markets, employees and the composition of ownership. In most respects the world economy had once again entered a period of free markets and a 'global level playing field' comparable to the late nineteenth century, the previous highpoint of the liberal economy.

1.5 Capitalism's Two-edged Sword

The drive to make profits has stimulated human ingenuity over millennia. This intense force operates even more powerfully in the epoch of the 'Global Business Revolution' than in previous epochs. It is a force that human beings themselves have created. However, this force is double-edged. As well as liberating them, it also enslaves them. Through the force of the pursuit of profit, mankind is allowed to win ever-greater mastery over nature, and achieve ever-greater levels of consumption, but at a high price. Mankind may even stand at a crossroads in which the very existence of the human species is threatened through the 'magical' forces that it has itself conjured up.

Capitalist Rationality in the Epoch of the Global Business Revolution

2.1 Capitalism and Cooperation

The Invisible Hand

Economists have long marvelled at the independently functioning market, which allows the actions of market participants to be 'magically' coordinated without any apparent guiding hand. Writing on the eve of the Industrial Revolution, Adam Smith produced the most famous of all analyses of the division of labour and the impact upon cooperation among people. For Smith the peculiar wonder of the autonomous-functioning market mechanism was that it produced deep cooperation without any sense of benevolence for one's fellow human beings, but achieved this instead through the pursuit of self-interest: 'It is not from the benevolence of the butcher, the brewer, or the baker, that we expect our dinner, but from their regard for their own interest. We address ourselves not to their humanity but to their self-love, and never talk to them of our own necessities but of their advantages' (Smith, 1976b: 18).

The Visible Hand

In the late nineteenth century in the United States and Europe, the 'modern firm' emerged. These complex internal business relationships became monitored and coordinated by salaried employees rather than by the market mechanism. The boundaries of the firm had shifted (Coase, 1988). Goods and services that had formerly been purchased through the 'anonymous' market were instead produced within the firm. Instead of an arms-length inter-firm relationship mediated through price, large areas of business transaction were internalised within the firm, and became subject to the 'visible hand' of planned resource allocation within the vertically and horizontally integrated firm (Chandler, 1977).

The External Firm

In the current capitalist epoch, the functions of control and coordination exercised by systems integrator firms have extended across the boundaries of the legally defined firm, facilitated by recent developments in information technology. The boundaries of the large corporation have not only 'shifted', so that a wide range of goods and services is procured from outside the firm, but the very boundaries of the firm have become blurred. If we define the firm not by the entity which is the legal owner, but, rather, by the sphere over which conscious coordination of resource allocation takes place, then, far from becoming 'hollowed out' and much smaller in scope, the large firm can be seen to have enormously increased in size during the global business revolution.

2.2 Competition, Industrial Concentration and Technical Progress

The epoch of the global business revolution has seen a dramatic rise in levels of industrial concentration. Through the impact of the 'cascade effect', oligopoly has penetrated ever-further down into the supply chain. Most economists, including both mainstream and non-mainstream, predicted that oligopoly would stifle competition and technical progress, and lead to price increases based on the exercise of market power. Instead, the epoch has witnessed intense oligopolistic competition, which has been responsible for this epoch's extraordinary technological dynamism. This reality has hardly begun to be absorbed and analysed by economists.[3] For Marx or Schumpeter, the nature and consequences of the global business revolution would be unsurprising.

The impact of this process upon technical progress has been striking. The world's research and development expenditure is highly concentrated. In 2003, the top 700 firms between them spent US$ 366 billion on research and development, an average of US$ 522 million per firm (DTI, 2004). These firms constitute the core of global technical progress. Between them they had revenue of US$ 8806 billion, constituting the core of the entire global economy. Even within the top 700 firms, there is a high degree of concentration in R&D expenditure. In 2003, the top 300 firms together spent US$ 291 billion on R&D, accounting for 80 per cent of the world total for the top 700 firms. The top 33 firms, with an R&D expenditure of over US$ 3 billion each, spent a total of US$ 147 billion on R&D, accounting for 40 per cent of the total for the top 700 firms. The top 17 firms spent an average of US$ 6 billion each on R&D, accounting for 25 per cent of the total for the top 700 firms. Between 1995 and 2002, the R&D expenditure of the top 300 firms rose by almost two-thirds, from US$ 177 billion to US$ 291 billion, a growth rate of more than 7 per cent per annum (*FT*, 25 June 1999 and 15 September 2003).

The increased focus on core business among the world's leading systems integrators and sub-systems integrators has enhanced the effectiveness of R&D expenditure, allowing benefits from economies of scale and scope. Technical progress in the instruments of R&D, especially IT hardware and software, has further enhanced the effectiveness of R&D spending. In addition, the world's leading firms are rapidly increasing their R&D bases in low and middle-income countries, which enables them to obtain greater amounts of knowledge per dollar spent on R&D.

Meaningful measurement of technical progress has eluded economists.[4] The pace of technical progress during the epoch of the global business revolution cannot be unambiguously compared with previous periods of rapid technical progress. However, it is self-evident that the epoch has seen one of the fastest periods of technical progress in human history, led by the oligopolistic firms that dominate the apex of global supply chains, which have in turn powerfully stimulated technical progress at lower levels in the supply chain. I shall examine briefly technical progress in four sectors in the past two decades:

Information Technology

The IT revolution has been at the heart of technical progress in all sectors. The IT hardware and software sector is by far the most important in terms of global technical progress. In 2003, 180 of the world's top 700 firms by R&D spending were from this sector, accounting for 26 per cent of the total spending on R&D by the world's top 700 companies (DTI, 2004). In 2003, IT hardware and software firms within the top 700 companies together spent US$ 94 billion on R&D, and had combined revenues of US$ 966 billion (*FT*, 25 October 2004). A group of 22 information technology companies in the top 700 (each with spending of more than US$ 1 billion) spent a total of US$ 62 billion on R&D, which amounted to 66 per cent of the total spending on R&D by the 180 IT firms among the world's top 700 companies (*FT*, 25 October 2004, and DTI, 2004).

The massive spending of the world's leading IT companies over the past two decades has stimulated a revolution in information generation and transmission. The revolution in IT has transformed both the nature of capital goods and the nature of a large fraction of final consumption. Goods and services in almost every sector have been comprehensively changed by this technical revolution, from complex engineering products, including aeroplanes, automobiles, farm equipment, and all types of manufacturing machinery, to almost every imaginable service, including mass media, retail, banking, insurance, tourism, transport, and marketing. The IT revolution has universally lowered costs and prices of IT goods and services. It has allowed a dramatic fall in the cost of global communications, transformed the cost and nature of R&D, and facilitated the profound change in the nature of the global firm and its relationship to the surrounding value chain.

Automobiles

The epoch of the global business revolution has witnessed dramatic changes in technology in almost every sector. For example, in the automobile industry, both passenger and commercial vehicles have altered radically, with huge reductions in weight, due mainly to advances in technologies embodied in steel, aluminium and plastics; large increases in fuel economy, due both to weight reduction and advances in engine technologies; large increases in vehicle safety, comfort, ease of use, reliability and longevity; and large reductions in polluting emissions.

Aerospace

In the aerospace industry, enormous changes have taken place in the nature of passenger aircraft. Large weight reductions per passenger carried have taken place due to advances in aircraft design, through improvements in each type of construction material, and through increased use of composite materials; large advances have taken place due to continuous progress in engine technologies, including weight reduction, increased fuel efficiency, reduced engine noise, increased engine reliability, and advances in ease of engine maintenance; and large advances have taken place in aircraft safety, due to advances in avionics and flight control systems, and advances in the design and reliability of aircraft components, including seats, engines, landing gear, avionics, and tyres.

Beverages

In the beverage industry, including both soft drinks and beer, quite limited changes have taken place in the nature of the product, but enormous technical progress has taken place in the nature of the processes involved in producing and distributing beverages. Filling machinery has greatly increased in speed, reliability, and fuel efficiency, alongside reductions in variability of filling height and bottle damage. Packaging technologies have altered radically. Metal cans and PET bottles have joined glass bottles to constitute the three main forms of primary packaging. Introduction of metal cans and PET allowed enormous changes in the appearance of primary packaging, increasing customer satisfaction through increased ease of use and attractiveness of designs. Improved packaging technologies have increased longevity of beverages at peak condition. All three types of primary packaging have achieved large reductions in package weight, which economises on use of raw materials, reduces weight in transport and improves ease of use by the final customer. These advances have occurred through intense interaction between leading beverage companies and the suppliers of packaging materials (including steel, aluminium, PET and glass), as well as with the firms that make machinery to produce primary packaging. Large advances have taken place in the machine building industry to produce 'PET pre-forms', PET blowing equipment, can-making machinery and glass bottle machinery. They have increased speed and reliability, reduced raw material and fuel consumption per unit, and improved packaging design capabilities. Distribution of beverages is enormously intensive in the use of road transport. Improvements in commercial vehicle technologies have greatly increased fuel efficiency in the distribution of beverages.

As these four examples indicate, increased focus on core business and increased firm size among both systems integrators and suppliers has increased economies of scale and scope at every level in the value chain. This applies to almost every sector. Alongside dramatic advances in product and process technologies, there has taken place a near universal decline in unit costs and an advance in product quality.

Consumers in high-income countries dominate final demand globally. They have benefited massively from the decline in prices since the 1970s. This has occurred in part due to the huge increase in production of goods (and, increasingly, services) in low and middle-income countries, but it has occurred also due to the remarkable technical progress that has resulted from oligopolistic competition among the global giant firms that dominate the global business revolution.

2.3 Finance and Development

Policy Shift

In the epoch of the global business revolution a consensus grew up among the 'Bretton Woods' institutions (the World Bank and the IMF), which argued that there are large benefits for both rich and poor countries alike to be gained by liberalisation of international capital flows, including freedom of movement on the capital account. The so-called 'Washington Consensus' argued that 'the size of the financial sector alone, regardless of its sophistication, has a strong causal effect on economic performance' (Wolf, 2004: 285). Underlying the Washington Consensus' approach is a simple proposition: 'Free markets are more efficient, [and] greater efficiency allow[s] for faster growth' (Stiglitz, 2002: 66). A variety of arguments supported this proposition.

Allowing free access to international finance and international financial institutions is the most immediate and powerful way to stimulate 'financial deepening' in developing countries, whose financial systems not only were 'repressed' by government intervention, but also very small compared to those of the high-income countries. Measures which stimulate the development of national financial systems will enhance productivity by facilitating transactions and leading to improved resource allocation (Singh, 2002). Capital account liberalisation leads to global economic efficiency, by allocating savings to those who can use them most productively. Citizens of countries with free capital movements can benefit from diversifying their portfolios, and thereby increase their risk-adjusted rate of return. It enables firms to raise capital at lower cost in international markets (Singh, 2002).

Pressure from global capital markets serves as an important discipline on government macro-economic and other policies 'which improves overall economic performance by rewarding good policies and penalising bad' (quoted in Singh, 2002). Removal of restrictions on the international movement of capital acts as a pressure on the state in developing countries to 'force review and reform of the financial sector', including breaking 'the connections between financial institutions and borrowers', and 'establishing an effective bankruptcy regime', which might thereby help to provide foreign capital with 'protection of its property rights' (Wolf, 2004: 287-8). In addition, capital controls are costly to enforce and are a source of corruption (Wolf, 2004: 287).

The Washington Consensus argued that it is beneficial for developing countries to allow free access to international financial firms, in order to benefit from their size and associated economies of scale and skill. However, it is agued that the only way to attract them and to benefit from their size and skills was to allow them 'to repatriate their capital and remit earnings…[and have] access to global financial markets' (Wolf, 2004: 284-6).

The Outcome

Foreign direct investment. Liberalisation of international capital flows since the 1970s has facilitated a large rise in foreign direct investment in developing countries. The stock of FDI in developing countries rose from US$ 307 billion in 1980 to US$ 2340 billion in 2002, an average annual growth rate of almost 10 per cent (UNCTAD, 2003: 257). The subsidiaries established by multinational firms in developing countries have a powerful influence on the modern sector of the local economy. Large manufacturing assembly facilities owned by multinational firms tend to stimulate the development of clusters of supplier companies, often encouraging other multinationals to invest to meet the needs of their global customers, contributing to the technical upgrading of the whole supply chain. Multinational firms tend to produce globally standardised products, whether they are final consumer goods for the global middle class or capital goods for other companies, making use of standard global machine tools, components and capital-labour ratios. Consequently, FDI in developing countries contributes to the spread of global production technologies, management systems and employee skills. Multinationals in developing countries also can take advantage of global procurement to lower unit costs of inputs of goods and services. Global oligopolistic firms also tend to carry their intense competition into developing countries, whether in the production of final consumer goods or capital goods for intermediate customers.

Stock markets. The epoch of the global business revolution has seen a significant expansion of the role of stock markets in developing countries' economies. The number of firms floated on stock markets in low and middle-income countries rose from fewer than 8000 in 1990 to 21 000 in 2003 (WB, WDI, 2004: 268). Total stock market capitalisation in low and middle-income countries increased from US$ 375 billion in 1990 to US$ 1837 billion in 2003, and stock market capitalisation as a share of GDP rose from 18.8 per cent to 33.3 per cent (WB, WDI, 2004: 268).

Although the total stock market capitalisation of low and middle-income countries is still only a small fraction of that of the high-income countries (less than 9 per cent in 2003), the expansion of stock markets has played an important role in stimulating economic development in low and middle-income countries. In order to attract both domestic and international capital, standards of corporate governance of firms in developing countries have needed to rise. International equity holders now constitute an important fraction of share ownership in many developing countries that were formerly substantially closed to multinational equity investors, and these have had a substantial influence on the nature of corporate governance. The expansion of stock markets has stimulated savings and channelled them into investment. They have provided a mechanism for facilitating mergers and acquisitions, and thereby allowing benefits from economies of scale. They have contributed to social stability by providing pension funds with a channel through which to diversify their investments.

Financial firms. The period of the global business revolution has seen a powerful process of merger and acquisition in this sector, driven by a number of factors. The obstacles to mergers and acquisitions have greatly reduced across the boundaries of different segments of the industry, across regions within large countries (especially in the United States), and across national boundaries.[5] Customers, both business and private, increasingly seek global financial services. There are large economies of scale and scope derived from procurement of IT hardware and software, in branding and marketing, and in human resource acquisition. Through a revolutionary period of mergers and acquisitions, a group of super-large financial firms has emerged. In the banking sector these include Citigroup,[6] Deutsche Bank,[7] HSBC,[8] J. P. Morgan Chase,[9] and Bank of America.[10] The industry has become increasingly bifurcated into a small group of immensely powerful large firms and a large number of small firms serving local markets and global niche markets.

Following financial liberalisation in most developing countries, global giant financial firms rapidly increased their acquisition activity. By 2001, within Latin America, the share of foreign banks in total bank assets had risen to 90 per cent in Mexico, 62 per cent in Peru, 61 per cent in Argentina and Chile, 59 per cent in Venezuela, and 49 percent in Brazil (Chang Song, 2005). In Mexico, the four leading banks that had been acquired by international banks alone accounted for around nine-tenths of the entire country's banking assets (*FT*, 18 September 2002).[11] By 2001, in Eastern Europe the share of foreign banks in total bank assets stood at 99 per cent in Estonia, 90 per cent in the Czech Republic and Poland, 89 per cent in Hungary, 86 per cent in Slovakia, 78 per cent in Lithuania, and 75 per cent in Bulgaria (Chang Song, 2005).

The penetration of developing countries' financial markets by global financial firms has brought powerful benefits for both individuals and businesses. The threat of competition from global banks can force local banks to improve their operating mechanisms. Global giant banks can spread risk across numerous markets. They have access to vast global assets and possess sophisticated IT systems with which to evaluate risk. They have also established a culture built around strict internal control systems, and have long experience of operating under the sophisticated financial regulation within the high-income countries. Global giant banks operate according to rigorous and systematic procedures, so that lending tends to be based on strict commercial criteria to a much greater extent than in many developing countries' banking systems. This increases the possibility that loans will be made to firms that are able to employ them effectively. This may tend to help more effective use of savings and thereby stimulate growth, as well as tending to reduce the risk of bad loans and of a financial crisis. Financial reforms in developing countries have often found it difficult to break the link between bankers and local political power holders. The entry of global banks can tend to break the link more effectively. Multinational firms tend to find that working with global banks can stimulate their growth in developing countries, by enabling them to benefit from lower-priced and higher quality services supplied to them on a global basis. Local depositors may also benefit from the presence of global banks, by having greater security for their deposits and more opportunity to benefit from global wealth management. Local pension funds may benefit by having access to the global asset management services of global banks.

The World Bank believes that those 'transition economies' that have been more willing to 'cede majority control of their banks to foreign interests' have enjoyed higher growth rates than their neighbours (WB, WDR, 2002). It is widely argued that 'countries with a higher proportion of foreign-owned banks are...less prone to financial crises, perhaps because foreign banks are better regulated, better managed or merely more immune to pressure for imprudent lending' (Wolf, 2004: 285).

Global Financial Risk

The global financial system has undergone tremendous change in the past two decades. The financial system has 'deepened' across much of the developing world, gradually supplanting the former 'repressed' financial structures. Advances in information technology and in financial instruments have greatly improved risk control in commercial banks. New financial instruments have distributed risk widely throughout the economic system. Banks have diversified risk as never before, via derivatives such as structured credit which can be used to transfer risk to insurance companies, pension funds, hedge funds and others outside the banking system. Alan Greenspan believes that there is a 'new paradigm' of 'active credit management' which makes the global financial system far more robust. Credit derivatives permit risks to be unbundled and transferred to those players who are best able to absorb them. Hedge funds' arbitrage activity makes markets more efficient and 'keeps the financial system fluid and flexible' (*FT*, 16 February 2005). The global financial system demonstrated its newly-found robustness by surviving intact a series of severe bouts of turbulence since the 1980s, including the Mexican Tequila crisis, the Asian Financial Crisis, the Russian and Argentinian financial crises, and 9/11. In the view of many financial experts, the global financial system is now so 'thick' as to be nearly indestructible. The IMF believes: 'Short of a major and devastating geopolitical incident undermining in a significant way, consumer confidence, and hence financial asset valuation, it is hard to see where systemic threats could come from in the short-term' (quoted in *Financial Times*, 16 February 2005).

2.4 Capitalist Globalisation and Freedom

The spread of global capitalism since the 1970s has stimulated accelerated growth among low and middle-income countries. Population growth rates in low and middle-income countries also fell sharply in this period. The average annual growth of GDP per capita increased from 1.5 per cent in 1980-90, to 2.4 per cent in 1990-2000, and reached 3.6 per cent from 2000-2004.[12] Not only have growth rates accelerated, but the explosive technical progress in this period has also helped to stimulate widespread progress in terms of fundamental freedoms for the mass of the world's population, especially for those living in developing countries.

Freedom from the Tyranny of Nature

a. Energy availability

Fossil fuels. It is widely thought that the prospects for fossil fuel supply are strictly limited. At today's level of consumption, it is predicted that there are only forty more years of oil reserves, and seventy years of gas reserves, while coal reserves may last for 200 years. In addition, the rate of increase of demand for primary energy in the low and middle-income countries is accelerating, so that the prospects for global energy supply and demand look even bleaker. However, the reserves of fossil fuel are not absolutely fixed. At higher prices, it becomes worthwhile using technologies that enable the extraction of a higher proportion of oil, gas and coal from existing fields. Higher prices also mean that sources of fossil fuel that used to be uneconomic become economically viable, such as tar sands, shale oil and 'gas in crystals'.[13]

Nuclear power. After years of stagnation, the increased price of oil, fears of national energy security and concerns over global warming, have led to a widespread reconsideration of the place of nuclear energy within the energy portfolio in all countries. Technical progress has greatly reduced the construction and operational costs of nuclear power stations, and increased their safety. Fast breeder reactors will greatly reduce the demand for uranium, so that there will be almost unlimited availability of the basic raw material for energy generation. In addition, nuclear fusion, which uses ordinary sea water as its fuel, and hence has virtually limitless fuel availability, may become commercially viable within a few decades.

Renewable energy. *Hydro power* accounts for less than 7 per cent of global electricity generation and it is unlikely that its share will increase significantly (Mottershead, 2005). In recent years there has been a large increase in investment in *wind turbines*, with consequential declines in the costs of production, installation and operation. However, *solar power* is the main potential source of renewable energy The influx of solar energy is equivalent to about 7000 times today's global energy consumption. Solar energy can be harnessed through growing plants. *'Biomass'* is increasingly being used in new types of power stations and domestic heating equipment. It has the major advantage that it is 'carbon neutral', since the emission of carbon dioxide when it is burned, either as a primary fuel or as a secondary fuel (such as ethanol) is counterbalanced by its absorption of carbon dioxide during its growth. *Solar cells and photovoltaic cell* technologies have been advancing rapidly, allowing rapid advances in the effectiveness of capture of solar energy and declines in the price of harnessing solar energy.

b. Energy efficiency

Technical progress in automobile engines, power generation equipment, building design and packaging, have contributed to large advances in energy efficiency. The impact has been especially large in low and middle-income countries, in which GDP per unit of energy use rose from US$ 3.1 (at constant PPP prices) per kilogram of oil equivalent in 1990 to US$ 4.2 in 2001 (World Bank, WDI, 2006: Table 3.8).

c. Global warming

It can be seen that there is an almost limitless availability of fossil fuels. However, the use of greatly increased amounts of fossil fuels threatens the environment through the impact of global warming, principally through the production of carbon dioxide. However, there are numerous ways in which the projected rise in global output could be achieved without increasing global carbon dioxide output. There are large opportunities for the more general use of carbon sequestration technologies so that extensive use can continue to be made of the world's massive coal reserves without contributing to global warming. A variety of possibilities exist through which technical progress might allow large increases in vehicle use to take place without substantial growth of carbon dioxide emissions (Oliva, 2005).[14]

BP has identified seven 'one billion ton wedges' that could form part of the 'stabilisation triangle' which might stabilise global carbon dioxide output without any major technological breakthrough. Each one gigawatt 'wedge' is the equivalent to 'taking 250,000 vehicles off the road'. The 'wedges' could include 700 1GW nuclear power stations; improving building techniques so that the amount of energy used to heat buildings remains constant (40 per cent of primary energy is used to heat buildings); a fifty-fold increase in global wind turbine capacity; doubling the rate of re-forestation; 2500 fossil-fuelled hydrogen power stations, which sequester carbon dioxide in oil fields; a 700-fold increase in photovoltaic cells; and re-powering 1400 GW of coal-fired power stations with gas.

d. Health

Technical advances in medicines and medical equipment, increasing real consumption levels, improvement of national and international government agencies' delivery systems, improved food security, as well as advances in infrastructure provision and better access to reliable drinking water,[15] and improved sanitation,[16] have contributed to improvements in health, helping to free people from the threat of illness, pain and premature death. In developing countries between 1970 and 2002, infant mortality rates fell from 108 per thousand live births to 61 per thousand, and under-five mortality rates fell from 166 per thousand to 89, while fertility rates fell from 5.4 births per woman in 1970-75 to 2.9 per woman in 2002-5 (UNDP, 2004: 155 and 171). Life expectancy at birth in developing countries rose from 56 years in 1970-5 to 65 years in 2000-5 (UNDP, 2004: 171).[17] Even in the least-developed group of countries, life expectancy rose from 44 in 1970-75 to 51 in 2000-5.

e. Communications

Mobility. Technical progress in transport has revolutionised the choices facing people in terms of personal movement. Since the 1970s the real price of automobiles and air travel has fallen tremendously, which has allowed people with ever lower income levels to acquire cars and make long journeys on aeroplanes. In low and middle-income countries, the number of passenger cars per 1000 people rose from 16 in 1990 to 35 in 2003, as automobile ownership began to penetrate lower income groups (World Bank, WDI, 2006: Table 3.12).

Telecommunications. Revolutionary technical advances, especially in semi-conductors, have contributed to enormous progress in the nature and real price of electronic consumer durables. The transformation of the telecommunications industry has been especially significant for advances in the standard of living of people in developing countries. Increases in average incomes in developing countries have helped to stimulate growth of expenditure on telecommunications goods and services. In developing countries between 1990 and 2002, the number of telephone mainlines per 1000 people rose from 29 to 96 and the number of cellular phone subscribers rose from zero per 1000 people to 101 (UNDP, 2004: 183). By 2002, for every 1000 people in developing countries, there were 257 radios, 190 TV sets and 28 personal computers (World Bank, WDI, 2004: 296). The technical and business transformation of the global media industry, as well as liberalisation of national controls, has hugely widened the range of broadcast information to which people of almost all segments of the income distribution can have access.[18] These developments have helped to provide people with enormously enhanced freedom of choice both for entertainment and knowledge acquisition.

Freedom from Control by Others

Urbanisation. The advance of market forces in pursuit of profit has been associated with rapid urbanisation and decline in rural living during the epoch of the global business revolution. The share of the urban population in low and middle-income countries rose from 24 per cent in 1965 (World

Bank, 1990: 39) to 42 per cent in 2002 (World Bank, WDI, 2004: 154). The total urban population in developing countries rose from 782 million in 1975 to 2.04 billion in 2002 (UNDP, 2004: 155).[19] The transformation in the living and working environment from a rural, isolated setting, with limited connection to markets, negligible opportunities for occupational and residential change, and a restricted, unchanging set of inter-personal relationships, to an urban capitalist environment, intimate engagement with the market for one's labour power, wide opportunities for occupational and residential change, and access to a wide and changing set of inter-personal relationships, has comprehensively changed the outlook of the new generation of urban dwellers. The new generation of urban dwellers operating in a capitalist environment is vastly more independent than their forbears, with far greater opportunities to resist pressures from parents and kin groups, and (in the case of wives and female children) from husbands, fathers and brothers.

Democratisation. In the political realm, the global business revolution, the accompanying process of capitalist urbanisation and the transformation of consciousness of the urban population has seen a powerful growth of demands for political liberties, paralleling the movements that emerged in Europe is the nineteenth century as capitalist urbanisation advanced. Across the developing world, the epoch saw large advances in political liberties. Whereas in 1985 38 per cent of the world's population lived in the world's 'most democratic countries', by 2000, the share had risen to 57 per cent (UNDP, 2002: 15). The share living in 'authoritarian regimes' had fallen from 45 per cent to 30 per cent (UNDP, 2002: 15).

Freedom from Poverty and Famine

Poverty. During the period 1975-2002, output per person in developing countries rose by around 2.3 per cent per annum, and in the years 1990-2002, the period in which globalisation intensified, the growth rate accelerated to 2.8 per cent per annum (UNDP, 2004: 187). The rapid increase in output per person during the period of the global business revolution has contributed to a massive reduction in global poverty. Between 1990 and 2000, the UNDP estimates that the proportion of people living on less than US$1 per day fell from around 33 per cent to 17 per cent in the East Asia and the Pacific regions, and from around 44 per cent to 30 per cent in South Asia (UNDP, 2004: 130).

Inequality. Studies which measure global inequality, using country averages weighted by population totals, have found that there has been a marginal decline in the global Gini coefficient during the last quarter of a century (Sutcliffe, 2002: 14).[20] This is mainly explicable by the fact that per capita incomes have grown faster in developing countries than in high-income countries.

Famine. In low-income countries, population grew by 2.2 per cent per annum between 1980 and 2002 (from 1.6 billion to 2.5 billion), while the amount of arable land per person shrank from 0.23 hectares to just 0.17 hectares in the same period. (World Bank, WDI, 2004: 40). Without large improvements in agricultural productivity in this period, food output per person would have declined and developing countries' susceptibility to famine would have greatly increased. In fact, this period saw unprecedented advances in agricultural technology and rapid farm modernisation in developing countries, including seeds, farm equipment, transport infrastructure and information technology.[21] Consequently, per capita food output in low-income countries grew by 0.8 per cent per annum (WB, WDI, 2004: 40 and 126). The improvement in agricultural performance in developing countries has played a central role in confining famines to Sub-Saharan Africa, whereas formerly they affected large parts of the developing world.

Freedom from War

After 1945 the international community established a group of organisations under the UN that provided mechanisms for mutually accepted conduct of international relations, principally, but not exclusively, in the economic sphere. The trend in all these organisations has been towards international harmonisation and 'deep integration' of conditions across countries. Through these steadily advancing arrangements, individual countries sacrificed their autonomy in the interests of establishing their own markets as part of a unified global capitalist market.

Since the 1970s, national governments across the world have abandoned protectionist, state-led strategies. Support for a 'national bourgeoisie' has almost disappeared as barriers to international capital flows have been universally dismantled. For the first time, production systems were established by firms across national boundaries on a global basis, with closely integrated international division of labour within the supply chain of large firms. Liberalisation of international capital flows means that firms from capitalist countries are more deeply embedded than ever before in each other's business systems. Foreign trade increased from 27 per cent of global GDP in 1980 to 52 per cent in 2002

(World Bank, WDI, 2004), so that global prosperity is more reliant than ever before on the maintenance of friendly relations between trading partners. The current period resembles the high-point of nineteenth century liberalism in its focus on the international rather than the national economy, the free flow of capital around the world, the spread of English as the common global language, and the construction through the market of a common global culture.

Few people now believe that there is any possibility of a global military conflict. For almost everyone, it is unimaginable that a global economy, with deeply intertwined economic relations and a global culture could have a global military conflict. The world can now look back upon more than half a century of peaceful relations among the leading capitalist countries. Increasingly, the period from 1914-1945 appears as an aberration in the long march towards global unification achieved by the modern capitalist market economy. The stresses in the international political system that existed in this period can be viewed as the outcome of strains arising from the nation-based pattern of industrialisation that was specific to a particular epoch in capitalist development (Hobsbawm, 1990: 25). As the capitalist world economy begins finally to take shape after a delay of one hundred years, we may be witnessing today the beginnings of the global government structure that was envisioned by nineteenth century liberal economists as the natural consequence of the global economy.[22] In such an environment, the possibility of major international military conflict would cease to exist, thanks ultimately to the 'cement' produced by the international capitalist economy.

3. Capitalist Irrationality in the Epoch of the Global Business Revolution

3.1 Human Psychology and Social Relationships

Smith and Mill

In the late eighteenth and nineteenth century, the political economists Adam Smith and John Stuart Mill were both deeply preoccupied with the psychological and social consequences of the market economy. They each believed that the market economy[23] was the most powerful force available for advancing the productive forces. However, they both considered that the very force that stimulated economic progress also damaged people psychologically and harmed their social relationships. They considered that the market economy deeply distorted people's essential nature, stimulating selfishness and inhibiting their capacity for cooperation. They both considered that the pursuit of material prosperity and social status diverted people from leading a tranquil and happy life.

[T]he disposition to admire, and almost to worship, the rich and powerful, and to despise, or at least, to neglect persons of poor and mean condition, though necessary to maintain the distinction of ranks and the order of society, is at the same time, the great and most universal cause of the corruption of our moral sentiments (Smith, 1976a: 61).

Happiness is tranquillity [sic] and enjoyment...[T]he pleasures of vanity and superiority are seldom consistent with perfect tranquillity, the principle and foundation of all real and satisfactory enjoyment (Smith, 1976a: 149-50).

The deep-rooted selfishness which forms the general character of the existing state of society, is *so* deeply rooted only because the whole course of existing institutions tends to foster it (Mill, 1998: xvii).

[T]he idea is essentially repulsive of a society only held together by the relations and feelings arising out of pecuniary interests, and there is something naturally attractive in a form of society abounding in strong personal attachments and disinterested self-devotion (Mill, 1998: 133).

Both Mill and Smith considered that the fundamental principle for individual happiness and social harmony was 'benevolence'. They believed that education was fundamental to the attainment of a society in which benevolence was the guiding principle of social relationships. They were optimistic that over time, through education, the values necessary for a benevolent and cooperative society could be established.

[T]o feel much for others and little for ourselves, to restrain our selfish, and to indulge our benevolent affections, constitutes the perfection of human nature; and can alone among mankind produce that harmony of sentiments and passions in which consists their whole grace and propriety (Smith, 1976a: 25).

All the members of human society stand in need of each others assistance...Where the necessary assistance is reciprocally afforded from love, from gratitude, from friendship, and esteem, the society flourishes and is happy. All the different members of it are bound together by the agreeable bonds of love and affection, and are, as it were, drawn to one common centre of mutual good offices (Smith, 1976a: 85).

Mill regarded benevolence as the essence of a Communist society.

> The one certainty, is that Communism, to be successful requires a high standard of both moral and intellectual education in all members of the community - moral, to qualify them for doing their part honestly and energetically in the labour of life under no inducement but their share in the general interest of the association, and their feeling of duty and sympathy towards it; intellectual, to make them capable of estimating distant interests and entering into complex considerations, sufficiently at least to be able to discriminate, in these matters, good counsel from bad (Mill, 1998: 426).

> Now I reject altogether the notion that it is impossible for education and cultivation...to be made the inheritance of every person in the nation; but I am convinced that it is very difficult, and that the passage to it from our present condition can only be slow. I admit that in the points of moral education on which the success of Communism depends, the present state of society is demoralising, and that only a Communist association can effectually train mankind for Communism. It is for Communism, then, to prove by practical experiment, its power of giving this training (Mill, 1998: 426-7).

Social Darwinism

In the United States, the 'Gilded Age' at the end of the nineteenth century witnessed a tremendous concentration of wealth and income. The idea that 'freedom' essentially meant freedom of contract became the bedrock of 'liberal' thinking. The true realm of freedom was regarded as 'the liberty to buy and sell...where and how we please, without interference from the state' (Foner, 1998: 120). Social Darwinism became the dominant political philosophy, strongly opposing state interference with the 'natural' workings of society. It was only with the onset of the Great Depression that US policy-makers questioned these ideas, and the role of the state in ensuring social justice was greatly enhanced.[24] These ideas remained as the mainstream of US political thought for long into the post-war world, reinforced by the massive task of economic and social reconstruction in war-ravaged Europe.

In the 1950s, a group of conservative thinkers set out to 'reclaim the idea of freedom'. By the 1990s, the dominant view equated 'freedom' with individual choice in the market place and minimal interference from the state. The idea that the free market is a moral concept stands at the centre of US political discourse at the start of the twenty-first century. In the National Security Strategy document of 2002, President Bush stated: '*The concept of "free trade" arose as a moral principle even before it became a pillar of economics.* If you can make something that others value, you should be able to sell it to them. If others make something that you value you should be able to buy it. *This is real freedom, the freedom for a person - or nation - to make a living'* (Bush, quoted in *Financial Times,* 21 September 2002).

In the epoch of the global business revolution, the stimulation of selfishness and greed has reached a new intensity. This has powerfully affected people's lives as both producers and consumers. From the perspective of people as producers, business leaders' daily lives are built around a remorseless global struggle for competitive success in the pursuit of profit. The commercial battlefield governs their lives. New information technology has allowed this abstract force to dominate their existence at every hour of the day. Pressures from globally integrated markets unavoidably feed through into the lives of the workforce in companies at every level in the global value chain. From the perspective of human beings as consumers, new information technologies, new marketing techniques and increasingly powerful global mass media companies ever more effectively stimulate increased individual consumption of goods and services as the path through which people seek individual satisfaction.

The dangers identified by Smith and Mill as fundamental to the market economy have been realised on a far grander scale than they could have imagined. Capitalist globalisation raises a profound ethical and spiritual challenge in the early twenty-first century.

3.2 Energy and the Environment

Ecological Transition in Developing Countries

The ability to provide a clean environment is closely related to levels of per capita income. In the high-income countries most measures of environmental standards have steadily improved since the 1970s. However, in fast-growing developing countries, ecological conditions have deteriorated seriously, and it will be a huge challenge for policy-makers to prevent further environmental degradation. The most likely prospect is that the low and middle-income countries will endure a long period of output growth in which they continue to be heavily polluted before they can become rich and clean.[25]

Urban air quality in fast-growing developing countries has deteriorated seriously since the 1970s. Levels of particulates, sulphur dioxide, and nitrogen dioxide, in the major cities in China and India are now far above those in the industrialised world, posing enormous challenges to the health of their citizens. For example, the level of particulates in Paris is 15 micrograms per cubic metre and 22-23 micrograms in London and New York, compared with 99 in Beijing, 115 in Jakarta, 137 in Chongqing, 145 in Calcutta, 159 in Cairo, and 177 in New Delhi (World Bank, WDI, 2006, Table 3.13).

Environmental degradation in developing countries is not confined to the cities. Across the low and middle-income countries, between 1990 and 2005 the forested area declined by an annual average of 91 million sq. km., compared with an annual increase of 7 million sq. km. in the high-income countries (World Bank, WDI, 2006, Table 3.4). Numerous species of mammals, birds and plants in fast-growing developing countries are threatened with extinction. For example, the proportion of mammal species threatened with extinction is estimated to be 16 per cent in China, 20 per cent in India and 22 per cent in Indonesia (WB, WDI, 2006, Table 3.4).

Global Warming

Energy consumption. Global energy use is rising rapidly. Between 1990 and 2003, the world as a whole increased its consumption of primary energy by 22 per cent (World Bank, WDI, 2006, Table 3.7). The prospects are for continued rapid growth of global primary energy consumption. In 2003, levels of per capita energy use in low-income countries still stood at only 501 kg., compared with 1373 kg. in middle-income countries and 5410 kg. in the high-income countries. In 2003, the number of motor vehicles per 1000 people still stood at just 47 in the low and middle-income countries, compared with 623 in the high-income countries and 808 in the United States (WB, WDI, 2006, Table 3.12). As developing countries achieve increases in per capita incomes, they will move steadily towards the levels of primary energy use of today's high-income countries. Moreover, even the high-income countries are still expanding their consumption of primary energy. Between 1990 and 2003, their total primary energy consumption rose by 23 per cent, and accounted for over one-half of the total global increase (WB, WDI, 2006, Table 3.7).

Greenhouse gases. It is now accepted by almost everyone that the production of carbon dioxide has caused an increase in the earth's temperature through the impact of the 'greenhouse effect'. The vast bulk of primary energy worldwide is from fossil fuels. Automobiles almost entirely use fossil fuels. In 2003, nuclear power and hydropower each accounted for only around 16 per cent of global primary energy for electricity generation, or less than one-third of the total (World Bank, WDI, 2006, Table 3.9). Coal accounted for 40 per cent, gas for 19 per cent and oil for just 7 per cent. The increased production of carbon dioxide is attributed primarily to increased burning of fossil fuels, and secondarily to cement production.[26]

The level of carbon dioxide in the earth's atmosphere is estimated to have risen from around 260 parts per million (ppm) before the Industrial Revolution[27] to 315 ppm in 1958, increasing still further to 397 ppm in 2005. If current trends in the use of fossil fuel were to continue then it is predicted that levels would rise to 400 ppm by 2015 and 800 ppm by 2100 (King, 2005).

It is now widely accepted that the rise in the level of carbon dioxide in the earth's atmosphere has contributed to an unprecedented increase in average global temperatures. If this continues it will pose 'a real threat to our global civilisation' (King, 2005). The threat will take the form of a rise in the global sea level, increased extreme weather events, and damage to agriculture.[28] It is thought likely that the Arctic Ice Cap will 'disappear completely by 2060' whatever action is taken in the next few years, since it takes many years for carbon dioxide to disperse from the atmosphere. Managing the consequences of global warming will pose a large challenge even for high-income countries, but for poor countries, especially those in Asia, the challenge will be even more serious. In the view of the United Kingdom's Chief Scientific Officer, Sir David King, a 'global turning point has been reached' and 'a choice must be made within this decade' if a disaster for the earth is to be avoided.

Lock-in. Under capitalist globalisation consumers are locked in to a pattern of final consumption organised around packaged and processed goods, which in their turn support a global packaging industry that uses plastics, steel and aluminium. The intermediate and final products are distributed mainly by road-based commercial transport systems. Roads require a network of supplier industries, including cement and steel. The production of commercial vehicles requires a global network of supplier industries, including steel, aluminium, plastics, and glass. Individuals have exercised their freedom of choice by demanding individualised transport systems in the shape of the automobile. Low and middle-income countries have, without exception, allowed the same pattern of development in their transport systems and the same freedom of individual consumer choice as exists in the high-income countries. Technical progress has reduced the consumption of energy and other inputs per unit of final product. However, the pace of growth of final consumption, based around the locked-in pattern of production and distribution, is producing large rates of increase in the consumption of primary energy, including oil.

Energy: International Relations and the Competition for Exhaustible Resources

There is little prospect of renewable energy replacing fossil fuels in the coming decades. Coal is likely to remain the most important source of primary energy for electricity generation for the foreseeable future. However, oil is critically important for transport, which is growing at a high rate, especially in developing countries.

Global consumption of oil is increasing rapidly. Total oil consumption increased by 19 per cent from 1995-2005, with increases of 17 per cent in the United States and 33 per cent in the Asia-Pacific Region (BP, 2006: 11). The United States consumes 25 per cent of the world total, compared with 29 per cent in the Asia-Pacific Region (BP, 2006: 11).[29]

Oil production in the United States is falling and oil production in the Asia-Pacific Region is stagnant. Consequently, oil imports in both regions are rising rapidly. Global oil imports rose by 24 per cent from 1998-2005 (BP, 1999: 19; and BP, 2006: 20-1). The United States accounted for 33 per cent of the increase and the Asia-Pacific Region for 49 per cent (China accounted for 25 per cent of the total world increase and the rest of the Asia-Pacific Region, excluding Japan, for 24 per cent).[30]

As developing countries raise their level of per capita income, and expand their transport systems, their demand for oil will expand greatly. For most of the Asia-Pacific Region, increased oil consumption will need to be satisfied mainly through increased imports.[31] However, the United States is likely to remain the most important importer of oil for a long period ahead. By 2004, the United States' net oil imports amounted to 58 per cent of its total oil consumption (BP, 2005), and it is predicted that by 2025 oil imports will account for as much as 68 per cent of US consumption (Klare, 2004: 76).

As the United States' dependency on imported oil has become ever larger, so the importance of secure access to oil has risen ever higher on the US foreign policy agenda. The Middle East is at the centre of the United States' search for energy security. Not only does it have over two-thirds of the world's oil reserves, but its share of global output is predicted to rise from 27 per cent in 2002 to 43 per cent in 2030 (Klare, 2004: 76). The share of the Gulf countries in world oil trade is predicted to rise from 41 per cent to 70 per cent in 2030 (Klare, 2004: 77-8). The United States Government's National Energy Policy document of 2001 concluded: 'Middle East oil production will remain central to world oil security…[and] the Gulf will be a primary focus of US international energy policy' (quoted in Klare, 2004: 78).

Oil has been a key part of past international relations conflicts. Many commentators have voiced concern at the prospect of conflict between the United States and the large oil-importing regions of the world as demands accelerate in the period ahead. Many US policy-makers believe that 'China is increasingly active in striving for energy resources in ways that portend direct competition for energy resources with the United States', and that 'this is producing a possibility of conflict between the two nations' (USCESRC, 2005:

171). Henry Kissinger, former US Secretary of State, has warned that the global battle for the control of energy resources could become the equivalent of the nineteenth century 'great game', which involved intense conflict between Britain and Russia for control of central Asia (*FT*, 2 June 2005).

The Environment

With only 16 per cent of the world's population, the high-income countries account for 52 per cent of the world's carbon dioxide production.[32] Despite technical progress to increase the amount of GDP generated per unit of energy use,[33] low and middle-income countries are fast increasing their production of carbon dioxide as their per capita income advances.[34] India and China together increased their production of carbon dioxide by 54 per cent from 1990-2002, and their share of global carbon dioxide production rose from 14.5 per cent in 1990 to 19.4 per cent in 2002 (World Bank, WDI, 2006: Table 3.8). However, their levels of carbon dioxide production per person are still far below those of the high-income countries.

Under the Kyoto Protocol, the main body of high-income countries agreed to attempt to restrict their carbon dioxide emissions by the year 2010 to roughly the level of 1990.[35] It is by no means certain that the signatories will achieve their intended goal. The carbon trading system only went into force in 2005, which is just five years before the expiry of the Kyoto Agreement. It is uncertain what form of agreement, if any, will operate after 2010.

The United States refused to participate in the Agreement. Under President Clinton, the United States Senate refused, by a majority of 95-0 to ratify the Treaty. The United States produces 24 per cent of global carbon dioxide emissions (World Bank, WDI, 2006, Table 3.8). Its level of emissions rose by 21 per cent between 1990 and 2002, accounting for 21 per cent of the total global increase. The rise was largely due to the increase in the number of motor vehicles and the distance travelled per person.[36]

The developing countries were not signatories to the Kyoto Agreement. Fast-growing developing countries are strongly committed to using motor vehicles as the core of their transport systems both for people and goods.[37] By the year 2002, the emissions of carbon dioxide from the low and middle-income countries stood at 48 per cent of the world's total emissions (World Bank, WDI, 2006, Table 3.8). However, in 2002 per capita carbon emissions in low and middle-income countries amounted to just 2.2 metric tons, compared with 12.8 metric tons in the high-income countries, and 20.2 in the United States. In the absence of extremely rapid technical progress and/or fundamental changes in the nature of economic development, the process of catch-up in developing economies will lead to globally unsustainable increases in carbon dioxide emissions.

There are possibilities for deep conflicts of interest between different segments of the world population over an issue of fundamental importance to the sustainability of human life on the planet.

3.3 Inequality

Capitalist globalisation is contributing to large changes in the distribution of income, wealth and life chances in both rich and poor countries.

The Global Elite

Those employees who work in the upper reaches of the value chain of globalising firms inhabit an increasingly homogenised global environment, with a common culture and high global incomes that broadly reflect their scarce skills. The international firm is, indeed, increasingly multinational in the origin of its employees, even at high levels. It is increasingly common even for CEOs of giant global firms to be drawn from nationalities other than those in which the company is headquartered. The global elite is a tiny fraction of the world's population that is made conscious of its special position through many symbols. It shares a common language (English). Its members move their place of residence frequently from country to country. They share common values. They read the same newspapers. They stay in the same global hotels. They communicate across their respective companies continuously, connected by ever-advancing new information technologies, the latest of which is the ubiquitous 'handheld Blackberry' device. They buy the same globally branded luxury goods - Prada, Gucci, Mont Blanc, Mercedes, Lexus and Ferrari. They are experts in global high quality wines. Their children attend the same international private schools and finish their education at the same global elite universities. They share a common culture of charity, care for poor people and concern for the global environment. Their companies' leaders attend the Davos Economic Forum. Their homes are increasingly physically isolated from those of ordinary people. They have less and less attachment to a particular country, both at the level of the company and as a social group. The members of the global elite typically own residences in several countries.

The differences between the life led by the members of this elite group and the mass of poor people are astronomical. Whereas close to three billion people live on less than US$ 2 per day, a few tens of millions of people[38] in the global elite live on upwards of US$ 200 per day. There is little evidence that allows robust calculation of changes in global inequality in the last two decades, since this requires good data not only on average incomes in different countries, but also on the distribution of income within countries across the world. Rough and ready calculations by Sutcliffe (2002), using data for a limited number of countries that have data on changes on the internal distribution of income, indicate that the global Gini coefficient of income distribution has altered little in the past two decades, remaining fairly constant at around 0.63-0.67 throughout this period.[39] His calculations confirm that the global distribution of income has been immensely uneven throughout the period of modern globalisation. In addition to an extremely high overall Gini coefficient, Sutcliffe's data show that in 2000, the richest 5 per cent of the global population had around 115-30 times the income of the poorest 5 per cent, the richest 10 per cent had around 60 times that of the poorest 10 per cent, and the richest 20 per cent had around 20-30 times that of the poorest 20 per cent (Sutcliffe, 2002: 28). The only conclusive trend is that the income share of the richest one per cent of the world population (around 60 million people) has enormously increased compared with the poorest one per cent, from a multiple of around 200 in 1980 to a multiple of around 400 in 2000 (Sutcliffe, 2002: 28).

Inequality in Developing Countries

Lewis phase. During the early phase of industrialisation, for a significant period of time the distribution of income typically becomes more unequal (the 'Kuznets curve'). During this phase, the majority of the workers in developing countries are under-employed in the farm sector on close to subsistence levels of income. As the modern sector expands, the growing army of rural-urban migrants is pulled into permanent wage employment, but mostly on low incomes in unskilled occupations. This is the so-called 'Lewis' phase of 'economic development with unlimited supplies of labour'.

On the one hand, rural-urban migration to permanent wage employment contributes to the decline in absolute poverty in many developing countries in recent decades. On the other hand, although a growing fraction of the urban workforce gradually moves into higher income occupations, a fundamental constraint is set to the growth of real incomes for urban unskilled labour by the availability of unlimited supplies of under-employed rural labour.

A large fraction of rural-urban migrants work as unskilled 'lumpen' labour in the urban 'informal' sector, unprotected by trade unions, health and unemployment insurance, effective minimum wage legislation or government supervision of conditions of work. Several hundred million people work in this sector in low and middle-income countries, often in arduous, physically dangerous and psychologically insecure conditions. The huge numbers of people who work in the informal sector across the developing world are employed mainly in a vast number of small-scale establishments. Conditions in the 'informal' mining, manufacturing, construction, agricultural wage labour, transport and service sectors, and the associated family living conditions, are frequently little different from those described in Frederick Engels' study the *Condition of the English Working Class*, published in the 1840s, during the early phase of British industrialisation.

International firms. Unlike most previous experiences of late industrialisation, today the world's leading firms have established production systems across the developing world within the fast-growing low and middle-income countries. During the global business revolution, low and middle-income countries have opened themselves to the free flow of foreign direct investment at a point in history at which levels of global industrial concentration and barriers to entry have never been higher. Within the fastest-growing parts of low and middle-income countries, leading multinational firms, almost all headquartered in the high-income countries, have established production systems that dominate large swathes of the host economy.

Development economists used to believe that multinational firms would adjust their 'factor proportions' (capital to labour ratios) to the conditions of developing countries, employing relatively large amounts of labour for each unit of capital. In fact, the epoch of globalisation has produced globally standard products using global standard technologies in the high value-added market for final and intermediate products. Global firms employ international workers at international income levels. Local employees of multinational firms in developing countries, whatever their skill level, tend to work at income levels considerably above those of comparably skilled local workers. Moreover, a disproportionate fraction of these are people with relatively high skill levels. Conditions of work also approximate those in high-income countries, even for manual work. Multinational firms must adopt global employment standards or their reputation will be damaged. Also, it is impossible to manage a multinational firm using a wide variety of different employment practices across different subsidiaries of the company in different locations. Insofar as local firms are able to compete with the global firms, they also must adopt global standards in order to competitively attract high quality local labour.

The presence of larger pockets of multinational firms within fast-growing low and middle-income countries has brought the 'twenty-first century' to these countries in terms of employment and remuneration, with pay and conditions of work determined by global standards. However, those employed in these conditions constitute only a small fraction of the non-farm population. Surrounding them is a vast and far larger 'sea' of urban informal sector employment, for whom pay and conditions of work are set by the standards of the rural under-employed masses, not by international markets.

In fast-growing low and middle-income countries during the epoch of globalisation, the combination of the Lewis phase of development with high-speed expansion of investment by international firms has led to a widespread increase in official measures of inequality. Many of these countries have seen the Gini coefficient of inequality in income distribution rise during this period from 0.2-0.3 to 0.4-0.6. The Gini coefficient of income inequality now stands at 0.44 in Turkey, 0.45 in China, 0.49 in Mexico and Malaysia, 0.53 in Argentina, 0.57 in Chile, and 0.58 in Brazil (World Bank, WDI, 2006: Table 2.8).

Inequality in High-Income Countries

Capitalist globalisation has led to large changes in the structure of inequality in the high-income countries. Nowhere is this more in evidence than in the United States. The central drive of American foreign policy in the epoch of globalisation has been the opening the global economy to free trade and free movement of capital:

> Promoting free and fair trade has long been a bedrock of American foreign policy...History has judged the market economy as the single most effective system and the greatest antidote to poverty. To expand economic liberty and prosperity, the United States promotes free and fair trade, open markets, a stable financial system, the integration of the global economy, and secure, clean energy development (Bush, 2006: 25).

Since the 1970s, this is exactly the system that has been established under US leadership, namely capitalist globalisation. There is an old saying: 'Be careful lest your wish is granted'. The United States' wish for a global free market has been substantially granted. However, the contradictions are far deeper than US policy-makers could ever have imagined.

The integration of global markets has had profoundly contradictory results for American people. Liberalisation of capital markets since the 1980s has opened up a vast world of low-priced labour across the 'transition' and 'developing' countries, including skilled and unskilled manual labour as well as scientists, engineers and managers. China is the largest single source of this greatly expanded labour supply to global markets. In the 'BRIC' countries (Brazil, Russia, India and China) alone, economic liberalisation since the 1980s has added around 1.7 billion people of working age to the international labour market. This is nearly three times the size of the labour force in the high-income economies.[40] China alone has a labour force of around 880 million, compared with 647 million in the high-income countries as a whole (World Bank, WDI, 2004: 38-40). In 2002, the average per capita gross national product in low and middle-income countries was US$ 1170 (4030 in PPP dollars), compared with US$ 26 490 (28 480 in PPP dollars) in the high-income countries (WB, WDI, 2004: 14-16). Previously, the labour markets of most low and middle-income countries were, to a significant degree, isolated from international markets by the operation of 'planned economies' or the protectionist, 'inward-looking' strategies of the developing countries in which most poor people lived. The levels of foreign trade and foreign investment before the 1980s were much lower than they are today.

Global labour markets are being integrated to some degree directly through some increases in international migration, but this remains only a small part of the integrative mechanism, since high-income countries retain tight controls over immigration. Rather, the process of integration has taken place indirectly, through the migration of capital to poor countries and through the export of goods and services from poor to rich countries. This places intense pressure for international equalisation of wages and conditions of work. These pressures add greatly to the impact of technological change, which has replaced a wide swathe of white-collar office jobs that demanded modest skills, while demand for unskilled jobs in the service sector, such as restaurants, retail and domestic help, has surged. It is now increasingly being recognised in the United States that the 'law of one price' operates in fully integrated markets. In this case, the 'market' is the global labour market:

> As China, India and the states of the former Soviet Union have commenced active participation in the global economy in the past ten to twenty years, the global market's workforce has doubled, placing major downward pressure on wages around the world. This is a function of what has been termed the 'law of one price', when capital is relatively unencumbered and the factors of production are mobile, capital will gravitate to regions with the highest rate of return. This has been occurring and continues to occur in China and elsewhere, and it is resulting in the movement of jobs, especially manufacturing jobs but increasingly service jobs as well, from the United States to China and to other countries offering higher returns on capital (USCESRC, 2005: 3).

One recent analysis (Blinder, 2006) has concluded that a wide range of occupations is susceptible to being outsourced from the United States to developing countries. The first round of vulnerable occupations is those in American manufacturing: 'The vast majority of [American] manufacturing workers produced items that could be put in a box, and so virtually all of their jobs were potentially movable offshore' (Blinder, 2006, 120). It emphasises that the information technology revolution means that a much wider range of occupations is capable of being outsourced than most people imagine, including a wide range of service sector activities: 'Eventually, the number of service-sector jobs that will be vulnerable to competition from abroad will likely exceed the total number of manufacturing jobs' (Blinder, 2006: 119). It concludes that the only occupations that will be untouched by this revolution in the global labour market will be 'personal services', as opposed to 'impersonal services' that can be 'delivered by wire'.

The study also emphasises that the threat to US occupational security exists at every level of skill and education. This process will have enormous political implications: 'As the transition unfolds, the number of people in the rich countries who will feel threatened by foreign job competition will grow enormously. It is predictable that they will become a potent political force in each of their countries' (Blinder, 2006: 127). Up until now, in the United States, job-market stress has been particularly acute for the uneducated and the unskilled. However, 'the new cadres of displaced workers, especially those who are drawn from the upper educational reaches, will be neither as passive nor as quiet. They will also be numerous' (Blinder, 2006: 127).

American workers are being forced to work longer hours, accept reduced rates of overtime pay, and accept reduced company contributions to health insurance and pensions. There are now 45 million Americans without health coverage, many of whom are full-time workers. During the epoch of capitalist globalisation, US income disparity has greatly increased. The income share of the top decile of the US population was stable at around 32-33 per cent from the 1960s to the early 1980s, but thereafter it rose to around 43-44 per cent in 2000-2, which was the same income share that they received in the 1920s and 1930s. The share of the top one per cent of the distribution rose from less than 8 per cent in the late 1960s and 1970s to around 15-17 per cent at the end of the 1990s (Piketty and Saez, 2006). The stagnation of median wages during the US economy's powerful growth since 2000 has become a central topic of US economists' attention. Between 2000 and 2006, the median US household income fell by 3 per cent while the share of corporate profits in GDP rose from 7 per cent to 12.2 per cent (*FT*, 10 June 2006). Alongside the growing inequality in income, America's social mobility is lower than in every other developed country except for the United Kingdom.[41]

There is 'widespread public angst' at the stagnation in median wages and the growing inequality. Former Harvard President Larry Summers believes that 'the most serious problem facing the United States today is the widening gap between the children of the rich and children of the poor' (quoted in *New York Times*, 24 May 2005). Alan Greenspan, then Head of the Federal Reserve warned of the dangers of current trends in the distribution of income in the United States: 'For the democratic society, that is not a very desirable thing to allow to happen' (quoted in *New York Times*, 5 June, 2005). The newly appointed chairman of the Federal Reserve, Ben Bernanke, said: 'We want everybody to participate in the American dream. We want everyone to have a chance to get ahead. And to the extent that incomes and wealth are spreading apart, I think that is not a good trend' (quoted in *Financial Times*, 25 July 2006).

3.4 The Firm and the Nation

Globalisation and Industrial Concentration

Economists have long debated the basic tendencies of capitalism. The main body of mainstream, 'neo-classical' economists, has considered that the basic driver of progress under capitalism is competition among the mass of anonymous small and medium-sized firms. Following Marshall, they consider that large firms do not grow indefinitely. Instead, like the 'trees in the forest', beyond a certain point they tend to atrophy and die, so that the forest canopy always remains at a certain height.[42] Most non-mainstream economists since Karl Marx have believed that the basic law of capitalism is the 'tendency to concentration'.[43] The period since the 1970s has provided an ideal opportunity to test competing theories of the basic tendencies of capitalism once the constraints are removed.

This period has seen a large change in the nature of business organisation, amounting to nothing less than a 'business revolution'. As global markets have opened up, multinational companies typically have responded by divesting their 'non-core' businesses to focus on a small array of closely related products in which they have global leadership, achieved through the possession of a combination of superior brand and technology, and through economies of scale and scope. The large size and business focus of leading firms has enabled them to benefit greatly from economies of scale in procurement. Leading global firms have increasingly outsourced manufacturing and 'non-core' service functions, to focus on the 'brain' functions of design, product development, final assembly, marketing and financing. Alongside the growth of outsourcing, they have also developed skills in systems integration and coordination of their supply chain. Leading global firms have also been able to attract the best employees in the international 'battle for talent'.

In almost every sector, the period since the 1970s has seen an unprecedented amount of merger, acquisition and divestment, with leading firms using this to consolidate their position at the centre of global markets by achieving focus and scale. Levels of global industrial consolidation within each sector have advanced remorselessly. The process has affected almost every sector, from the world's most sophisticated, high technology capital goods, to the simplest consumer goods. It is as though a law has come into play, under which in every sector, the top half dozen systems integrator firms, with superior brands and/or technologies account for over one-half of the entire global market in the particular product.[44]

The explosive advance in industrial consolidation among systems integrator firms has produced a powerful consequential impact on industrial structure, which has been termed the 'cascade effect' (Nolan, 2001). The global industry leaders in each sector have used their procurement power to exert intense pressure on their supply chains, typically requiring leading firms in the upper tiers of the supply chain to supply inputs on a 'just-in-time' basis to production sites around the world. This has intensified the pressure upon supplier firms to build global networks to feed the needs of global customers. The leading systems integrators place intense pressure on their suppliers to achieve technical progress in order to supply inputs of improving technical quality so that they can meet the demands of final customers. Moreover, they exert remorseless pressure on their suppliers to lower prices for a given product quality. This has, in turn, resulted in intense pressure upon supplier firms themselves to merge and acquire, and to divest non-core business, in order to gain scale and focus, enabling them to achieve economies of scale in research and development, procurement, human resources, and subsystems integration.

Globalisation and the Firm from the Perspective of the Low and Middle-Income Countries

From the perspective of developing countries, the 'global level playing field' appears to be extraordinarily uneven. Developing countries have liberalised their economies in the midst of the most dramatic process of industrial concentration ever witnessed. This presents an immense challenge to their indigenous firms.

In the epoch of the 'global level playing field', the landscape of industrial competition is very uneven indeed. The high-income economies contain just 15 per cent of the world's total population. Firms headquartered in these countries account for 94 per cent of the companies listed in the '*Fortune 500*', which ranks firms by sales revenue. They account for 96 per cent of the firms in the '*FT 500*' list of the world's leading firms, ranked by market capitalisation. There is not a single firm from the low or middle-income countries in the list of the world's 'top 100 brands' (Sorrell, 2004). The world's research and development expenditure is highly concentrated among firms from high-income countries. In 2003, just four of the top 700 firms by R&D expenditure, which constitute the core of global technical progress, were from low and middle-income countries, two from China and two from Brazil.[45] The world's leading firms are rapidly increasing their R&D bases in low and middle-income countries, which enables them to obtain greater amounts of knowledge per dollar spent on R&D.

The United States sits at the centre of capitalist globalisation. Despite China's rise, the United States still accounts for over 26 per cent of global manufacturing output (excluding production in overseas subsidiaries of firm headquartered in America) compared with around 6 per cent for China.[46] The United States is by far the world's most powerful stock market. Its share of the total value of global stock markets rose from 33 per cent in 1990 to 47 per cent in 2003 (World Bank, WDI, 2004: 268). In 2004, firms headquartered in North America accounted for 175 of the *Fortune 500* companies (ranked by sales revenue) (*Fortune*, 26 July 2004). In the same year there were 247 North American firms in the *FT 500* companies (ranked by market capitalisation), accounting for 55 per cent of the total market capitalisation of *FT 500* firms (*FT*, 27 May 2004). The vast bulk of global technical progress takes place in a relatively small number of giant firms. Among these firms, those from North America are dominant. In 2005, out of the world's top 1000 firms ranked by R&D expenditure, 440 were headquartered in North America (DTI, 2005). The so-called 'BRIC' countries (Brazil, Russia, India and China), with a combined population of 2.7 billion (43 per cent of the world's total) between them had a mere nine firms among the world's top 1000 firms ranked by R&D expenditure.[47]

As developing countries have liberalised the conditions for investment by international firms, global systems integrators and the leading parts of their supply chains have established oligopolistic positions in local markets for products which have high value-added, embody high technology and carry powerful brands. For example, in Brazil, which has US$ 175 billion of FDI, in 2001 multinational firms accounted for fourteen of the top 25 'Brazilian' firms.[48] In the critically important banking sector, following liberalisation in Latin America and Eastern Europe global giant financial firms quickly achieved dominant positions.

Globalisation and the Firm from the Perspective of the High-Income Countries

The United States government has taken the lead in promoting the liberalisation of international capital flows, both directly and through its leading role in international institutions. The results have exceeded expectations. Global stocks of FDI rose from US$ 699 billion in 1980 to US$ 7123 billion in 2002, of which stocks of FDI in developing countries rose from US$ 307 billion to US$ 2340 billion in the same period (UNCTAD, 2003: 257-9). The very success of this endeavour, has brought its own challenges for the political economy of the high-income countries.

The giant firms which dominate the epoch of globalisation may have their headquarters in a given high-income country, but the share of assets, employment and revenue generated outside their home country has risen remorselessly in the epoch of capitalist globalisation. For a large number of firms, the international economy is now more significant than the economy of the country in which they were originally based.[49] Liberalisation of international capital flows means that a large shift has taken place in ownership structures. It is increasingly likely that foreigners will own a substantial share of the equity of a firm headquartered in a given country. These developments mean that firms from leading capitalist countries are more deeply embedded than ever before in each other's business systems, and in the business systems of developing countries, and less embedded in the political economy of their home country.

A large body of the citizens of the home countries believe that the interests of the international firms based in their country of citizenship are substantially divorced from the interests of the home country. These fears were crystallised in Samuel Huntington's book *Who are we?* (2004). Huntington believes that the United States faces serious threats to its national identity and unity from various directions, including the rise in domestic social inequality, and the 'globalisation' of the American elite. The large changes in the distribution of income and in the nature of work in the United States are perceived by many US citizens to be linked closely to the internationalisation of the large 'American' firm. In Europe also, there are deep fears among ordinary people about the increasing divorce of the international firm from the nation. Many leading global firms have expressed the view that in the long term their largest markets, the main location for their assets and employment, will be the giant 'BRIC' group of countries (Brazil, Russia, India and China).

3.5 Finance

Inherent Instability of Financial Markets

Keynes (1936: Chapter 12) attacked the idea that financial markets are inherently efficient, and based on rational expectations. He emphasised the influence of speculation in determining prices in financial markets: 'Speculators may do no harm as bubbles on a steady stream of enterprise. But the position is serious when enterprise becomes the bubble on a whirlpool of speculation. When the capital development of a country becomes a by-product of the activities of a casino, the job is likely to be ill-done' (Keynes, 1936: 159). He believed that speculation is 'a scarcely avoidable outcome of our having successfully organised "liquid" investment markets', and 'the risk of the predominance of speculation increases' as the organisation of investment markets improves (Keynes, 1936: 158-9).

Shiller has pointed out the shortcoming in 'many of the major finance textbooks today', which 'promote a view of markets working rationally and efficiently', and 'do not provide arguments as to why feedback loops supporting speculative bubbles cannot occur' (Shiller, 2001: 67). In fact, they 'do not even mention bubbles or Ponzi schemes': 'These books convey a sense of orderly progression in financial markets, of markets that work with mathematical precision' (Shiller, 2001: 67). Shiller (2001) has shown that bubbles in financial markets are 'so natural that one must conclude that 'if there is to be debate about…speculative bubbles, the burden of proof is on the sceptics to provide evidence as to why [they] cannot occur' (Shiller, 2001: 67). The initiating factor is often the optimism generated by a feeling that the economy has entered a 'new era'. Once the speculation process gets under way, powerful positive feedback loops drive markets ever higher. Credit is extended on the basis of increased collateral asset prices, which supports still further increase in asset prices, and still further credit expansion (White, 2006: 9).

The counterpart of the powerful tendency of financial markets to produce self-reinforcing 'bubble' effects is the tendency to produce self-reinforcing market collapse: bubbles tend to burst, rather than slowly deflating (Shiller, 2001).

Alan Greenspan commented on the 1987 US stock market crash and the Asian Financial Crisis as follows: 'At one point the economic system appears stable, the next it behaves as though a dam has reached a breaking point, and water (read, confidence) evacuates its reservoir' (Greenspan quoted in Singh, 2002). The tendency for financial bubbles to collapse has been heightened by modern sophisticated measures of internal risk management, which operate through daily, price-sensitive risk limits, with the same techniques used by all market participants. Consequently, they will respond simultaneously and in the same way to an initial fall in asset prices, causing a vicious circle of asset price collapse.[50]

Financial Risk Today

The relationship between finance and the real world of production of goods and services is fundamental to economic activity. In the epoch of the global business revolution, this relationship has assumed a global character. The global financial system stands on the edge of a precipice. The world faces the possibility of a catastrophic financial crisis stemming from the operation of the capitalist free market in the realm of finance. The impending crisis has several inter-related elements.

Rate of interest. The rate of interest in the high-income economies has fallen to unprecedentedly low levels in the past decade. In part this has been due to government policy to serve as an anchor for consumer price inflation by limiting inflationary expectations. The low rate of interest has also been stimulated by the massive increase in foreign exchange reserves in East Asia and the oil-exporting countries. Between 1995 and 2005, world foreign exchange reserves tripled to more than US$ 4000 billion, with an accelerating rate of increase after the year 2000.

The devastating impact of the Asian Financial Crisis on economies in the region prompted intense efforts by East Asian economies in the subsequent period to follow 'mercantilist' policies, increasing export surpluses in order to expand their foreign exchange reserves, in the hope that this would insulate them from the impact of such a crisis in the future. It was hoped that the large accumulations of foreign exchange reserves would enable these economies to 'self-insure' against financial crisis rather than rely on international institutions such as the IMF (*FT*, 9 March 2006). In addition, the rise in oil and gas prices after the turn of the millennium stimulated increased export surpluses and foreign exchange reserve growth in the oil-producing economies.

These reserves have massively increased the supply of financial investments to global markets, especially the United States. The availability of such vast and rising foreign exchange reserves seeking a return on global financial markets, especially in the United States, means that the US government finds it relatively easy to borrow from international markets, and has helped to keep the rate of interest low. These developments in turn have helped to keep interest rates low and stimulated a long-term bubble in asset prices. The inflow of funds has also helped to prop up the US dollar.

Falling price of goods and services. The period of the global business revolution has seen falling prices of final goods and services. The cause of the decline is partly due to the entrance of a vast number of new workers at low wages from the former Communist planned economies and from the formerly inward-looking developing countries. The enormous increase in low-cost, low-price exports has underpinned the decline in the price of a wide range of goods and services. The decline has also been due to intense oligopolistic competition among giant firms, who compete by forcing down prices along their respective supply chains and by investing huge amounts in technical progress.

Asset price bubble. Alongside the decline in the prices of final goods and services has taken place an unprecedented asset bubble. The bubble has been stimulated by the feeling that the world has entered a new era of global markets and uninterrupted capitalist expansion across the world. The asset bubble has been self-reinforcing, with speculation driving up asset prices in a classic self-reinforcing cycle around the world. The asset bubble moved from the stock market in general to the IT sector. In the past few years, the asset bubble has increased dramatically in the property market, the market for oil, gold, silver, aluminium, platinum, nickel, and other metals, the bond market (forcing down bond yield), the market for agricultural products such as refined sugar and orange juice futures, and even to exotic areas such as the art market.

Property prices have surged across the world. Between 1995 and 2005, average house prices tripled in Australia, almost tripled in the United Kingdom, more than doubled in Spain, and almost doubled in the United States (*FT*, 17 April 2006). The underlying fundamentals of supply and demand for properties have not changed greatly in this period, and differ greatly from country to country, and region to region. What is common is the huge rise in property prices. The most plausible explanation for the explosive growth is that the liberalisation of credit markets in leading economies has allowed lenders to meet the demand for mortgages more easily. The period has seen a wide range of innovations in the range of mortgages on offer, including 'interest only', 'deferred payment of interest', and 'multi-generational mortgages'. House values have become the largest source of personal wealth,[51] and mortgages have become the largest source of household debt.[52]

For example, the price of copper surged from less than US$ 1000 per tonne (three-month forward) in 2001-02 to US$ 1800 in mid-2005, before achieving a 'near-vertical take-off', reaching US$ 8500 per tonne in May 2006 (*FT*, 24 May 2006). Between 2001 and 2005, global copper usage rose by less than one-fifth[53], alongside a more than eightfold rise in the price of copper. It is widely believed by experts in the field that 'momentum investors' have played a central role in the rise in the copper price, as indeed they have in the increase in other commodity prices.

National monetary authorities target consumer price inflation, not asset price inflation. They are afraid to puncture the asset price bubble through increasing the interest rate, for fear of the socio-economic consequences. However, the longer the asset price bubble continues, the more serious will be the final result when the bubble bursts. Some commentators believe the monetary authorities ought to concern themselves with asset price inflation as well as consumer price inflation. Preoccupation with consumer price inflation is likely to stimulate conditions that lead to asset price bubbles and the eventual collapse of asset prices, with large damaging effects on the economy and society (Eichengreen and Mitchener, 2003).

Sources of liquidity. The expansion of liquidity has been driven in part by the historically low rate of interest. However, it has also been driven by the self-reinforcing process of endogenous money creation: 'Monetary expansion is systemic and endogenous rather than random and exogenous...The fact is that money, defined as a means of payment in actual use, has been continuously expanded, and existing money has been used ever more efficiently in periods of boom to finance expansion, including speculation. This has occurred despite efforts of banking authorities to control and limit the money supply' (Kindleberger, 1996: 45). Kindleberger warns that 'the problem of "money" is that it is an elusive construct, difficult to pin down and to fix in some desired quantity for the economy' (Kindleberger, 1996: 48). Both the velocity of circulation and the invention of new forms of money make it extremely difficult to control the quantity of money. The Radcliffe Commission in Britain in 1959 claimed that in a developed economy there is an 'indefinitely wide range of financial institutions' and 'many hold highly liquid assets which are close substitutes for money, as good to hold and only inferior when the actual moment of payment arrives' (quoted in Kindleberger, 1996: 48). The period of the global business revolution has seen a proliferation of new financial institutions and new forms of debt.

New financial institutions. In the epoch of the global business revolution, the range of financial institutions has expanded beyond imagination. Traditional commercial banks now compete routinely with investment banks, credit card companies, insurance companies, and the financial branches of supermarkets, automobile companies, aircraft manufacturers, oil companies, and diversified conglomerates such as GE.

Hedge funds hardly existed before the 1990s. The amount of money invested in so-called 'hedge-funds'[54] had risen to around US$ 1500 billion by the middle of 2005, almost doubling in the previous two years, and rising from around US$ 170 billion ten years ago (*FT*, 23 May 2005). Hedge funds account for only around 2 per cent of total financial assets. Due to their high leverage, their use of derivatives and their active trading policy, they account for around two-fifths of daily trading in equity markets in the United Kingdom and the United States, and on some days as much as 70 per cent (*FT*, 29 September 2004). Investors in hedge funds are 'impatient for results'. They expect hedge fund managers to be 'more aggressive and to take larger bets in their search for much higher returns' (*FT*, 29 September 2004). The sector has been widely criticised for its aggressive use of leverage, pursuit of short-term momentum trading and heavy involvement in 'increasingly esoteric and illiquid markets in pursuit of high returns' (*FT*, 14 May 2005).

Endogenous money supply: new sources of debt. Moreover, the sources of debt have expanded into forms that were unimaginable before the global business revolution. For example, two decades ago, derivatives didn't exist.[55] A huge variety of derivative products has emerged in recent years, based on predictions of price changes in currencies,[56] interest rates, bonds, equities and equity indices, and commodities. The market for credit derivatives and the associated new types of debt[57] has exploded. Today, derivatives are a hugely important part of the global financial system. By 2004, the global total of outstanding notional amounts of all types of derivatives reached US$ 500 trillion (HSBC, 2005).[58] This compares with a global 'gross national income' of US$ 32 trillion in 2002 (World Bank, WDI, 2004). Investors now have 'a dizzying array' of corporate bond and debt instruments to choose from (*FT*, 17 June 2005).

The glut of global savings in search of high yield has stimulated investors into ever more risky asset classes in order to generate high returns. Important segments of risk are located in areas of the economy that are not regulated by financial authorities.[59] The new financial instruments are extremely complex, with risks that are often not fully understood by the investors. Derivatives often invest in each other's products, increasing the leverage and risk for end-investors, so that a collapse in one part of the system could rapidly spread to other parts (*FT*, 16 February 2005). Nor have they been tested in the face of acute economic stress. Financial instruments such as collateralised debt obligations (CDOs) which are widely dispersed throughout the economic system has spread risk widely. However, the fact that such a wide array of financial institutions, pension funds, banks, hedge funds, and insurance companies, have all 'piled into the sector', means that 'if a nasty accident did ever occur with CDOs it could ricochet through the financial system in unexpected ways' (*FT*, 19 April 2005).

Increased indebtedness in high-income economies. In the high-income economies, the asset prices bubble, especially that in property, has formed the foundation for an explosive growth of credit, both to fund speculation and to fund current consumption. Whereas East Asian economies have saved an extremely high share of income, in the high-income countries, based on a self-inflating asset bubble, levels of personal indebtedness have reached extraordinary heights. By 2004, the US population's savings rate stood at minus one per cent, compared with 35 per cent in China (Roach, 2005). The level of household debt in the Unites States has risen remorselessly, from 60 per cent of household income in the mid-1980s to over 120 per cent in 2004 (*FT*, 16 February 2005). In the United States, the share of consumption has risen from around 65 per cent in the early 1980s to 71 per cent in 2004 (Roach, 2005). The United States accounts for only around 5 per cent of global population, but it accounts for no less than 35-40 per cent of global consumption.

Consequences of asset bubbles. The consequences of the unprecedented asset bubble are extremely serious. They have led to a large redistribution of wealth in high-income economies towards those with higher incomes and those who already own larger asset holdings. They reward speculation over investment in production of goods and services. They encourage a culture of borrowing and indebtedness.

Most seriously, when the bubbles burst, it will lead to massive global consequences. It will cause a widespread financial sector crisis, penetrating deep into the sectors that have absorbed risk, which are now much more widely distributed throughout the economic system of the high-income economies than before the global business revolution. It will cause a collapse of people's consumption, as the wealth effect takes hold and people in high-income economies seek to rebuild their savings. It will cause widespread anger in high-income economies as people are forced to curtail their spending in the face of a collapse of their wealth. The impact on consumption growth will affect the growth of demand for exports from developing countries, which will affect their socio-economic stability.

Absence of global financial system regulation. The global financial system is now deeply integrated across national boundaries, far more deeply even than the integration of production systems. However, the transition from primarily national to global markets has not been accompanied by a strengthening of international regulatory governance. In the view of many financial experts, there is 'no-one in charge at the global level' (*FT*, 15 March 2002). The IMF, the institution that is supposed to guide the global financial system, has been described as a 'rudderless ship in a sea of liquidity' (Barry Eichengreen, speaking at an IMF meeting in September 2005 (quoted in

Financial Times, 26 September 2005). At the same meeting Fred Bergsten, Director of the Institute for International Economics, said that the IMF's Strategic Review had 'provided too few answers to the questions [it] raised'.

Moreover, the complexity of the new financial instruments has made it extremely difficult for regulatory authorities to understand fully the nature of systemic global financial risk. The problem for regulators has been exacerbated by the fact that the global financial system has now developed instruments of such great complexity and at such a high speed, that no-one understands how to regulate the whole system, even assuming that the political mechanisms existed to do so. The spread of financial innovation is so dramatic that 'regulators, lawyers and rating agency officials struggle to keep up' (*FT*, 19 April 2005). Moreover, the massive extent of repacking and sale of debt means that debt is far more deeply distributed throughout the economy than was the case before the global business revolution. This provides a source of stability and enhances the ability of the financial system to ride out relatively small-scale crises, but means that the whole global financial system is far more susceptible to a giant financial crisis should it erupt.

There is deep unease among policy makers: 'We are in uncharted territory. If a crisis hits, we think the market will absorb shocks smoothly, but the truth is, no one knows for sure' (quoted in *Financial Times*, 19 April 2005).

Central role of the United States. The United States stands at the centre of the global financial system. Growth of the US domestic and international imbalances cannot expand indefinitely. In 2004, Alan Greenspan warned:

> Net claims against residents of the United States cannot continue to increase forever at their recent pace…Continued financing of today's current account deficits as a percentage of GDP will, at some future point, increase shares of dollar claims in investor portfolios to levels that imply an unacceptable amount of concentration of risk. International investors will eventually adjust their accumulation of dollar assets, or, alternatively, seek higher dollar returns to offset concentration of risk (quoted in *Financial Times*, 20 November 2004).

The necessary adjustments may occur smoothly. However, it is *'quite likely that the ultimate adjustment will be both swift and brutal'* (Martin Wolf, *FT*, 8 October 2005).

Lessons of history. The lessons of history suggest extreme caution in considering the potential for a global financial crisis to erupt. The world's largest financial crisis occurred in the early 1930s, following a period of price stability, and, even, price deflation at the end of the decade. The period preceding the crisis was characterised by rapid technological innovation, rising productivity, rapid increases in the prices of equity and real estate, and strong fixed investment. Behind these developments were technical innovations in the financial sector, not least the much greater availability of consumer credit (White, 2006: 7).

Financial risk and developing countries. In the epoch of the global business revolution, greatly increased 'freedom' for the giant global financial firms to allocate capital across international markets has contributed to a rise in global financial instability. The instability has been especially serious for developing countries, where financial crises can cause deep downturns in economic activity and threaten social stability. These have, in their turn, frequently led to the overthrow of national governments.

The number of financial crises has sharply increased since widespread liberalisation of financial markets began in the 1980s. The period since then has seen a succession of huge financial crises among developing countries. These include the Mexican Tequila Crisis of 1994-95; the Asian Financial Crisis of 1997-98; the Russian Crisis of 1998; and the Argentinian Crisis of 2001-02. In addition, there have been numerous smaller financial crises.

There are strong grounds for believing that capital flows to developing countries might be especially volatile. Both internal (e.g. weak domestic financial systems; frequent economic shocks) and external factors, particularly the animal spirits of foreign investors, make these flows volatile. Empirical evidence suggests a close link between financial liberalisation and financial crises in developing countries. The volatility and the pro-cyclicality of private capital flows to developing countries is a well-attested feature of international capital movements during the last two decades. Such in-flows come in surges, often bearing no relationship to the economic fundamentals of the country and leave the country when they are most needed, i.e. in a downturn. Also, the early phases of industrialisation are bound to have a tendency towards social and political instability. This further amplifies the potential for financial instability inherent in naturally occurring speculative bubbles. Moreover, the Bank for International Settlements has concluded that financial instability in developing countries tends to be increased where international financial firms dominate the financial systems, as it 'exposes local banking more directly to changes in global conditions' (reported in *Financial Times*, 5 December 2005).

The Asian Financial Crisis has led to a substantial modification of the views of senior officials in the IMF, which formerly was firmly in favour of capital account liberalisation. An IMF study has concluded that there is little hard evidence that developing countries with open capital accounts grow faster than those with closed accounts (reported in *Financial Times*, 21 August 2006). They emphasise that countries 'need to develop well-functioning institutions and reasonably mature capital markets before they can benefit from capital account liberalisation'. They emphasise that they also need to have 'decent corporate governance', appropriate economic and exchange rate policies and 'openness to trade' if they are to avoid financial crises alongside capital account liberalisation.

3.6 The Nation State

The Persistence of Nationalism in the Epoch of Globalisation

People are still tightly bound into the framework of the nation state. Firms have become truly global, and many aspects of culture have become globalised, especially for the global ruling elite. However, the nation state remains the primary basis of identity and political activity for the mass of humanity. People remain bound to particular countries through the accident of their birth. Most people cannot and do not wish to migrate to another country. Far from weakening nationalist feelings, economic development greatly strengthens nationalist feelings, Indeed, national identity typically is weak prior to modernisation. The growth of national identity occurs through the development of a national language and through universal education, typically led by the central government, and by the development of mass media.

US Military Dominance

Nowhere is the persistence of the state felt more powerfully than in the military sphere. Already, in the late 1990s the United States accounted for almost two-fifths of total world military spending (IISS, 1999: 37). Since then, the military spending of NATO (Europe) has stagnated, while the US annual spending on weapons has risen to over US$ 400 billion (IISS, 2005).

The United States has a stock of 8000 active or operational nuclear warheads, with an average destructive power that is twenty times that of the Hiroshima bomb (McNamara, 2005). The US government regards nuclear weapons as central to its military strategy for 'at least the next several decades' (McNamara, 2005). In 2004, the former Secretary of Defense William J. Perry said: 'I have never been more fearful of a nuclear detonation than now...There is a greater than 50 per cent probability of a nuclear strike on US targets within a decade'(quoted in McNamara, 2005). Once a nuclear battle begins, there is no way to contain the resulting conflict. The effects of using a modern nuclear weapon are devastating, inflicting certain 'enormous destruction on civilian life and property', and 'there is no guarantee against an unlimited escalation once the first strike occurs'. McNamara characterises the US nuclear weapons policy as 'immoral, illegal, militarily unnecessary, and dreadfully dangerous...The risk of an accidental or inadvertent nuclear launch is unacceptably high' (McNamara, 2005).

American nuclear technology has advanced at high speed. The United States believes that it now has the ability to destroy the nuclear capability of any potential enemy without the risk of retaliation. Its potential enemies would 'have no warning at all of a US submarine-launched missile attack or a strike using hundreds of stealthy nuclear-armed cruise missiles' (Lieber and Press, 2006: 49).

Economic Crisis and Military Conflict

A random disturbance to the global system, such as a financial crisis, especially if it attacks the United States, has the potentiality to spiral at high speed into a global nuclear catastrophe. Such a possibility is increased by the deep uncertainties within the advanced capitalist countries, especially the United States, created by the growing inequalities of income and wealth, and the fact that the core of the economic system, the giant firm, has a greatly weakened allegiance to any particular country.

4. Groping for a Way Forward

The exercise of individual freedoms has been inseparable from the expansion of the market, driven by the search for profit. This force, namely capitalism, has stimulated human creativity in ways that have produced immense benefits. As capitalism has broadened its scope in the epoch of globalisation, so these benefits have become even greater. However, capitalist freedom is a two-edged sword. In the epoch of capitalist globalisation, its contradictions have intensified. As human beings have taken to new heights their ability to free themselves from fundamental constraints through the market mechanism, so they also have reached new depths in terms of the uncontrollability of the structures they have created. Global capitalism has created uniquely intense threats to the very existence of the human species at the same time that it has liberated humanity more than ever before from fundamental constraints on their lives. While different countries and regions can contribute to the solution of some of these contradictions, the deeply interdependent nature of capitalist globalisation means that the fundamental solutions can only be accomplished at a global level. The Astronomer Royal, Lord Rees, believes that 'the odds are no better than fifty-fifty that our present civilisation on Earth will survive to the end of the present century' (Rees, 2003: 8).

If humanity cannot find a 'mean', its prospects for survival are bleak. The destruction of human civilisation may arise either from the internal self-destructiveness of extreme free market individualism, or from the nihilistic response of those excluded and angered by the globalisation of the free market.

Relations between the United States and China will be central to the possibilities for cooperative global solutions to the contradictions of capitalist globalisation. If China can find solutions to its own challenges, and build a 'harmonious society' and a new path of sustainable economic development it can make a huge contribution to the challenges facing the world. It is critically important that the United States engages positively with China, permitting China's 'peaceful rise', so that the two countries can cooperate in finding solutions to the challenges facing the world, arising from the contradictory character of capitalist globalisation.

It may only be the approaching 'final hour' which finally forces human beings to grope their way towards globally cooperative solutions. The falling of the 'dusk', as humanity looks into the abyss, may be the final impulse to produce the cooperative solution that is immanent within the unfolding of global capitalism: 'The owl of Minerva spreads its wings only with the falling of the dusk' (Hegel, 1952: 13).

Notes

1. In the case of China, these included gunpowder, steel-making, the canal lock gate, the compass, the wheelbarrow, the windmill, mechanical clockwork, water-powered metallurgical blowing machines, water-powered trip hammers for forges, hemp spinning machines, gear wheels, power transmission by driving belt, the sternpost rudder, watertight compartments, and the crank (Needham, 1954-).
2. Including the Civil War and anti-Japanese Wars in China, the war in the Pacific, and the First and Second World Wars.
3. Indeed, the common response of most economists, both 'radical' and mainstream, is denial, and endless manipulation of data to attempt to 'prove' that industrial concentration is not in fact taking place, and to suggest that technical progress, insofar as it is acknowledged to be taking place, is the product mainly of small and medium-sized firms. However, the reality of the technical transformation of this epoch and the consequences of oligopolistic competition for real price declines, are obvious to most people through their daily lives.
4. Economists' reduction of 'technical progress' to the so-called 'residual' in the 'production function', which remains after account has been taken of the contribution to economic growth of increased inputs of 'capital' and 'labour', is embarrassingly superficial.

5. There remain barriers to cross-border acquisitions in certain East Asian countries. However, even these barriers are slowly falling, including the rapid growth of international acquisition of South Korean financial institutions. Some significant barriers remain to international mergers and acquisitions within the EU, especially those affecting Italian, German and French financial institutions. While EU-based financial services firms push strongly for the rest of the world, especially developing countries, to allow them free access to their markets for merger and acquisition, certain EU countries are reluctant to allow international financial firms to merge with and acquire local financial firms.

6. Formed from Salomon Brothers Investment Bank, Travellers Group, Citicorp, and Schroders' investment banking business.

7. Formed, inter alia, from Deutsche Bank, Morgan Grenfell and Bankers Trust.

8. Formed, inter alia, from HSBC Holdings, Republic New York, and Banque Hervet.

9. Formed, inter alia, from J. P. Morgan, Chase Manhattan, Robert Fleming and Bank One.

10. Formed, inter alia, from Bank of America and Fleet Boston.

11. Following the acquisition of Mexico's Bannamex by Citigroup, the *Financial Times* commented: 'The acquisition [of Bannamex] underscored the rapacious appetite of Citigroup…for assets in the developing world, and Citigroup executives made it clear that they will pursue similar deals in other emerging markets' (*FT*, 18 May 2001). Following its take-over of Poland's Bank Handlowy, Citigroup announced that increasing its operations in China was 'top of our radar screen' (*FT*, 18 January 2002).

12. Derived from WB, WDR, 2001, Tables 3 and 11, and WB, WDI, 2006, Tables 2.1 and 4.1.

13. At a price of around US$ 70 per barrel, there are at least 200 years of oil reserves contained in tar sands. Shale oil contains an estimated eight times more energy than in all other forms of fossil fuel combined, including oil, gas, coal, peat, and tar sands. Coastlines of most countries have huge amounts of gas contained within crystals. The total reserves of 'gas in crystals' are larger than all known reserves of fossil fuels added together, and the techniques for gaining access to these gases could be commercially viable within 15 years (Mottershead, 2005).

14. These include improvements in internal combustion engine technologies; the use of hybrid vehicles which combine the internal combustion engine with the addition of an electric motor; pure electric vehicles which may ultimately be powered with electricity generated from renewable sources, eventually from solar power, or from fossil fuels accompanied by carbon dioxide sequestration; and expanded use of biofuels, which are carbon dioxide neutral.

15. The proportion of the rural population of low-income countries with access to improved water sources (defined as 'the availability of at least 20 litres per person per day from a source within one kilometre of the dwelling) rose from 59 per cent in 1990 to 70 per cent in 2000 (WD, WDI, 2004: 134).

16. In low-income countries, the proportion of the urban population with access to improved sanitation facilities (defined as 'at least adequate excreta disposal facilities (private or shared but not public) that can effectively prevent human, animal and insect contact with excreta') rose from 58 per cent in 1990 to 71 per cent in 2000, while in the rural areas it rose from 20 per cent to 31 per cent in the same period (WB, WDI, 2004: 154).

17. In high-income countries, infant mortality fell from 22 per thousand live births in 1970 to 5 per thousand in 2002, while life expectancy at birth rose from 71 years to 78 years.

18. Even in low-income countries, by 2002 there were 139 radios per thousand people and 91 TV sets (UNDP, 2004: 298).

19. By 2002, developing countries contained 69 per cent of the total global urban population (UNDP, 2004: 155).

20. Using the data from these different international studies, Sutcliffe has calculated that the global Gini coefficient of the distribution of world income fell from around 0.58-0.62 in 1980 to around 0.52-0.56 in 1998 (Sutcliffe, 2002: 14). These studies all use 'purchasing power parity' (PPP) data.

21. In low-income countries, between 1979-81 and 2000-02 the amount of fertiliser applied per hectare of arable land rose from 289 grams to 717 grams, the number of tractors per square kilometre of arable land rose from 20 to 66 and irrigated land increased its share of total cropland from 19.8 per cent to 26.4 per cent (WB, WDI, 2004: 122-3).

22. For variants on this view see Ohmae, 1990, and Fukuyama, 1992.

23. The term 'capitalism' was not used until after both Smith and Mill died.

24. When he assumed the Presidency in 1933, Franklin D. Roosevelt proclaimed: 'For too many Americans, life is no longer free; liberty no longer real; men can no longer follow the pursuit of happiness' (quoted in Foner, 1998: 196).

25. Already, measured in PPP dollars, the low and middle-income countries account for 45 per cent of global Gross National Income, and their growth rate is over double that of the high-income countries (WB, WDI, 2006: Table 1.1). However, their per capita income is only 15 per cent of that of the high-income countries (in PPP dollars).

26. Burning oil releases about 50 per cent more carbon dioxide than burning natural gas, and burning coal releases about twice as much (WB, WDI, 2004: 147).

27. Throughout the period of human life on earth, levels of carbon dioxide in the atmosphere fluctuated between around 190 ppm (during 'Cold Periods') and around 260 ppm (during 'Warm Periods'). Human civilisation in its present form is usually thought to have begun with the onset of a Warm Period around 60 000 years ago (King, 2005)

28. The main negative impact is likely to take place in developing countries. In high-income countries it is possible that global warming could lead to increased yields.

29. Japan consumes 6.4 per cent of the world total, China consumes 8.5 per cent and the rest of the Region consumes 14.1 per cent (BP, 2006: 11).

30. Japan's oil imports were stagnant.

31. It is forecast that by 2020, China will be importing as much as three-quarters of its total oil consumption.

32. With 4.7 per cent of the world's population, the United States accounts for 24 per cent of the world's carbon dioxide production (WB, WDI, 2006: 3.8).

33. GDP (in PPP dollars) per kilogram of oil equivalent in low and middle-income countries rose from 3.1 in 1990 to 4.2 in 2003 (WB, WDI, 2006: 3.8).

34. The low and middle-income countries have already overtaken the high-income countries in terms of the production of nitrous oxide. In 2002, they accounted for 71 per cent of the global total (WB, WDI, 2006: Table 3.8).

35.   The agreement specifies that the signatories will ensure that in 2010 their carbon dioxide emissions will be 5.2 per cent below those of 1990 (Lomborg, 2001: 302). The principle mechanism through which they hope to achieve this is by trading carbon permits. These are allocated to production establishments in the main polluting industries, which can trade the resulting right to pollute, selling them if they produce less than the fixed target, and buying them if they over-pollute relative to the target for the particular establishment.

36.   The number of motor vehicles increased from 758 per 1000 people in 1990 to 808 per thousand in 2003. The distance covered by road traffic rose from 2.5 trillion vehicle kilometres in 1990 to 4.2 trillion in 2003 (WB, WDI, 2006, Table 3.12).

37.   It is predicted that the number of vehicles in China will rise from 24 million in 2005 to 100 million in 2020 (Bergston, et al, 2006: 54).

38.   We may very loosely define the globalised elite as those earning more than US$ 50,000 per year.

39.   It cannot be stressed enough that these data employ the PPP measure of income, with all the inadequacies that this entails, and have only flimsy data on a small number of countries for changes over time in income distribution.

40.   The workforce in the high-income countries in 2002 was 647 million, compared with 3.3 billion in the low and middle-income countries as a whole, and 1747 million in the four 'BRIC' countries (Brazil, Russia, India and China) (WB, WDI, 2004: 38-40).

41.   Recent research shows that an American child born in the bottom-fifth income group has just a one per cent chance of becoming 'rich' (defined as the top 5 per cent of American income earners), whereas a child born rich has a 22 per cent chance of remaining rich as an adult (*F T*, 3 May 2006).

42.   In recent years, many economists and sociologists have been influenced by the rise of outsourcing and the impact of new information technology. They consider that a new 'post-Fordist' paradigm has arisen in which networks of small and medium-sized firms have replaced the large corporation, and, indeed, the large corporation has been 'hollowed out'.

43.   Non-mainstream economists in the Austrian tradition, notably Joseph Schumpeter, but more recently including economists such as Edith Penrose, also believe that capitalism contains an inherent tendency towards growth in size of the large corporation and industrial concentration.

44.   These dramatic developments are consistent with the persistence in most sectors of a large number of small and medium-sized firms, which produce mainly non-branded, low technology products, supplying local markets, and which collectively occupy a small share of total global markets. These parts of the segmented industrial structure typically supply the lower groups within each country's income distribution.

45.   There were nine firms from Korea and seven from Taiwan (DTI, 2004).

46.   At current rates of growth China will not overtake the United States's manufacturing output until some time between 2020 and 2025 (WB, WDI, 2004, Section 4).

47.   A group of five small European countries (Denmark, Finland, The Netherlands, Sweden, and Switzerland) has a total of 92 firms in the world's top 1000 companies ranked by R&D expenditure (DTI, 2005).

48.   These include (in descending order of revenue within Brazil in 2001) Volkswagen (2), GM (3), Fiat (5), Unilever (7), Bunge Foods (9), Phillip Morris (10), Nestlé (11), Ford (12), Cargill (13), DaimlerChrysler (16), Siemens (20), Ericsson (21), BASF (22), and Motorola (24).

49. For example, Siemens, a 'German' firm, has 753 international affiliates, has 59 per cent of its assets and employment abroad, and generates 76 per cent of its sales from foreign markets. Proctor and Gamble, an 'American' firm, has 174 international affiliates, has 58 per cent of its assets, 55 per cent of its sales and 63 per cent of its employment abroad.

50. As long as market participants herd, which they have been doing for as long as markets have existed, the spread of sophisticated risk systems based on the daily evolution of market prices will spread instability, not quell it.

51. For example, in the United Kingdom by 2006 housing wealth had reached 59 per cent of personal wealth (*FT*, 25 July 2006). By 2006, letting of dwellings had become the largest single sector in the UK economy, exceeding sectors such as banking and finance, construction, and even health services (*FT*, 21 August 2006).

52. US mortgage debt has reached around US$ 12 000 billion (*FT*, 17 April 2006).

53. From 14.8 million tonnes to 16.4 million tonnes (*FT*, 24 May 2006).

54. In fact, the term 'hedge funds' is a misnomer in relation to hedge funds today. There is now little difference between the strategy employed by hedge funds and that employed by a traditional asset manager, except that the hedge fund manager is more aggressive. Contrary to popular myth, hedge funds are 'merely vehicles through which people invest in underlying assets: equities, bonds, currencies, commodities and real estate': 'The time has come to stop talking about hedge funds versus non-hedge funds, and to think about asset management as comprised of active and passive investors, with hedge funds as ultra-active management' (*FT* Editorial, 18 August 2005).

55. Derivatives products are so called because they derive from the price of another product.

56. Turnover on global foreign exchange markets has soared since the 1980s, driven by investor interest in currencies as an asset class. The foreign exchange market is 'by far the world's biggest financial market' in terms of trading volume. Trading on the world's foreign exchange markets soared to a record level of US$ 1900 billion per day in April 2004 from around US$ 1100 billion in 1995 (*FT*, 29 September 2004). The growth in the foreign exchange market includes currency bets by hedge funds, often in the form of 'macro funds' making big currency bets (*FT*, 29 September 2004). Turnover in currency and interest rate derivatives has also soared in recent years.

57. These include such structured credit instruments as 'residential mortgage-backed securities' (RMBS), 'commercial mortgage-backed securities' (CMBS), and numerous other 'asset-backed securities' (ABS) including 'collateralised loan obligations' (CLOs), and 'collateralised debt obligations' (CDOs). CDOs consist of re-packaged pools of credit derivatives based on dozens of corporate credits. Although each CDO includes hundreds of corporate names, the same firms appear in almost all CDOs.

58. In 2004, within the total derivatives market, interest rate derivatives accounted for 43 per cent of the total, currency derivatives accounted for 24.9 per cent of the total, commodity derivatives for 24.7 per cent, and various other types for the remaining 7.4 per cent (HSBC, 2005).

59. For example, most 'hedge funds' are based 'offshore' to minimise tax liabilities for the fund and the investors, and are 'unrestrained' (*FT*, 11 March 2005).

References

Bairoch, P., 'International industrialization levels from 1750 to 1980', *Journal of European Economic History* (Fall 1982)

BP, *World Energy Review* (London: BP, 1999)

BP, *World Energy Review* (London: BP, 2005)

BP, *World Energy Review* (London: BP, 2006)

Bergsten, F., B. Gill, N. R. Lardy and D. Mitchell, *China: The Balance Sheet* (New York: Public Affairs, 2006)

Bush, G.W., 'America's Security Strategy' (Washington DC: The White House, 2002)

Bush, G.W., *National Security Strategy of the United States of America* (Washington DC: The White House, 2006)

Chandler, A., *The Visible Hand* (Cambridge, Mass.: Harvard University Press, 1977)

Chang, Song, 'Consolidation and Internationalization in the Global Banking Industry since 1980s, and the Implication for Chinese Banking Reform' (Judge Business School, University of Cambridge: Doctoral Dissertation, 2005)

Coase, R. H., 'The nature of the firm', in R. H. Coase, *The Firm, the Market and the Law* (Chicago: University of Chicago Press, 1988) (originally published 1937)

Department of Trade and Industry, *The UK R&D Scoreboard, 2004* (London: DTI, 2004)

Department of Trade and Industry, *The UK R&D Scoreboard, 2005* (London: DTI, 2005)

Eichengreen, B., and K. Mitchener, 'The Great Depression as a credit boom gone wrong', *BIS Working Papers,* No 137 (2003)

Foner, E., *The Story of American Freedom* (New York: W.W.Norton, 1998)

Fukuyama, F., *The end of history and the last man* (Harmondsworth: Penguin Books, 1992)

Hegel, G. F, *The Philosophy of Right* (English edition, Oxford: Oxford University Press, 1952) (German edition originally published 1820)

Hobsbawm, E., *Nations and nationalism since 1780* (Cambridge: Cambridge University Press, 1990)

HSBC, Presentation to China Executive Learning Programme, Cambridge (2005)

Huntington, S. P., *Who are we?* (London: Simon and Schuster, 2004)

International Institute of Strategic Studies, *The Military Balance, 1998-99* (London: IISS, 1999)

International Institute of Strategic Studies, *The Military Balance, 2004-05* (London, IISS, 2005)

Keynes, J. M., *The General Theory of Employment, Interest and Money* (London: Macmillan, 1936)

Kindleberger, C.P., *Manias, crashes and panics* (London: Wiley, 1996)

King, D., 'The challenge of global warming', Presentation to China Executive Learning Programme, Cambridge (2005)

Klare, M., *Blood and Oil* (London: Hamish Hamilton, 2004)

Lewis, A., 'Economic development with unlimited supplies of labour', *The Manchester School* (May, 1954)

Lieber, K., and D. Press, 'The rise of China's nuclear supremacy', *Foreign Affairs* (March/April, 2006)

Lomborg, B., *The Skeptical Environmentalist* (Cambridge: Cambridge University Press, 2001)

Marx, K., and F. Engels, *The Communist Manifesto*, in Marx, K., and F.Engels, *Marx and Engels: Selected Works* (London; Lawrence and Wishart, 1968) (*The Communist Manifesto* originally published 1848)

McNamara, R., 'Apocalypse soon', *Foreign Policy* (May/June, 2005)

Mill, J.S., *Principles of Political Economy* (Oxford: Oxford University Press, 1998) (originally published 1848)

Mottershead, C., 'Energy and climate change' (London: BP, 2005)

Needham, J., *Science and Civilisation in China* (Cambridge: Cambridge University Press, 1954-)

Nolan, P., *China and the Global Business Revolution* (Basingstoke: Palgrave Macmillan, 2001)

Ohmae, K., *The borderless world* (London: Collins, 1990)

Oliva, P., 'Energy and the environment: the case of the automobile industry', Presentation to China Executive Learning Programme, Cambridge (2005)

Piketty, T., and E.Saez, 'The evolution of top incomes: a historical and international perspective', National Bureau of Economic Research, Working Paper 11955 (2006)

Rees, M., *Our Final Hour* (New York: Basic Books, 2003)

Roach, S., Presentation to China Executive Learning Programme, Cambridge, (2005)

Shiller, R., *Irrational Exuberance* (Princeton: Princeton University Press, 2001)

Singh, A., 'Globalisation and financial liberalisation', mimeo (2002)

Smith, A., *The Theory of Moral Sentiments* (Oxford: Oxford University Press, 1976a) (originally published 1761)

Smith, A., *The Wealth of Nations* (Chicago: University of Chicago Press, Cannan edition, 1976b) (originally published 1776)

Stiglitz, J., *Globalisation and its discontents* (Harmondsworth: Penguin Books, 2002)

Sorrell, M., 'The advertising and marketing services industry: outlook good and getting better' in WPP, *Annual Report, 2004* (WPP, 2005)

Sutcliffe, B., *A more or less unequal world? World income distribution in the 20th century* (Bilbao: University of the Basque Country, 2002)

UNCTAD, *World Investment Report, 200* (Geneva: UNCTAD, 2003)

UNDP, *Human Development Report, 2002* (New York: UNDP, 2002)

UNDP, *Human Development Report, 2004* (New York: UNDP, 2004)

US-China Economic and Security Review Commission (USCESRC), *Report to Congress* (Washington DC: US Government Printing Office, 2005)

White, W., 'Is price stability enough?', *BIS Working Papers*, No 205 (2006)

Wolf, M., *Why Globalisation Works* (London and New Haven: Yale University Press, 2004)

World Bank, *World Development Report* (WDR) (Washington DC: Oxford University Press, 1990)

World Bank, *World Development Report, 1999-2000: Entering the Twenty-First century* (Washington: Oxford University Press, 2000)

World Bank, *World Development Indicators* (WDI) (Washington DC: Oxford University Press, 2001)

World Bank, *World Development Indicators* (WDI) (Washington DC: Oxford University Press, 2004)

World Bank, *World Development Indicators* (WDI) (Washington DC: Oxford University Press, 2006)

Chapter 8

CAPITALISM, CONFLICT AND COOPERATION: US-CHINA RELATIONS UNDER CAPITALIST GLOBALISATION

Peter Nolan and Jin Zhang

Introduction

Since ancient times, the pursuit of profit by capitalists has stimulated human creativity in ways that have produced immense benefits. As capitalism has broadened its scope in the epoch of globalisation, these benefits have increased enormously. Human beings have been liberated to a far greater degree than hitherto from the tyranny of nature, from control by others over their lives, from poverty, and from war.

However, capitalist freedom is a two-edged sword. In the epoch of globalisation, its contradictions have intensified. Inequality has increased in both rich and poor countries. The threat to the natural environment has deepened. Capitalist globalisation has produced a high degree of instability in global finance. Its surging contradictions may even result in the obliteration of the human species through nuclear war. Capitalist globalisation has created uniquely intense threats to the very existence of the human species at the same time that it has liberated humanity more than ever before from fundamental constraints.

Since the late 1970s, under the leadership of the Chinese Communist Party, China's policy of reform and opening up has led to it becoming ever more deeply integrated with the capitalist global economy. This has enabled it to benefit from the 'advantages of the latecomer' and to the release of its latent productive forces based on a long history of capitalist development

(Xu Dixin and Wu Chengming, 2000). It has produced remarkable economic growth and transformation of Chinese people's standard of living. However, the very success of China's engagement with global capitalism has produced deep contradictions, including rising inequality, declining energy security, worsening ecological damage, and serious difficulties in competing with the world's leading firms. Resolving these contradictions is a central task for the Chinese leadership. This is a 'choice of no choice'. Sustainable development in China requires that it must achieve balanced development and establish a 'harmonious society'.

Capitalist globalisation has had a contradictory impact also on the United States. It has brought great benefits to American firms, American shareholders, and American consumers. However, it has also brought deep challenges. These include a sharp increase in inequality, a decline in energy security and an increased threat to the natural environment, erosion of national identity among leading American firms, and potential financial instability. China's rise is increasingly the scapegoat for American difficulties that arise from capitalist globalisation.

Despite its increasingly universal character in the epoch of globalisation, capitalism retains deep roots within individual nations, each with their own national interests and internal contradictions that influence their international relations. The tension between the universalising impulse of capitalism and the archaic structure of the nation state remains intense. The contradictory character of capitalist globalisation is crystallised in US-China relations. There is a serious possibility of deep conflict between them, which would be a catastrophe for humanity. Faced with such a terrible possibility, US-China cooperation is the only rational path for the leadership of the two countries to pursue. They can benefit from mutual support in resolving the stresses that capitalist globalisation brings to both countries and to the whole global community.

1. China

1.1 China's Rise

Since the 1980s, China's policies of experimental reform and opening-up ('groping for stones to cross the river') have produced a remarkable economic performance. From 1990 to 2002, China's growth rate of GDP averaged 9.7 per cent per annum, compared with 3.4 per cent among low and middle-income countries and 2.5 per cent for high-income countries (WB, WDI, 2004). China rose from being the world's seventh largest producer of manufacturing output in 1990 to the third largest in 2005. Its exports grew at over 13 per cent per annum between 1990 and 2001, and it rose from the world's fourteenth largest exporter in 1990 to the third largest in 2005. Global corporations view China as central to their long-term strategy. By 2002 it had overtaken the United States as the country with the largest FDI inflows (UNCTAD, 2003: Table B.1). Over the course of the past two decades, China's indigenous large enterprises have undertaken large-scale evolutionary institutional change. They have grown rapidly and absorbed a great deal of modern technology. They have learned how to compete in the marketplace. A large group of them has floated on international stock markets. The number of Mainland Chinese firms in the *Fortune* 500 increased from just three in the late 1990s to fourteen in 2004.

The explosion of market forces in China after the 1970s, alongside the progressive deepening of China's engagement with global capitalism, transformed people's lives. The World Bank estimates that the proportion of the rural population in poverty declined from 31 per cent in 1979 to 13 per cent in 1982, 'a speed and scale of poverty decline that is unprecedented in human history' (WB, 1986: 30). The share of urban dwellers in the total population rose from 17 per cent in 1975 to 38 per cent in 2002 (WB, WDI, 2004).[1] The nature of employment changed decisively, away from farming: the number employed in the non-farm sector rose from 118 million (30 per cent) to 412 million (56 per cent) in the same period (SSB, ZTN, 2003: 128).[2] The proportion of the population with access to sustainable improved sanitation rose from 29 per cent in 1990 to 40 per cent in 2000 (WB, WDI, 2004). The infant mortality rate fell from 85 per thousand live births in 1970 to 31 in 2002, and life expectancy at birth rose from 63 years in 1970-75 to 71 years in 2000-05. The rate of illiteracy fell from 23 per cent in 1982 to 7 per cent in 2000 (SSB, ZTN, 2003: 99). The number of mobile phone subscribers rose from a negligible level in 1990 to 161 per thousand in 2002 (WB, WDI, 2004), and the number of internet users increased from 20 million in 2000 to 110 million in 2005 (*FT*, 13 May 2006).

1.2 China's Globalisation Challenge

Alongside the immensely positive impacts, China's deep engagement with capitalist globalisation has been accompanied by surging contradictions.

Poverty and Inequality

Behind almost every aspect of China's development process in the early twenty-first century lies the harsh reality of the 'Lewis model' of economic development with unlimited supplies of labour (Lewis, 1954). China has a huge population of almost 1.3 billion, almost 70 per cent of whom still live in the countryside.[3] Chinese official data show that there are approximately 580 million rural dwellers (73 per cent of rural households) with less than US$ 360 per year (SSB, ZTN, 2002: 343).[4] The great extent of rural underemployment provides intense incentives for rural-urban migration, and severe downward pressure on non-farm wages in unskilled and low-skilled occupations. There are as many as 150 million rural migrants working in the urban areas. They are predominantly unskilled labour, earning US$ 1-2 per day.

Around 300 million Chinese workers, a large fraction of whom are illegal 'immigrant' workers, are now employed in the non-farm 'informal' sector, without the protection of trade unions, mainly in small enterprises with little regulation over conditions of work, and without unemployment or health insurance. Furthermore, around 40-50 million workers have lost their jobs due to reform in state-owned enterprises. On the other hand, large amounts of FDI by multinational firms is helping to produce clusters of modern businesses and residential areas, in which the relatively affluent urban middle class is isolated and protected from the surrounding mass of poor people.

The national Gini Coefficient rose from 0.30 in 1978 to 0.45 in 2002 (UNDP, 2005: 56-8). In 2002, the Gini Coefficient for the distribution of wealth reached 0.55, while that for the distribution of housing values was 0.74 and that for the distribution of the value of consumer durables was 0.84 (UNDP, 2005: 69). In 2002, the top ten per cent of the Chinese population accounted for 32 per cent of national income, 41 per cent of total wealth and 49 per cent of financial assets (UNDP, 2005: 69).

The Global Business Revolution

Since the 1980s, China has implemented industrial policies intended to nurture a group of globally competitive large indigenous firms. However, this period has witnessed a revolution in world business. It has seen a unique intensity of merger and acquisition. An unprecedented degree of global industrial concentration has been established. A veritable 'law' has come into play. Within the high value-added, high technology, and/or strongly branded market segments, a handful of giant firms, the 'systems integrators', occupy upwards of one-half of the global market (Nolan, 2001a and 2001b; Nolan et al, 2007). The process of concentration cascades across the value chain. The leading firms in each sector select the most capable suppliers, in a form of 'industrial planning', adopting 'aligned partners' who can work with them across the world. A 'cascade effect' has produced intense pressures upon first tier suppliers, forcing them to develop leading global positions, achieved through expanded research and development, and investment in global production networks. The result is a fast-developing process of concentration at a global level in numerous industries that supply the systems integrators.

This intense industrial concentration among both systems integrators and their supply chain, brought about through pressure from the 'cascade effect', presents a comprehensive challenge for Chinese firms. Not only do they face immense difficulties in catching up with the leading systems integrators, who occupy that part of the 'iceberg' that is visible 'above the water'. They also face immense difficulties in catching up with the powerful firms that now dominate almost every segment of the supply chain, the invisible part of the 'iceberg' that lies hidden from view.

Three years after China joined the WTO, a senior government official from the State-owned Assets and Administration Commission (SASAC) acknowledged: 'There is still a huge gap between China's large enterprises and the world's leading multinational companies, whether one looks at the comparison in terms of their number, scale or efficiency, or from the angle of strength of profits and innovative capability, or internationalisation'. Successful late-comer industrialising countries, from the United States in the late nineteenth century to South Korea in the late twentieth century, each produced a group of globally competitive firms. China is the first successful latecomer not to have done so. The fact that the world's sixth largest economy (the second largest in PPP terms) (WB, WDI, 2004) has not produced a substantial group of internationally competitive large firms is highly significant in the history of modern capitalist development.

Energy and the Environment

China's success in becoming the 'world's workshop' has been achieved at a high price in terms of environmental deterioration. Fast-growing developing countries typically experience a phase of environmental deterioration until average incomes rise beyond a certain point, at which point the environment begins to improve.[5] China is likely to remain for many years firmly locked into the phase of environmental deterioration unless drastic action is taken by the Chinese state.

The area affected by serious soil erosion has increased to include around 38 per cent of the entire country (UNDP, 2002: 70). The area of desert is increasing at the rate of around 2500 square kilometres per year, equivalent to the area of a medium-sized country. China's area of natural forests is falling at an alarming rate. There is 'rampant water pollution', and a serious and worsening shortage of fresh water. China's emission of organic water pollutants is as large as that of the United States, India, Russia and Japan combined (WB, 2004: Table 3.6). Recent Chinese provincial-level studies of 'Green National Product' estimate that there is only negligible 'real growth' when destruction of the natural environment is taken into account.

The country's explosive industrial growth since the late 1980s, which has been deeply integrated into capitalist globalisation, has been highly 'commodity-intensive' and highly energy-intensive. In 2005, China accounted for around four per cent of global GDP, but it consumed nine per cent of global crude oil, 20 per cent of aluminium, 30-35 per cent of steel, iron ore and coal, and 45 per cent of cement (*FT*, 23 May 2006). Between 1994 and 2004, China's total primary energy consumption increased by 71 per cent and its share of global primary energy consumption increased from 9.8 per cent to 13.6 per cent (BP, 2005).

China has large coal reserves, estimated to be around 13 per cent of the world total (BP, 2005). The relatively low cost of coal provides a strong incentive to continue to use coal as the main source of primary energy. It accounted for 69 per cent of China's primary energy consumption total in 2004 (BP, 2005). By the mid-1990s, China had overtaken the United States as the world's biggest coal producer, accounting for almost 30 per cent of global output. In the absence of large-scale technical change, such a high dependence on coal has enormous deleterious environmental implications, both for China and the world.

It is predicted that the number of automobiles in China will reach 50 million by 2010 (UNDP, 2002: 49). Solutions to urban air pollution, which is increasingly caused by automobile traffic, 'are sought through technical improvements rather than in alternative transport systems' (UNDP, 2002: 60). The rapid growth of passenger vehicles and trucks has significantly contributed to China's accelerating demand for oil. Between 1994 and 2004, China's oil consumption increased 113 per cent. However, China's oil reserves amount to only around 1.4 per cent of the world total (BP, 2005), and from 1994 to 2004 China's oil production only grew by 19 per cent. By 2004, China was importing 2.5 million barrels of oil per day, and the price of these imports has risen greatly since the mid-1990s. It is forecast that by 2020 China will be importing as much as three-quarters of its total oil consumption (USCESR, 2003: 8).

China is the world's second largest producer of carbon dioxide, standing at 50 per cent of the level of the United States, but its per capita emissions are still a mere 11 per cent of those of the United States (WB, WDI, 2004: Table 3.8). If China were to sustain its current growth path and at some point catch up with today's level of per capita income in the United States, and were to use similar technologies, China's emissions of carbon dioxide would be one-fifth greater than those of the entire world today.[6]

Today, China's per capita consumption of primary energy is only around one-ninth of that in the United States: the United States today consumes around eight metric tons (oil equivalent) of primary energy per person, compared with around 0.9 metric tons per person in China (WB, WDI, 2004: 140-2). If China were to climb to the United States' current level of per capita consumption of primary energy, it would consume more even than the current total world consumption (10 000 million metric tons) (WB, WDI, 2004: 142). There are many different scenarios for China's path of growth and for the role of technical progress both in energy production and consumption.[7] However, it is hard to imagine a scenario in which national energy security is not of central importance for China as its energy needs expand.

The Capability and Role of the State

China's outstanding economic performance since the 1980s is inseparable from the firm leadership and political stability provided by the Chinese Communist Party. However, the country's engagement with capitalist globalisation also poses deep challenges for the nature and function of the Chinese state.

China is a vast, poor country with urgent development needs, which can only be met by state action. Despite some increase in the government's fiscal strength in recent years, central government revenue still accounts for only around seven per cent of GDP (WB, WDI, 2004: Table 4.11). The share of central government revenue in GDP is below that of other large developing countries, such as India, Mexico, Pakistan, and Indonesia, as well as Russia. The state's fiscal weakness has forced it to look for drastically increased contributions from fees paid by individuals when they use health and education services. By the end of the 1990s, budgetary allocations covered just 46 per cent of actual expenditures on education (WB, 2002: 85). Between the late 1980s and mid-1990s, there was 'a substantial deterioration in the educational status of the poor' (WB, 2002: 42). The government budget funded just 11 per cent of total health expenditure, while 59 per cent came from out-of-pocket payments (WB, 2002: 43). By the year 2000, China ranked 61st out of 191 countries in overall quality of health, but it ranked 188th in terms of fairness in financial contribution to health expenditure (WB, 2002: iv).

The professional capability of the Chinese state has greatly increased since the early 1980s. However, in order adequately to serve China's development needs it requires comprehensive reinvigoration that goes far beyond improved technical competence. It needs substantially to expand its scope in order to undertake activities that the market is unable to provide. Improved public access to health and education is a central goal of the government's efforts to establish a 'harmonious society'.

Communist Party leadership is the foundation of China's modernisation. The Party is deeply intertwined with every aspect of socio-economic life. In the late 1980s and early 1990s, Deng Xiaoping warned repeatedly of the dangers of China collapsing into chaos. In his 2001 speech to celebrate the 80th anniversary of the founding of the Chinese Communist Party, Jiang Zemin stated: '[The Party] must address the two major historic subjects of enhancing the Party's ability of exercising state power and art of leadership, and resisting corruption and warding off risks...[W]e must be strict in Party discipline. We should have a deeper understanding of the loss of political power by some Communist Parties in the world that had long been ruling parties and learn a lesson from them'.

There has been widespread insider dealing and corruption during China's economic system restructuring, notably in the ubiquitous triangular relationship between the local Communist Party, the banks and the 'development' of publicly owned land, as well as the process of privatising state-owned enterprises. In recent years, the level at which Party members were tried and sentenced for corruption has risen to include many in high positions. These include a former deputy governor and former mayor of Shijiazhuang, Hebei's largest city; the mayor of one of China's largest cities, Shenyang; a former vice-minister of public security; a former chief of military intelligence; and a deputy chairman of the National People's Congress. Official reports to the National People's Congress in early 2003 declared that in the previous five years, the war against graft had been substantially stepped up, with a total of almost 13 000 prosecutions of government officials (*South China Morning Post*, 11 March 2003).

Financial Institutions

Engagement with the international financial system is, arguably, the most sensitive and difficult aspect of China's involvement with global capitalism. The Asian Financial Crisis provided a deep insight into the fragility of China's financial institutions. China appeared to escape any effects of the crisis, due to the fact that the *renminbi* was not fully convertible. In fact, the crisis had a deep impact through the medium of Hong Kong and the massive debts accumulated there by Mainland 'trust and investment' and 'red chip' companies, and other Mainland-based entities operating in Hong Kong. The most visible of these were GITIC (Guangdong Trust and Investment Company) and GDE (Guangdong Enterprises) which included five floated 'red chip' companies. During the Asian Financial Crisis, GITIC went into bankruptcy while GDE was insolvent and comprehensively restructured. Prior to the crisis, they each had been regarded as model institutions by international lenders. GITIC's bankruptcy and GDE's restructuring allowed the outside world to look closely inside large Chinese companies for the first time. The investigations revealed comprehensive failure in corporate governance, including disastrous lending practices: a large fraction of their loans were made to firms and institutions that were unable or unwilling to repay their debts. A substantial part of their 'investments' were highly speculative, including heavy participation in the property boom in Guangdong Province and Hong Kong.

After the Asian Financial Crisis, the central government began a massive 'clean up' of the country's financial institutions. The clean up revealed shocking evidence about the state of corporate governance in China's main banks. In early 2002, it was revealed that five bank officials at the Bank of China's branch in Kaiping city (Guangdong) had stolen the equivalent of nearly US$ 500 million. The problems penetrated to the apex of the country's banking system. Zhu Xiaohua, who held top positions in China's financial sector, including deputy governor of the People's Bank of China, head of China's foreign exchange reserves and head of China Everbright Bank, was arrested in 1999, and subsequently sentenced to fifteen years imprisonment. Wang Xuebing, formerly head of the China Construction Bank and then of the Bank of China, was arrested in 2002 and subsequently sentenced to twelve years imprisonment.

Since the late 1990s, the Chinese government has taken on a large fraction of the stock of non-performing loans (NPLs) in the state banking sector by establishing asset management companies to dispose of NPLs and recapitalise the banks, using bank profits and injecting cash from the state's coffers. Despite progress in reducing the stock of NPLs, especially in the four big state-owned banks, the level of NPLs remains a matter of serious concern. Many experts have drawn attention to the possibility that new NPLs may have replaced the old ones during the explosive growth of credit in the past few years. In 2006 Ernst & Young, PwC and McKinsey all produced reports saying that China's original stock of bad loans had not been fully dealt with and that a huge stock of new NPLs had been created in the meantime (*FT*, 4 May 2006).[8]

China's financial firms face escalating international competition under the terms of the WTO Agreement. Since the 1980s the world's leading financial firms have been through a period of unprecedented merger and acquisition. The period saw the emergence of super-large financial services firms, such as Citigroup, JP Morgan Chase, Bank of America and HSBC. They have rapidly acquired dominant positions in Latin America and Eastern Europe. After its acquisition of Banamex, one of Mexico's largest banks, Citigroup proclaimed: 'China is top of our radar screen' (Nolan, 2004: 57). If China's indigenous large financial firms cannot achieve their own self-reform, then the global giants are likely to assume an increasing role in the commanding heights of China's financial sector.

2. The United States

Capitalist globalisation has stimulated America's economic progress, but also produced deep internal policy challenges for the United States. These challenges are increasingly perceived within the United States as being linked with China's rise, rather than intrinsic to the contradictions of capitalist globalisation.

2.1 America's Dominance of Globalisation

The United States sits at the centre of capitalist globalisation. Despite China's rise, the United States still accounts for over 26 per cent of global manufacturing output (excluding production in overseas subsidiaries of firm headquartered in America) compared with around six per cent for China and at current rates of growth China will not overtake the US manufacturing output until some time between 2020 and 2025 (WB, WDI, 2004: Section 4). The United States is by far the world's most powerful stock market. Its share of the total value of global stock markets rose from 33 per cent in 1990 to 47 per cent in 2003 (WB, WDI, 2004: 268). In 2004, firms headquartered in North America accounted for 175 of the *Fortune* 500 companies (ranked by sales revenue) (*Fortune*, 26 July 2004). In the same year there were 247 North American firms in the *FT* 500 companies (ranked by market capitalisation), accounting for 55 per cent of the total market capitalisation of *FT* 500 firms (*FT*, 27 May 2004). The vast bulk of global technical progress takes place in a relatively small number of giant firms. Among these firms, those from North America are dominant. In 2005, out of the world's top 1000 firms ranked by R&D expenditure, 440 were headquartered in North America (DTI, 2005). The so-called 'BRIC' countries (Brazil, Russia, India and China), with a combined population of 2.7 billion (43 per cent of the world's total) between them had a mere nine firms among the world's top 1000 firms ranked by R&D expenditure.[9]

2.2 The De-stabilising Impact of Capitalist Globalisation upon the United States

Social Contradictions

Liberalisation of capital markets since the 1980s has opened up a vast world of low-priced labour across the 'transition' and 'developing' countries, including skilled and unskilled manual labour as well as scientists, engineers and managers. China is the largest single source of this greatly expanded labour supply to global markets. Global labour markets are being integrated mainly by migration of capital to poor countries rather than migration of workers to rich countries. This places intense pressure for international wage equalisation.

American workers are being forced to work longer hours, accept reduced rates of overtime pay, and accept reduced company contributions to health insurance and pensions. There are now 45 million Americans without health coverage, many of whom are full-time workers. During the epoch of capitalist globalisation, US income disparity has greatly increased. The income share of the top decile of the US population was stable at around 32-33 per cent from the 1960s to early 1980s, but thereafter it rose to around 43-44 per cent in 2000-02, which was the same income share that they received in the 1920s and 1930s. The share of the top one per cent of the distribution rose from less than eight per cent in the late 1960s and 1970s to around 15-17 per cent at the end of the 1990s (Piketty and Saez, 2006). Alongside the growing inequality in income, America's social mobility is lower than in every other developed country except for the United Kingdom.[10] Former Harvard President Larry Summers believes that 'the most serious problem facing the United States today is the widening gap between the children of the rich and children of the poor' (*New York Times*, 24 May 2005).

As consumers, American people have benefited enormously from globalisation, with an unprecedented fall in the price of most goods and services. However, as producers, they have faced greatly increased pressures. Ordinary Americans increasingly believe that the interests of nominally US-based multinational corporations and their shareholders are divorced from the interests of American citizens. 'One clear danger is that people will increasingly cast round for scapegoats' (Edward Luce in the *Financial Times*, 3 May 2006).

Energy and the Environment

The United States is by far the world's largest consumer of primary energy. Between 1990 and 2001 its consumption of primary energy rose by over 18 per cent, and by 2001 its share of the world total had increased to 22.8 per cent (WB, WDI, 2004: 142). The US oil production fell from 8.4 million barrels per day in 1990 to 7.2 million in 2004, while its oil consumption rose from 17.7 million barrels per day to 20.5 million barrels in the same period (BP, 2005). Net oil imports rose from 45 per cent of total consumption in 1994 to 58 per cent in 2004 (BP, 2005). Oil accounts for over two-fifths of total American primary energy consumption, and it is critically important for the country's transportation system. In President George W. Bush's words, America is 'addicted to oil'. Energy security has become a more important issue than ever in US foreign policy.

US policy-makers believe that 'China is increasingly active in striving for energy resources in ways that portend direct competition for energy resources with the United States', and that 'this is producing a possibility of conflict between the two nations' (USCESRC, 2005: 171). Richard D'Amato, chairman of the US-China Economic and Security Review Commission argues that 'it is critical to persuade China to abandon its mercantilist spree to lock up attractive energy supplies wherever it can, and instead to participate [in planning] for sharing oil in the case of supply disruptions and begin relying on free markets to promote energy security for everyone' (USCESRC, 2005: 171).

The United States is deeply locked in to a growth pattern that uses fossil fuels as the main source of primary energy. Between 1990 and 2000, it accounted for 46 per cent of the total global increase in carbon dioxide emissions, and in 2000 it accounted for 24 per cent of total world carbon dioxide emissions (WB, WDI, 2004: 146-7). The United States' per capita emissions of carbon dioxide are 22 times the average level of those in low-income countries, and nine times those of China (WB, WDI, 2004: 146). The United States was unprepared to join the Kyoto Protocol without matching action being taken by the world's poorest countries. This provides an ominous signal for the possibility of the world achieving the collective solutions necessary for global survival under US leadership in the decades ahead.

In the last few years in the high-income countries there has developed a gathering hysteria over the perceived threat to human civilisation from burning fossil fuels. China is increasingly perceived by Americans as the major threat to the global environment in the coming century. Jared Diamond's book *Collapse* paints a nightmare vision of the environmental implications for the world of 'China's rise'. He forecasts that if current trends continue, then by the year 2050 China will become the world leader in carbon dioxide emissions, accounting for 40 per cent of the world's total emissions.

China will soon overtake Japan as the world's largest importer of tropical timber. Diamond argues that China is, in effect, 'conserving its own forests' by 'exporting deforestation to other countries, several of which (including Malaysia, Papua Guinea, and Australia) have already reached or are on the road to catastrophic deforestation' (Diamond, 2005: 372). Diamond argues that several of China's 'exports' pose a severe environmental threat to the United States: '[T]he three best-known pests that have wiped out numerous North American tree populations – the chestnut blight, the misnamed "Dutch" elm disease, and the Asian long-horned beetle – all originated in China or else somewhere nearby in East Asia' (Diamond, 2005: 371). He believes that the Chinese grass carp, 'now established in rivers and lakes of 45 US states', competes with 'native fish species and causes large changes in aquatic plant, plankton, and invertebrate communities' (Diamond, 2005: 371).

Diamond is concerned at yet another threat to the United States from China's rise: 'Still another species of which China has an abundant population, which has large ecological and economic impacts, and which China is exporting in increasing numbers is *Homo Sapiens*. For instance, China has now moved into third place as a source of legal immigration into Australia and significant numbers of illegal as well as legal immigrants crossing the Pacific reach even the US' (Diamond, 2005: 371).

Jared Diamond's *'Collapse'* is a bestseller in the United States. It both reflects and helps to nurture popular sentiment, especially in the United States, about the perceived dangers of 'China's rise'. Its popularity spans a wide political canvas, from right-wing anti-immigrant groups to left-wing environmentalists. By linking closely China's rise with people's deep fears about the survival of the planet, the sentiments expressed in Diamond's book are immensely potent politically.

Financial Contradictions

The vast and growing size of the United State' fiscal and current account deficits, international borrowing and level of personal debt, stand at the heart of the unfolding global financial fragility. The United States and China present mirror images of each other. China has become a 'supply engine' of the global economy, while the United States has become the world's 'demand engine'. Each is growing in a deeply unbalanced fashion (Roach, 2005).

A large fraction of the demand stimulus for Chinese growth has come from exports, which grew from less than ten per cent of GDP in the early 1980s to around 36 per cent in 2004. Its export growth has been critically important in sucking low-skilled workers into non-farm employment, which has made a large contribution to poverty reduction. After decades of high levels of welfare security under the planned economy, the transition to the market economy has produced high levels of personal insecurity. In addition, the fact that the distribution of income has become markedly more unequal, has helped to stimulate a high rate of savings in China. The share of consumption in China's GDP fell from around 53-54 per cent in the early 1980s to 42 per cent in 2004, while the share of fixed asset investment in GDP climbed from around 30 per cent in the early 1980s, already a high level, to around 45 per cent in 2004 (Roach, 2005).

In the United States, on the other hand, the share of consumption has risen from around 65 per cent in the early 1980s to 71 per cent in 2004 (Roach,

2005). The United States accounts for only around five per cent of global population, but it accounts for no less than 35-40 per cent of global consumption. Despite having over 20 per cent of the world's total population, China accounts for less than one per cent of global consumption. The United States is 'addicted to shopping', while China is 'addicted to saving' (Roach, 2005). By 2004, the US population's savings rate stood at minus one per cent, compared with 35 per cent in China (Roach, 2005).

The level of household debt in the Unites States has risen remorselessly, from 60 per cent of household income in the mid-1980s to over 120 per cent in 2004 (*FT*, 16 February 2005). This has been made possible by the low level of US interest rates, which have in their turn been made possible by the willingness of central banks of East Asia and the Islamic oil-exporting countries, to buy US Government debt. China has used a large share of its rapidly rising foreign exchange reserves to purchase US Government debt. The increase in household debt has been stimulated also by the bubble in the US housing market, which has greatly increased household wealth. If house prices ceased to rise, or, even worse, if the house price bubble burst, there would be a large effect on US household balance sheets.

Growth of the US domestic and international imbalances cannot continue indefinitely. In 2004, Alan Greenspan warned: 'Net claims against residents of the United States cannot continue to increase for ever at their recent pace…Continued financing of today's current account deficits as a percentage of GDP will, at some future point, increase shares of dollar claims in investor portfolios to levels that imply an unacceptable amount of concentration of risk. International investors will eventually adjust their accumulation of dollar assets, or, alternatively, seek higher dollar returns to offset concentration of risk' (quoted in *Financial Times*, 20 November 2004). The necessary adjustments may occur smoothly. However, it is *'quite likely that the ultimate adjustment will be both swift and brutal'* (Martin Wolf, *FT*, 8 October 2005).

If the dollar was 'dumped', the consequences would be a sharp rise in US interest rates, a major US recession, and a surge in American protectionist sentiment (Wolf, 2005a). Current asset price bubbles, including that in the housing market, are largely sustained by low interest rates, so that the impact of such a crisis would flow through the entire political economy of the United States and that of the whole world. The Asian Financial Crisis demonstrated that the 'fire' of a financial crisis moves at high speed, and swiftly shifts into the economic, social and political sphere. This time, the setting would be truly global. Deep international integration has brought many benefits. It also means that it is harder for any part of the global political economy to avoid the destructive effects of a global financial crisis.

3. Resolving the Contradictions: Conflict or Cooperation?

The United States and China will be by far the most important actors in the global political economy in the first decades of the twenty-first century. The prospect for global sustainable development hinges around the relationship between these two mighty forces. Despite their respective immense strengths, each of them has its own internal contradictions, brought about by the impact of capitalist globalisation on the two economies and societies, one aspect of which is their deepening mutual economic integration. Their growing interaction may end in terrifying conflict. However, the prospect, literally, of the end of the world, may encourage the evolution of a cooperative relationship based on enlightened self-interest, which attempts to resolve through collective action the immanent contradictions of capitalist globalisation, in respect both to their internal development, and to their mutual relationship and their joint role in the international political-economy.

3.1 Conflict?

Despite the overthrow of communism in the USSR and Eastern Europe, and the rise of a market economy in China, the United States still feels deeply insecure. Its feelings of vulnerability were increased greatly by 9/11. It seeks to reduce its vulnerability through military and other forms of spending to protect its territory from attack, as well as by trying to nurture a world in which American values dominate. In the epoch of the global market economy, which has a central impulse towards universalism that breaks down international economic, social and cultural differences, it is remarkable that the United States spends so much on instruments designed to wound and kill human beings from other countries.

America's Need for Enemies

Samuel Huntington has done more than anyone to shape the American establishment's view of international relations, notably through his book *The clash of civilisations* (Huntington, 1996). Huntington's latest book *Who are we?* (2004) identifies the choices that he considers the United States faces today.

Huntington believes that the United States faces serious threats to its national identity and unity from various directions. These include the rise in domestic social inequality, the rapid expansion of 'Hispanisation' of American culture, and the 'globalisation' of the American elite. Historically, the existence of an external enemy has played a central role in helping to create American national unity out of a people who came to the country from all over the world. America's sense of national unity was undermined by the collapse of the 'evil empire' of the former USSR: 'The absence of a significant external threat reduced the need for a strong national government and a coherent, unified nation' (Huntington, 2004: 265). Much of American foreign policy debate since then has involved identifying the new 'enemy': 'The ideal enemy for America would be ideologically hostile, racially and culturally different, and militarily strong enough to pose a credible threat to American security' (Huntington, 2004: 266).

For Huntington, there are two possible enemies who might fulfil this role, namely the 'Muslim' world and China: '[China is] still communist in theory if not in economic practice, clearly a dictatorship with no respect for political liberty, democracy, or human rights, with a dynamic economy, an increasingly nationalistic public, a strong sense of cultural superiority, and among its military and some other elite groups, a clear perception of the United States as their enemy' (Huntington, 2004: 267).

There is a powerful set of interests in the United States that believes serious conflict with China is unavoidable. In the early days of the George W. Bush administration, Joseph Cirincione, of the Carnegie Endowment warned: 'There are many people in this [Bush junior] administration who think that a war with China is likely, perhaps even inevitable, in the next 20 or 30 years. [They think] China will challenge us [and] we'd better be ready for it' (quoted in *Financial Times*, 20 August 2001). Henry Kissinger warned: the hawks see China 'as a morally flawed inevitable adversary' and believe that the United States should act 'not as a strategic partner, but as it treated the Soviet Union during the cold war, as a rival and a challenge' (quoted in Nolan, 2004: 38). General Brent Scowcroft, former security advisor to two republican administrations (Gerald Ford and George Bush senior), commented: 'If there is a real division within this [Bush junior] administration, it is probably on China. There is a division between those who see China as inexorably developing into the primary security threat to the US, and those who feel China is transforming rapidly but…that it has been overwhelmingly positive' (quoted in *Financial Times*, 20 August 2001). These divisions persisted throughout the first and second Bush administrations. 'Realists' in American policy-advice circles, such as John Mearsheimer of Chicago University, argue that the United States will 'seek to contain China and ultimately weaken it to the point where it is no longer capable of dominating Asia' (Mearsheimer, 2005). Mearsheimer considers that 'the USA is likely to behave towards China much the same way it behaved towards the Soviet Union in the Cold War'.

The United States fears that China's rise will transform fundamentally the balance of world economic and military power. President Bush warned China: 'In pursuing advanced military capabilities that can threaten its neighbours in the Asia Pacific region, China is following an outdated path that, in the end, will hamper its own pursuit of greatness. It is time to reaffirm the essential role of American military strength. We must build and maintain our defences beyond challenge...Our forces will be strong enough to dissuade potential adversaries from pursuing a military build-up in hopes of surpassing, or equalling, the power of the US' (quoted in *Financial Times*, 21 September 2002). Following 9/11, the consensus among the inner core of the Bush administration shifted to the view that 'in the long-term the US would only find security in a world in which US values were widely held and spread' (*FT*, 6 March 2003).

As the world moves towards unified markets and global capitalism, the possibility of military conflict increases rather than diminishes. The world is in the middle of one of the 'great historic changes in relative power', and 'historically such changes have mainly led to conflict' (Wolf, 2005a). Martin Wolf warns: 'Ours is the second era of globalisation since the dawn of the industrial revolution. The first began in the second half of the nineteenth century and ended with a series of political and economic disasters in the first half of the twentieth century. If such calamities are to be avoided, much will depend on relations between the US and a rising China....Peaceful and cooperative relations are perfectly possible...[b]ut they are not inevitable' (Wolf, 2005b).

America's Nuclear Arsenal

In 1999, the US military budget stood at US$ 253 billion, compared with just US$ 135 billion for NATO Europe (IISS, 1999: 37). In the wake of September 11, the US military budget rose to over US$ 400 billion by 2005, while the military spending by NATO Europe stagnated. In 2006, President George W. Bush requested Congress to increase US military spending to a record level of US$ 439 billion in fiscal year 2007 (*FT*, 7 February 2006).[11] Moreover, this figure did not include requests for US$ 9.3 billion to maintain the US nuclear arsenal, or US$ 50 billion in emergency spending to fund the wars in Afghanistan and Iraq. When all forms of military expenditure are included, it is estimated that the United States is 'on a path to spend US$ 2 billion per day by the end of [the Bush administration's] tenure' (*FT*, 7 February 2006).

The United States has a stock of 8000 active or operational nuclear warheads, with an average destructive power that is twenty times that of the Hiroshima bomb, which killed around 200 000 people (McNamara, 2005). Of these nuclear weapons, 2000 are on hair-trigger alert, ready to be launched on 15 minutes warning. The United States has never endorsed the policy of 'no first use':

> We have been and remain prepared to initiate the use of nuclear weapons – by the decision of one person, the president – against either a nuclear or non-nuclear enemy whenever we believe it is in our interest to do so...On any given day, as we go about our business, the president is prepared to make a decision within 20 minutes that could launch one of the most devastating weapons in the world. To declare war requires an act of congress, but to launch a nuclear holocaust requires 20 minutes' deliberation by the president and his advisors (McNamara, 2005).[12]

The world has never faced a greater risk of nuclear warfare.

The US Annual Report to Congress on 'The Military Power of the People's Republic of China' (2005) concluded that China will not be ready to fight even a 'moderate-sized adversary' until 2010, and that the PLA is 'presently unable to compete directly with other modern military powers'. China has a limited nuclear arsenal. China possesses no long-range bombers or modern submarine-based nuclear weapons. China's medium-range bomber force is 'obsolete and vulnerable to attack'. China's entire intercontinental nuclear arsenal consists of 18 stationary single-warhead ICBMs: These are 'not ready to launch on warning'. Their warheads are 'kept in storage' and 'the missiles themselves are unfuelled' (Lieber and Press, 2006: 49).[13] The lack of any advanced early warning system adds to the vulnerability of China's ICBMs: 'It appears that China would have no warning at all of a US submarine-launched missile attack or a strike using hundreds of stealthy nuclear-armed cruise missiles' (Lieber and Press, 2006: 49).

American military analysts claim that the United States has succeeded in its explicit goal of nuclear primacy. Russia can 'no longer count on a survivable nuclear deterrent'. Despite 'much talk about China's military modernisation', the odds that China will acquire a survivable nuclear deterrent in the next decade are 'slim' (Lieber and Press, 2006: 48-9). The fact that for many years to come the United States may have the capability to destroy the nuclear weapons systems of either Russia or China without risk of nuclear retaliation can be seen as a force for global stability. It may also be viewed as a dangerous encouragement to the United States to threaten or, even, to use nuclear violence in the event of international confrontation.[14]

The US Government regards nuclear weapons as central to its military strategy for 'at least the next several decades' (McNamara, 2005). This provides an intense incentive for other nations to either expand their existing arsenal or develop nuclear weapons if they do not already possess them. McNamara characterises the US nuclear weapons policy as follows: '[It is] immoral, illegal, militarily unnecessary, and dreadfully dangerous. The risk of an accidental or inadvertent nuclear launch is unacceptably high'. The only rational policy, in his view, is to 'move promptly towards the elimination – or near elimination – of all nuclear weapons'.

Fears of 'China's rise' are now deeply embedded in the US intellectual and government elite in relation to China's perceived impact on inequality, conditions of work, energy security, ecology, and financial security, not to speak of the perceived threat to the US's global economic, cultural and military dominance.[15] It requires little imagination to visualise the innumerable different ways in which the contradictory impact of capitalist globalisation upon both China and the United States could erupt into a military conflict.

3.2 Cooperation?

Deepening Inter-connection of US and Chinese Political Economy

In the 1980s, the prime goal of American foreign policy was the overthrow of the 'evil empire' in the Soviet Union. This goal was pursued through acceleration of the arms race and numerous channels of influence upon Soviet policy-makers. US policies played a significant role in the collapse of Soviet communism and the disintegration of the USSR. 'Regime change' resulted in state disintegration, with disastrous consequences for the economy and for the welfare of most Russians. The Soviet economy had only negligible linkages to the US economy. The USSR accounted for a tiny fraction of American exports and there was no investment in Russia by US multinationals. Soviet exports to the United States were trivial in scale. The collapse of the Soviet economy had a negligible impact on the US economy other than the short-term fall in military expenditure.

During the explosive development of capitalist globalisation since the 1980s, the Chinese and US economies have become deeply inter-twined. US consumers benefit from the explosive growth of low-priced Chinese exports.[16] US companies and shareholders benefit from China's absorption of booming American investments and from American companies' access to the low-cost manufacturing supply-chain in China. US primary product producers (including food, oil and mining companies) benefit from exports to China, both directly from the United States and, increasingly, from production bases in other countries.[17] US high technology firms benefit from the export of products such as aeroplanes, medical equipment, telecomms equipment, power equipment, semi-conductors, and software. US retailers benefit from low-cost sourcing in China. The US government benefits from Chinese government purchase of its debt. This in its turn helps to keep US interest rates low, which helps to sustain the US housing bubble. This helps to underpin the growth of US personal consumption through the wealth effect and the ability of US consumers to borrow against the value of their housing wealth.

'System disintegration' in China, such as the United States helped bring about in the USSR, Afghanistan and Iraq, and may help to bring about in Iran (and, in its turn, perhaps more widely in the Islamic world), would have severe economic consequences for the United States. It is in the interests of US business and the mass of US citizens, not to speak of the rest of the world, to support the efforts of China's Communist Party leadership to achieve the country's 'peaceful rise'.

China's deep engagement with global capitalism has resulted in an economy that is far more open to the international economy than were other latecomer countries. By 2003, the ratio of the stock of inward investment to GDP was 35 per cent, compared with 8 per cent in Korea, 5 per cent in India and just 2 per cent in Japan (Wolf, *Financial Times*, 14 September 2005). In 2004, the ratio of China's trade to its GDP reached 70 per cent. China's economy is far more open to trade than any other large economy. The foreign trade ratios of the United States and Japan are both less than 25 per cent (Wolf, 2005b).

The United States is extremely important for the Chinese economy. The United States has become the largest source of foreign direct investment (FDI) inflows into China, amounting to over 10 per cent of total inflows (excluding Hong Kong) by 2002 (SSB, ZTN, 2003: Table 17.15).[18] There are large positive externalities from American FDI in China. Leading global 'systems integrator' firms from the United States stimulate other international firms (both from the United States and elsewhere) within their supply chain to establish production facilities in China. They bring their own managements skills and technologies to China, and exert intense pressure on the whole supply chain within China to advance its business and technical skills (Nolan *et al.*, 2007). By 2002, the United States had become much the most important market for China's exports, totalling US$ 70 billion, which amounted to 22 per cent of China's total exports, compared with 18 per cent for the whole of Europe and 15 per cent for Japan (SSB, ZTN 2003: Table 17.7). China's imports from the United States amounted to only 9.2 per cent of China's total imports in 2002. However, these imports consist predominantly of high technology products, which play an important role in upgrading the technological base within China. A serious downturn in the US economy, or the rise of American protectionism, would have large deleterious economic consequences for China.

State and Market

The interpretation of 'freedom' has been the object of intense debate in the United States since Independence. At the heart of the struggle for the meaning of 'freedom' in the United States was the battle over the role of the state, and its function in the achievement of 'negative' and 'positive' freedoms.

In the nineteenth century, the United States achieved explosive industrialisation behind protectionist barriers. The 'Gilded Age' at the end of the century witnessed a tremendous concentration of wealth and income.[19] The idea that 'freedom' essentially meant freedom of contract became the bedrock of 'liberal' thinking. The true realm of freedom was regarded as 'the liberty to buy and sell...where and how we please, without interference from the state' (Foner, 1998: 120). Social Darwinism became the dominant political philosophy, strongly opposing state interference with the 'natural' workings of society. The leading Social Darwinist, Prof William Sumner (Yale) argued that freedom meant the 'abnegation of state power and a frank acceptance of inequality'.[20]

The 1890s saw deep class struggle in the United States, stimulating the emergence of powerful critiques of free market fundamentalism in the years leading up to the First World War. The founder of the American Economics Association, Richard T. Ely, wrote: 'We regard the state as an educational and ethical agency whose positive assistance is one of the indispensable conditions of human progress (quoted in Foner, 1998: 130). Leading Progressive thinker John Dewey argued: 'Effective freedom [is] far different from the highly formal and limited concept of autonomous individuals that need to be protected from outside restraint' (quoted in Foner, 1998: 153). William F. Willoughby argued that Progressivism 'looks to state action as the only practicable means now in sight, of giving to the individual, all individuals, not merely a small economically strong class, real freedom' (quoted in Foner, 1998: 153). However, it was only with the onset of The Great Depression that such ideas came into the mainstream of US politics. When he assumed the Presidency in 1933, Franklin D. Roosevelt proclaimed: 'For too many Americans, life is no longer free; liberty no longer real; men can no longer follow the pursuit of happiness' (quoted in Foner, 1998: 196). These ideas remained as the mainstream of US political thought for long into the post-war world, reinforced by the massive task of economic and social reconstruction in war-ravaged Europe.

In the 1950s, a group of conservative thinkers set out to 'reclaim the idea of freedom'. For them, freedom meant de-centralised political power, limited government, and a free market economy.[21] By the 1990s, the dominant view equated 'freedom' with individual choice in the market place and minimal interference from the state. As the US business system became increasingly powerful globally, the idea gained force that the United States should lead the world towards a single universal free market. The collapse of the USSR deeply reinforced Americans' confidence in the free market, and in the country's duty to lead the world towards this as a universal form of socio-economic organisation. By the 1990s, in the United States there was no serious intellectual challenge to the economic philosophy of the free market: 'Market utopianism has succeeded in appropriating the American faith that it is a unique country, the model for a universal civilisation which all societies are fated to emulate' (Gray, 1998: 103-5).

The idea that the free market is a moral concept stands at the centre of US political discourse at the start of the twenty-first century: 'The concept of "free trade" arose as a moral principle even before it became a pillar of economics. If you can make something that others value, you should be able to sell it to them. If others make something that you value you should be able to buy it. This is real freedom, the freedom for a person - or nation - to make a living' (Bush, quoted in *Financial Times*, 21 September 2002). President Bush's National Security Strategy document of September 2002 was entitled 'How the US will lead freedom's triumph'. It states that freedom is the 'non-negotiable demand of human dignity; the birthright of every person - in every civilisation': 'Today, humanity holds in its hands the opportunity to further freedom's triumph over all [its] foes. The US welcomes [its] responsibility to lead in this great mission' (quoted in *Financial Times*, 21 September 2002).

However, the roles of state and market are already beginning to be re-thought in the United States in the light of the surging contradictions of capitalist globalisation, and their impact. The wisest voices in US political discussion realise that the answer to these contradictions is not to blame 'China's rise', but, rather, to return to an older tradition that attempts to establish a more sophisticated understanding of the appropriate role of state and market. If the United States encounters severe financial turmoil it may impel a re-assessment of the role of state and market, and the meaning of 'freedom' in a way comparable with that at the end of the nineteenth century and following the Great Depression.

China also is searching for its own balance of state and market. Under the extremes of Maoist administrative direction, the economy failed to meet the aspirations of Chinese people: 'direction' rather than real planning, which steps in where the market fails, deadened economic life. China is now looking back to its own history for inspiration about the appropriate role of state and market (Nolan, 2004). Throughout its own long history the Chinese state both stimulated and regulated the market economy. Alongside vibrant market development, the Chinese state guided economic activity through such mechanisms as control over the money supply, commodity price stabilisation, constructing irrigation and transport infrastructure, organising famine relief, regulating urban planning, and spreading knowledge. In periods when the state operated effectively, the economy and society functioned harmoniously.

China and the United States have entered the epoch of capitalist globalisation from fundamentally different starting points. However, they are both groping their way towards a sustainable development path. Despite the huge discrepancy in their levels of development, they are both experiencing profound system de-stabilisation arising from the surging contradictions of raw capitalist globalisation. The United States and China can both learn enormous amounts from their respective political-economic histories. Both countries are trying to 'use the past to serve the present'. China is trying to find a new centre of gravity after the extremes of the Maoist 'instruction economy', and to search in its own long history for inspiration. In the United States it is increasingly recognised that the country needs to learn from its own history about the way in which to control the market in the broad social interest. A financial crisis in the United States may lead to war, or, it may lead to a return to a deeper role for the state comparable with that after the Great Depression, and in the post-war period of global reconstruction, when America's leaders tried to build a 'Great Society'.

Science and Technology

The United States is at the centre of global technical progress. Its firms are by far the most powerful in terms of R&D, with 43 per cent of the world's top 1000 companies by R&D expenditure (DTI, 2005). In 2002, US companies spent around US$ 21.2 billion on R&D undertaken in other countries. Of this total around US$ 2.7 billion was in developing countries, of which around US$ 650 million was undertaken by US companies in China (UNCTAD, 2005: 294). By 2003, foreign companies are estimated to have accounted for around 24 per cent of total R&D spending in China (UNCTAD, 2005: 292).[22] Of this, American companies accounted for around 31 per cent (UNCTAD, 2005: 292-4).

US tertiary education in technical subjects[23] is greatly exceeded by that in China, India and Russia. In 2000-01, there were 2.6 million students enrolled in tertiary education in these subjects in China, 2.4 million in Russia, 1.9 million in India and 1.7 million in the United States (UNCTAD, 2005: 296). In 2006, the US National Academies[24] published the report 'Rising Above the Gathering Storm', which argued for a large increase in both the size and effectiveness of government intervention in US science and technology if the country is to sustain its technological lead. It argued that the American government needed to greatly increase its involvement in science and technology. The report makes a number of recommendations, for ways in which the United States can attract an even larger share of the world's most able young scientists and engineers to work there, including easing visa requirements, providing priority to doctoral level scientists and engineers in obtaining US citizenship, and providing international students and researchers in the United States with access to information and research equipment in US industrial, academic, and national laboratories comparable with the access provided to US citizens and permanent residents in a similar status (The National Academies, 2006).

China was at the centre of global technical progress right up until the Industrial Revolution in the late eighteenth century. [25] Although the pace of technical progress may have slowed down somewhat after China's medieval 'industrial revolution', a steady stream of significant technical advances was made thereafter through until the nineteenth century, without making the leap to a full-fledged modern 'Industrial Revolution'.

Although Chinese firms still face an intense struggle on the 'global level playing field', Chinese people are already making a large and rapidly-growing contribution to global technical progress. Chinese engineers and scientists constitute a large and growing fraction of the research force of leading global firms, working both in the high-income countries, and, increasingly, within research institutes established by global firms in China. American firms are in the vanguard of global technical progress, and, already, Chinese scientists and engineers are making a large contribution to new knowledge within those firms.

There are numerous areas in which science needs urgently to produce solutions in order to allow global sustainable development. Nowhere is the challenge more intense than in China. These challenges include improving human physical and mental well-being, overcoming the exhaustion of non-renewable resources, producing food in sustainable ways, and shifting the structure of consumption towards sustainable paths. China cannot simply replicate the growth pattern of today's high-income countries. Due to its vast size and explosive growth, these challenges are of unique intensity in China. The very survival of China and the world depends on meeting these challenges. By contributing to solutions to these burning problems, Chinese science and technology can make a massive contribution towards global sustainable development. The achievement of global sustainable development is in the long-run interests of US business and the mass of US citizens.

Energy and the Environment

The energy sector is a critical area of inter-action between the United States and China. Perceptions of the importance of energy security have dramatically increased in the United States in recent years. In March 2006, the Chairman of the Senate Foreign Relations Committee, Richard Lugar warned: 'No-one who is honestly assessing the decline of American leverage around the world due to energy dependence can fail to see that energy is the albatross of US national security' (quoted in *Financial Times*, 14 March 2006). He compared President Bush's 2006 State of the Union speech, in which the former oil executive warned that the United States was 'addicted to oil', with 'President Nixon using his anti-communist credentials to open up China'. He said that the United States needed to expand international coordination of energy issues, 'especially with India and China', to address the growing global competition for energy resources. He argued that resolving US energy security required 'extraordinary international diplomacy'.

In some ways, China and the United States face common problems and have common incentives to solve their respective energy problems. Both of them have huge coal reserves. There is tremendous potential for them to cooperate in technologies to convert coal to oil (USCESRC, 2005: 171). China's investments in coal liquefaction, using US-South African technology, are already well advanced.[26] China can benefit from American technology in a number of areas that enable it to increase the efficiency of its energy consumption and thereby tend to reduce its reliance on oil. These include energy intensity use reduction through employment of advanced machinery, clean coal technologies, and combustion efficiency improvements (USCESRC, 2005: 172). The United States and China could also work together to develop and implement utilisation of 'next generation fuels' such as hydrogen. The United States and China have a common interest in political and social stability in Islamic countries in order to ensure stability of oil supplies.

Finance

By early 2006, global economic imbalances had reached a record level. The US current account deficit had increased from 0.4 per cent of world GDP in 1997 to around 1.9 per cent in 2006 (*FT*, 24 April 2006). In 1997, 'Emerging Asia' had a current account deficit, amounting to 0.1 per cent of global GDP, while Japan and the Oil Exporters each had a surplus amounting to around 0.2 per cent of global GDP. The experience of the Asian Financial Crisis was searing for Emerging Asia. The region resolved to try to insure itself against another financial crisis by generating large export surpluses and accumulating large foreign exchange reserves. By early 2006, the region had achieved a current account surplus amounting to 0.6 per cent of global GDP, compared with 0.4 per cent for Japan, and, largely due to rising oil prices, 0.8 per cent for the Oil Exporting Countries. By early 2006, the net foreign assets of

Emerging Asia and the Oil Exporters had each reached 3 per cent of global GDP and those of Japan had reached 4 per cent, while the United States' net negative balance in terms of foreign assets had quadrupled from 2 per cent of global GDP in 1997 to 8 per cent in early 2006 (*FT*, 24 April 2006).

China's current account surplus and its role in the overall growing global imbalances was smaller than that of Japan, Germany or the Oil Exporting Countries. However, its role is politically the most sensitive. The debate over the worsening international imbalances is focused disproportionately on the US-China relationship, with an intense confrontation between the two governments over their respective responsibility for global financial fragility stemming from international imbalances: 'Up to now, the debate has been narrowly bilateral, with China insisting the US must address its low savings rate and the US insisting that China should revalue the *renminbi*. Partly as a result, neither has been able to diminish what has been described as a global "financial balance of terror"' (*Financial Times*, Editorial, 25 April 2006). Clearly, the problem of international imbalances embraces far more than simply the United States and China, and cannot be solved at a purely bilateral level.

By early 2006, fears intensified that global international economic imbalances might unwind dramatically. There was wide anxiety at the absence of international coordination of the emerging global imbalances. The agency that had been established precisely to deal with international financial coordination, namely the IMF, was widely perceived to have failed in its coordination function precisely when it was most needed. The Governor of the Bank of England, Mervyn King, warned that the IMF 'could slip into obscurity' if it 'failed to reclaim its role as the umpire of the global economy' (quoted in *Financial Times*, 28 April 2006). Against all predictions, in April, 2006, the IMF announced significant changes in its role: 'Even the most sceptical finance ministers and central bank governors viewed the IMF meeting as a great success' (*FT*, 24 April 2006). There was finally 'a shared understanding [that] huge trade gaps represent the biggest threat to the world economy', and crucially, there was 'a willingness to do something about it' (*FT*, 24 April 2006).

The IMF meeting of April 2006 decided to initiate 'a process that goes beyond analysis and description of problems, and engage in discussions with the specific governments about the linkages and spillovers of the macroeconomic situation, and in relation to the global economy' (Rodrigo Rato, Managing Director of the IMF, quoted in *Financial Times*, 24 April 2006). This meant that the IMF would henceforth report publicly on the effects of, for example, Chinese policies on the US trade deficit, and call together the relevant countries to see whether an agreement on policy changes could be reached. It would decide which countries were relevant for any given issue, and provide a forum to see if agreement could be reached. The Fund decided that where problems arose it would have the right to call 'multilateral consultations', forcing groups of countries to explain how their domestic policies were compatible with Article IV of the IMF and to try to secure agreement on policy changes.[27]

At the same meeting it was decided to initiate major changes to the IMF's methods of operation. The meeting approved a plan to give big emerging market economies a greater stake in the Fund. It was agreed that emerging market economies should greatly increase their role in the IMF's decision-making processes. China, along with South Korea, Mexico and Turkey, were to be granted an 'ad hoc' quota increase to raise their shareholding. It was agreed that this first step would be linked to 'near-term completion of broad second step reforms'. Under the new system, quotas for the IMF would be calculated on the basis of GDP rather than a complex range of variables as at present. It was agreed that there would be a further increase in emerging market representation, and a shake-up of the current board structure. At present, of the 24 IMF executive directors, nine are European, and the convention is that there is always an American director of the World Bank and a European managing director of the Fund. It was hoped that these changes would increase the IMF's legitimacy and 'bind rising economic powers more tightly into the multilateral financial system' (*FT*, 24 April 2006).

Faced with the threat of global financial disaster, at the final hour it appeared to many people that, with the agreement of both rich and poor countries, the IMF was finally assuming the role for which it was originally intended: 'In Washington last weekend, there was unanimous agreement that all IMF members shared collective responsibility for global issues and mutual responsibility to each other, and for the first time also committed to addressing the fund's governance issues' (Gordon Brown, UK Chancellor of the Exchequer, quoted in *Financial Times*, 28 April 2006).

Harmonious Society

Capitalist globalisation has contributed to surging inequality of income and life chances in both China and the United States in recent years. In China, there has been a surge of policy debate about the explosive growth of inequality, not only in income, but also in education, health and life chances. The country's leaders have declared their intention to try to establish a 'harmonious society' based on a just distribution of income and life chances. In the United States also there has been a surge of publications about the rapidly growing disparity of income and life chances, with parallels being drawn with the 'Gilded Age' in the late nineteenth century. Today, as then, many Americans, from widely differing political backgrounds, feel that the US government must play a much larger role in income redistribution if American society is to remain stable and just, and if 'freedom' is to mean more than simply the 'freedom' to buy and sell.

From ancient times to the present day, philosophers have sought to find a 'middle way' between competing extremes as the ethical foundation for the good society. If they are to cooperate internationally to solve the challenges created by capitalist globalisation, human beings must find a common ethical ground from across the different world civilisations, 'using the past to serve the present' to form a common ethic for global survival, which answers people's deep spiritual needs from the basis of a simple rational philosophy that all people can understand.

In their search for a good society, China and the United States can look to their respective intellectual traditions and to those key elements that constitute common ethical foundations for social life. The most influential thinkers of all cultures have addressed the fundamental issues of the ethical foundations for human survival. Among the most enduring of these are Confucius (1979), Aristotle (1976) and Adam Smith (1976 and 1982).[28] Each of them is deeply spiritual, attempting to address human beings' fundamental fears and needs. Each of them is based on humanistic rationality, which is complementary to, rather than substitutes for, the main religious belief systems.[29] At the core of their common search for an ethic to guide human beings towards a good life has been the concept of benevolence. They agree that the pursuit of wealth, social position and ever-increasing consumption is not the path to human happiness. They share the view that a good society is one in which social harmony is achieved through the whole people sharing a common view of social justice. They each believe that education is critically important for inculcating the ethics that form the foundation of the good society. They share the view that the only rational human goal is happiness, and that this is most completely achieved through the search for tranquillity, not the relentless pursuit of material consumption and pleasure.

Conclusion

The essence of capitalism is its propensity towards universalism. In the pursuit of profit, capitalism has always pushed beyond local boundaries, whether village, town, region or country. However, there has always been a tension between capitalism's universal impulse, and the nation. In the process of constructing modern capitalism, the national state has both propelled capitalism forward and reinforced the sense of national identity and interests, through the mechanisms of mass education, the mass media and government ideology (Hobsbawm, 1990). The rise of modern capitalism in the late nineteenth century erupted into the international conflict that dominated much of the twentieth century. Even in the epoch of capitalist globalisation, there persists a profound tension between the national state and international impulse of capital. The tension is crystallised today in the relationship between the United States and China. This relationship is central to the prospect for human survival.

Against almost all predictions, the combination of political stability under the leadership of the Chinese Communist Party, and experimental economic system reform and opening up, resulted in the most remarkable epoch of development the world has ever seen. China has been unique among large latecomer countries in its degree of openness to trade, international capital and business, and international culture. China's ever-deepening incorporation into global capitalism has transformed the country's productive forces and social relationships, producing enormous benefits for Chinese people. However, it has also led to wide-ranging challenges that threaten the entire social, economic and political system. These include the growth of inequality, deterioration in the physical environment, the harsh challenge of the 'global business revolution' for large Chinese firms, widespread corruption, and the reform of China's financial sector.

The Chinese government is working hard to devise polices that can meet the intense internal challenges. These include policies to equip the country's leading firms to meet the challenge of the global business revolution, to mitigate the unequal distribution of income, to improve health and educational provision for the mass of the population, to improve energy efficiency, to reduce environmental pollution, and to tackle corruption. No sector is more vital to the government's reform efforts than finance. China is groping for a way to avoid socio-political upheaval in the midst of immense internal challenges and to ensure 'harmonious development', which establishes a balance between China's inland and coastal regions, urban and rural areas, society and economy, and nature and man. This is a 'choice of no choice' for China's sustainable development.

Capitalist globalisation has also brought enormous benefits to the United States. China's increasing involvement in the global capitalist economy has contributed greatly to US prosperity. US firms benefit from their investments in China. US high technology companies benefit by their sales to China and by employing large numbers of Chinese scientists and engineers. US consumers benefit from China's cheap exports. The US Government benefits from China's bond purchases. However, global capitalism has also given rise to intense contradictions within US capitalism in respect to social inequality, energy, the environment, and financial fragility. There is a growing perception that China's rise threatens the dominant position of its firms, as well as its social stability, the identity of American firms, its energy security, its natural environment and its financial stability. These perceptions may influence decisions taken by the leadership or be made use of by them in a time of socio-economic crisis.

Capitalist globalisation has produced intense contradictions within both China and the United States, as well as in their inter-relationship. The possibility that, through a variety of channels, these contradictions might result in the final conflict for humanity is attracting increased attention from commentators across a wide spectrum of political persuasions. The degree of inter-connectedness in world affairs is now so deep that it is no longer possible even for the strongest political economy in the world to establish 'national' security within its own borders.

If the United States seeks long-term security, it faces a 'choice of no choice'. It must cooperate with Communist China to support the construction of a harmonious society internally within China. The areas of necessary cooperation include resolving China's energy needs, its ecological difficulties, its financial system reform, and reform of its health and education systems, and supporting China's efforts to establish a just distribution of income. In other words, it must accept and contribute to China's 'peaceful rise', even if that means accepting that the resulting system of political economy will look very different from that of the United States today. China and the United States have no choice but to cooperate to solve the global challenges produced by capitalist globalisation.

Within the evolving fabric of capitalist globalisation there are innumerable institutions, both governmental and non-governmental, local, national and international, through which people strive to assert collective control over the global economy. Although they are far from fully developed, numerous mechanisms are emerging to stimulate behavioural responses by businesses, in order to meet collective human needs for system survival.

The challenges that are faced by human beings are the product of people's own purposive activities, expressed mainly through the economic system. It is within their collective power to resolve these contradictions. The very depth of the challenges they now face may shock them into the action necessary to ensure the survival of the species. Alongside human beings' competitive and destructive instincts, which are expressed through and nurtured by capitalism, are their instincts for species survival through cooperation. However great the challenge may be, human beings have the capability of solving the contradictions that are of their own making.

Notes

1.   If the proportion of unregistered urban dwellers were to be included, the share of urban population would be even higher. The absolute number of officially registered urban dwellers rose from 193 million in 1980 to 482 million in 2002.

2. Of these, the number employed in manufacturing and construction rose from 61 million to 122 million, and the number employed in transport, wholesale and retail, and catering, rose from 19 million to 71 million (SSB, ZTN, 2003: 128).

3. Many of these now work in the non-farm sector, albeit that they reside in villages.

4. Of course, in terms of PPP dollars, the income level is somewhat higher.

5. Lomborg (2001) provides an extended account of this argument.

6. Of course, technical changes will tend to reduce the amount of energy used per unit of final product, but the remorseless growth of output, combined with the prospect of further population growth, and the strong incentive to rely on fossil fuels, make it virtually certain that China's emissions of carbon dioxide will continue to grow to the point that China is the world's largest producer of carbon dioxide.

7. The most obvious issues include the contribution of coal liquefaction from domestic coal supplies and the pace of advance in the energy efficiency of machines, especially transport equipment.

8. In 2006, Ernst & Young published a report which estimated that China's NPLs exceeded US$ 900 billion, over a third of which were from the big four state-owned banks. However, it quickly issued a statement disclaiming the estimate in its own report, saying that its estimate of bad debts for the country's big four state banks 'cannot be supported and...is factually erroneous' (FT, 16 May 2006). The estimate in its published report was at odds with its own audit of the balance sheet of the Industrial and Commercial Bank of China. Ernst & Young withdrew the original report, and announced that they would publish a revised report in due course.

9. A group of five small European countries (Denmark, Finland, The Netherlands, Sweden, and Switzerland) have a total of 92 firms in the world's top 1000 companies ranked by R&D expenditure (DTI, 2005).

10. Recent research shows that an American child born in the bottom-fifth income group has just a one per cent chance of becoming 'rich' (defined as the top five per cent of American income earners), whereas a child born rich has a 22 per cent chance of remaining rich as an adult (FT, 3 May 2006).

11. The 2006 budget proposals also included cuts totalling US$ 65 billion in government spending on health insurance for the elderly and other welfare entitlement programmes over the next five years.

12. For the detailed procedures, see McNamara, 2005.

13. China's ICBMs use liquid fuel, which corrodes the missiles after 24 hours. Fuelling them is estimated to take two hours.

14. Even though China is far weaker then the United States in both nuclear and conventional weapons, in the epoch of modern information technology, there are new forms of warfare that may to some degree outweigh ordinary military superiority, including attacks against IT networks in finance, power distribution, telecommunications, and the mass media.

15. The views of the mass of US citizens and the diverse components of the US business community are more difficult to evaluate.

16. By 2003, China accounted for 16 per cent of total US imports. Its share of US imports of toys and games stood at 77 per cent, while its share of office equipment etc, stood at 24 per cent and its share of clothing stood at 17 per cent (Glyn, 2006: 91).

17. We know of no estimate of the total amount of revenue for US firms derived from their production from their branch plants in China and from their sales to China of food and raw materials from their operations in other countries. If these figures

were added together, they would greatly reduce the 'real' Chinese balance of trade surplus with the United States. If the contribution of US firms exporting to the United States from their production bases in China were also included, then the 'real' Chinese export surplus to the United States would be even further reduced.

18. By 2002, the flow of FDI from the United States into China stood at US$ 5.4 billion, compared with US$ 4.1 billion from Europe, and US$ 4.2 billion from Japan (SSB, ZTN 2003: Table 17.15). Inflows from Hong Kong totalled US$ 17.9 billion, but it is impossible to disentangle the proportion of this that is accounted for by re-investment in China by Chinese Mainland firms' operations outside China, especially in Hong Kong, and by firms from other parts of the world operating through Hong Kong (Taiwan is especially important in this process, due to the restrictions on direct investment in the Mainland).

19. By 1890, the richest one per cent of the population received the same total income as the bottom 50 per cent, and owned more wealth than the bottom 99 per cent (Foner, 1998: 117).

20. In his view society faced only two possible alternatives: 'liberty, inequality and the survival of the fittest; not-liberty, equality, survival of the unfittest' (quoted in Foner, 1998: 122).

21. The immediate intellectual origins of the movement can be traced back to the publication in 1944 of Friedrich Hayek's book , *The Road to Serfdom*. The theme of the book was simple: 'planning for freedom' was an oxymoron, since 'planning leads to dictatorship' (Foner, 1998: 235).

22. The comparable proportions for other selected countries were: South Korea=1.6 per cent (2002); Japan=3.4 per cent (2001); Mexico=33 per cent (2001); Brazil=47.8 per cent (2003); and Singapore=59.8 per cent (2003) (UNCTAD, 2005: 292-3).

23. Science, engineering, and mathematics.

24. National Academy of Sciences, National Academy of Engineering, and Institute of Medicine.

25. Among the most significant examples of technical progress in pre-modern China were gunpowder, steel-making, the canal lock gate, the compass, the wheelbarrow, the windmill, mechanical clockwork, water-powered metallurgical blowing machines, water-powered trip hammers for forges, hemp spinning machines, gear wheels, power transmission by driving belt, the sternpost rudder, watertight compartments, and the crank (Needham, 1954-).

26. Shenhua Coal Group plans to invest around US$ 20 billion on coal liquefaction technologies over the next few years.

27. Article IV allows IMF member countries to choose their own economic and exchange rate policies, so long as they 'avoid manipulation of payments adjustment or to gain unfair advantage over other members'.

28. See Nolan (2004: 145-55) for an analysis of the common ethical ground in Confucius and Adam Smith.

29. For example, at the height of early Islamic civilisation, from the tenth to the twelfth century, Muslim scholars preserved the intellectual heritage of Aristotle, and combined this with their own commitment to Islam and the Koran (Braudel, 1993: 81-4). Muslim philosophy was 'trapped between Greek thought on the one hand and the revealed truth of the Koran on the other' (Braudel, 1993: 82)

References

Aristotle, *Ethics* (Harmondsworth: Penguin Classics edition, 1976)

BP, *World Energy Review* (London: BP, 2005)

Braudel, F., *A History of Civilisations* (Harmondsworth: Penguin Books, 1993)

Bush, G. W., *National Security Strategy of the United States of America* (Washington DC: The White House, 2003)

Bush, G. W., *National Security Strategy of the United States of America* (Washington DC: The White House, 2006)

Confucius, *The Analects (Lun Yu)*, translated, with an Introduction by D.C.Lau (Harmondsworth: Penguin Books, 1979)

Department of Trade and Industry, *R&D Scoreboard, 2005* (London: DTI, 2005)

Diamond, J., *Collapse* (Harmondsworth: Penguin Books, 2005)

Foner, E., *The Story of American Freedom* (New York: W. W. Norton, 1998)

Glyn, A., *Capitalism Unleashed* (Oxford: Oxford University Press, 2006)

Gray, J., *False Dawn* (London: Granta Books, 1998)

Hobsbawm, E., *Nations and nationalism since 1780* (Cambridge: Cambridge University Press, 1990)

Huntington, S.P., *The Clash of Civilizations and the Remaking of World Order* (New York: Simon and Schuster, 1996)

Huntington, S.P., *Who are we?* (London: Simon and Schuster, 2004)

International Institute of Strategic Studies, *The Military Balance, 1998-99* (London: International Institute of Strategic Studies, 1998)

Lewis, A., 'Economic development with unlimited supplies of labour', *The Manchester School* (May, 1954)

Lieber, K., and D. Press, 'The rise of China's nuclear supremacy', *Foreign Affairs* (March/April, 2006)

Lomborg, B., *The Skeptical Environmentalist* (Cambridge: Cambridge University Press, 2001)

McNamara, R., 'Apocalypse soon', *Foreign Policy* (May/ June, 2005)

Mearsheimer, J. J., 'Better be Godzilla than Bambi', *Foreign Policy* (January/ February, 2005)

Needham, J., *Science and Civilisation in China* (Cambridge: Cambridge University Press, 1954-)

Nolan, P., *China and the Global Business Revolution* (Basingstoke: Palgrave Macmillan, 2001a)

Nolan, P., *China and the Global Economy* (Basingstoke: Palgrave Macmillan, 2001b)

Nolan, P., *China at the Crossroads* (Cambridge: Polity Press, 2004)

Nolan, P., J. Zhang and C. Liu, *The Global Business Revolution and the Cascade Effect: Systems Integration in the Global Aerospace, Beverage and Retail Industries* (Basingstoke: Palgrave Macmillan, 2007)

Nolan, P., *Coca-Cola and the Transformation of the Chinese Business System* (Basingstoke: Palgrave Macmillan, 2008) (forthcoming)

Office of the Secretary of Defense, *The Military Power of the People's Republic of China: Annual Report to Congres,* (Washington DC: Department of Defense, 2005)

Piketty, T., and E. Saez, The evolution of top incomes: a historical and international perspective', National Bureau of Economic Research, Working Paper 11955 (2006)

Roach, S., Presentation to China Executive Learning Programme, 24 October 2005 (London: Morgan Stanley, 2005)

Smith, A., *The Theory of Moral Sentiments* (revised edition) (Indianapolis: Liberty Classics edition, 1982) (originally published 1761)

Smith, A., *The Wealth of Nations* (2 Vols) (Chicago: University of Chicago Press, Cannan edition, 1976) (originally published 1776)

State Statistical Bureau (SSB), *Chinese Statistical Yearbook, (Zhongguo tongji nianjian)* (ZTN) (Beijing: Statistical Bureau Publishing House, various years)

United Nations Conference on Trade and Development (UNCTAD), *World Investment Report 2003* (Geneva: UN Publications, 2003)

United Nations Conference on Trade and Development (UNCTAD), *World Investment Report 2005* (Geneva: UN Publications, 2005)

United Nations Development Programme (UNDP), *China Human Development Report 2002: Making Green Development a Choice* (Washington DC: Oxford University Press, 2002)

United Nations Development Programme (UNDP), *China Human Development Report 2005: Towards Human Development with Equity* (Beijing: China Development Research Foundation, 2005)

US-China Economic and Security Review Commission (USCESRC), *Report to Congress* (Washington DC: US Government Printing Office 2005)

US National Academies, *Rising Above the Gathering Storm* (2006)

Wolf, M., Presentation to China Executive Learning Programme (Cambridge, 2005a)

Wolf, M., 'China's rise need not bring conflict', *FT*, 14 September 2005 (2005b)

World Bank (WB), *China: Long-term Development Issues and Options* (Washington DC: World Bank, 1986)

World Bank (WB), *World Development Report, 2002: Building Institutions for Markets* (Washington: Oxford University Press, 2002)

World Bank (WB), *World Development Indicators* (WDI) (Washington: Oxford University Press, 2004)

Xu Dixin and C. Wu, *Chinese Capitalism, 1522-1840* (edited and annotated by Charles Curwen) (Basingstoke: Macmillan, 2000)

INDEX

DATE DUE

GAYLORD   PRINTED IN U.S.A.